GOD'S
HERETICS

THE ALBIGENSIAN CRUSADE

GOD'S
HERETICS

THE ALBIGENSIAN CRUSADE

AUBREY BURL

SUTTON PUBLISHING

First Published in 2002 by
Sutton Publishing Limited · Phoenix Mill
Thrupp · Stroud · Gloucestershire · GL5 2BU

British Library Cataloguing in Publication Data
A catalogue record for this book is available from the British Library

ISBN 0-7509-2572-8

Typeset in 11/14·5pt Sabon.
Typesetting and origination by
Sutton Publishing Limited.
Printed and bound in England by
J.H. Haynes & Co. Ltd, Sparkford.

Contents

DEDICATION

*To the schoolmasters and lecturers who taught me
that history is about men and women*

'The Cathars believe that there are two gods. One is good and a
saviour, the Father of good spirits, in which they believe. The other
created the world and human beings, and they have no faith in him.
The Father of spirits was light. The creator of the world was, for
them, the Prince of darkness.'

Evrard de Béthune, twelfth century *Liber Anti-heresis*.

Acknowledgements

I am indebted to many people for their guidance and assistance in the writing of this book: to Janet Shirley for her translation of the *Chanson de la Croisade*; Mervyn and Gunilla Elliott for the luxury of their gite in a vineyard near Limoux; Richard Parsons-Jones of Tanners Wine Merchants, Shrewsbury, for his information about the history of wine-growing in the south of France; Mme Andrée Cancel of Lavaur for her generous provision of historical material about the town; and the two ladies who did the same for Muret; Rosemary Baker for her discovery of two elusive articles; and Michael Costen for his warnings about driving along the backroads of the Languedoc with insufficient petrol and, also, for the equal warning of the challenge of Montségur.

I am also very grateful to the staff of Sutton Publishing, in particular to Catriona Belk, Sarah Flight and my editor, Christopher Feeney, for their sensitive repairs to an ailing typescript. And, as always, this book owes much to my wife, Judith, who despite her enthusiasm for open-air markets was always happy to endure a climb to yet another ruinous castle in the clouds.

On our wanderings in search of the barbarities and tragedies in the towns and villages of Occitania the only mutilation we inflicted was slight, some minor misuses of the lovely French language.

Preface

This is a book about an agonising tragedy. Worse, the tragedy endured over lifetimes in one of the loveliest regions of France. The medieval story of the region is like a cleverly crafted mosaic, attractively coloured and patterned but out of it, if one stares with intensity, the image of a devil's face emerges.

The region of the 'Languedoc', literally, the language of Occitania, is four hundred miles from Paris in the deep south-east of France. It is a world of its own. To the south are the Pyrenees with their snows and alpine meadows. Below them are expanses of limestone plateaux, '*causses*', some transformed for the grazing of cattle, others harshly wild with infertile soils.

On the lower plains, Languedoc is a quiet countryside of quiet rivers, the Garonne, Tarn, Hérault, and of noisy cities: Albi at the north, that gave its name to the crusade; Toulouse to the west that was besieged three times; Carcassonne at the centre; Béziers in the east, that suffered the first insanity of slaughter.

In the north are the Aubrac mountain roads with their lines of winter poplars like the upturned broomsticks of witches. In the south, jagged ravines writhe through the landscape, like the fantastic otherworld of the precipitous Gorges de Galamus above St Paul de Fenouillet, where the narrow, twisting, rock-hung road is a triumph of French engineering. At the rich heart of Languedoc are the vineyards of the Corbières, wind-blown Minervois and Roussillon. The entire region is an idler's paradise.

There are architectural wonders: the late eleventh century cloisters at Moissac, the delicate traceries of the pink marble tribune-cum-choir at Serrabone. The visitor needs to absorb the half-timbered romance of the square at Mirepoix and wander around circular bastides, like Montauban, with their chessboard-planned streets. To these pleasures can be added explorations of the old quarters of Toulouse with their glow of golden-red brick; a tour of the sombrely reconstructed parapets and ramparts of Carcassonne; and sight of the awesome dominance of the 'recently' completed St.-Just cathedral in Narbonne. There are also the literally breathtaking ruins of castles on the crest of steeply approached mountains: Roquefixade, Quéribus, Montségur among them.

Occitania is a vast area, a pentagon like the gable end of a house of some 30,000 square miles with Gueret at its apex, the 'roof' sloping down to Bordeaux at the west and the Rhône at the east, and the bottoms of the walls at Auch and Narbonne.

Languedoc, '*langue d'oc*', was the part of southern France where a Latin-based Romance language was spoken. The langue d'Oïl in northern France used 'oui' as a corruption of the Latin '*hoc ille*' meaning 'yes'. Closer to the Latin was the 'oc' of Occitania. Even today the region has a dialect of its own, understandably partly Spanish with that country only forty miles away across the mountains. The speech is a little like Catalan. The price of cushions in the open-air Sunday market of Espéraza near Limoux sounded like only five francs but was actually a hundred; the French '*sahn*' for 'cent' became '*sang*' in the local patois. The 's' is soft, consonants hard – so Lauragais is 'low-rag-ace'. No one speaks pure Occitan today, but it is preserved in the literature of the Languedoc and in the accents of local people.

The Languedoc is a visitor's wonderland. But it is also a land of blood. It is not the great cities with their traffic and their crowds that so starkly evoke the pain and the tragedies. It is the small town, the village: the courtyard of Villerouge-Termenès castle, where a pyre of straw and vine-leaves burned an unbeliever to death; the broken walls of the well under the cliffs at Minerve, overlooked today by a replica of the *trebuchet* that smashed and shattered the covered path descending to that vital source of water; the immense cavern at Lombrives, where steps and ramps trudge uneasily up to an inner gallery in which, it is said, seven centuries ago, fellow Christians walled up the faithful to die of starvation. Perhaps the saddest, because so simple, is the memorial stone at the edge of Lavaur where Guirauda, the deeply-loved châtelaine of that fortified town, was savagely murdered. These are the places where the grim memories of the Albigensian Crusade most grievously survive.

The horror began in 1209 when the Catholic Pope, Innocent III, ordered a crusade against the obstinate heretics known to outsiders as Cathars, 'the pure ones'. They believed in two gods, one spiritual and Good, the other earthly and Evil, and denied the physical reality of the Crucifixion. The Catholic church pronounced an anathema, demanding the extermination of the ungodly.

With a fanaticism like that of sixteenth-century Spanish conquistadors slaughtering the heathen Aztecs and Incas of the Americas, or Second World War German troops annihilating *untermenschen* in Poland and Russia, the French crusaders destroyed towns, massacred inhabitants, mutilated opponents and condemned scores, sometimes hundreds, of Cathars, men and women, to the murderous flames of mass-pyres with the indifference of bigotry.

It was a conflict between two quite different societies, one from the north of France, the other from the much more languorous south. To underline the linguistic differences, in this book the Christian names of crusaders are given in their normal French spelling such as Guillaume and Pierre. In contrast the southerners, equally Christian, are called by the anglicised forms of William and Peter.

Early monkish contemporaries like Guillaume de Tudela and the Cistercian monk, Pierre des Vaux-de-Cernay, as well as the later, less reliable Guillaume de Puylaurens, chronicled the campaigns; those events, the sieges, ambushes and battles have been described in many subsequent works, the most accessible being listed in the Bibliography. The present book is not just one more military history of the crusade. It is as much concerned with the people and places involved, what happened, where, and what can still be seen today of that terrible period.

What is surprising in this account of bloodshed, battles and brutality is the number of women who appear in it, often not as mere footnotes but as important figures: Guirauda of Lavaur; Esclarmonde, the Cathar noblewoman; Béatrice of Planisolles; Hildegard of Bingen, the nun; Alice de Montmorency, wife of Simon de Montfort; Blanche of Castile, Queen-Regent of France.

Most unexpected of all must be Mary Magdalene, who probably died in Judaea, two thousand miles from southern France and over a thousand years before the Albigensian Crusade. Whether, instead, she was buried in the Languedoc, and whether she arrived there with a priceless Christian secret, are part of the controversy about the treasure of Montségur and Rennes-le-Château.

To go to the Languedoc, even in today's tranquillity, is to be faced with the painted memories of the past. This is not a guidebook nor is it a sentimental diary of the many villages that have been visited. It is a record of who lived there and what happened in those apparently ordinary settlements.

Many placenames form a roll of dishonour: Béziers, Bram, Casseneuil, Marmande, Moissac, Puisserguier. The people are a mixture of the good and the bad, exhibiting extremes of behaviour from that of the gentle piety of Guilhabert of Castres to the ruthless persecutions of the military genius, Simon de Montfort. One woman, Béatrice of Planisolles, is mentioned often in this book. She lived in Montaillou, a village afflicted in the early fourteenth century by the Inquisition. She appears in chapters preceding that episode as a revelation of the status of women in medieval France, that period of the supposed non-emancipation of womanhood.

It is hoped that the book will lure readers to explore the loveliness of the Languedoc, and to enjoy the ever-changing scenery: the coast, plains and mountains, the abbeys and old towns, the castles, the markets, the food and wine – but also to find and feel regret at those sad places where so many innocent people suffered. If the book succeeds in this wish its writing will have been justified.

It begins with a hilltop village that, despite its former castle, had little to do with the crusade: Rennes-le-Château.

INTRODUCTION

Rennes-le-Château

The story of the brutal and tragic Crusade in the Languedoc can be told through the histories of just seven towns, cities and villages: Rennes-le-Château, Béziers, Lavaur, Toulouse, Montségur, Montaillou and Villerouge-Termenès. The first must be Rennes-le-Château about which much has been written. A mysterious, hidden treasure made it famous; and it was that controversial fortune that linked it with the Cathars.

On its hill near Limoux in the south of the Languedoc, the village of Rennes-le-Château has been claimed to be the place where the enormous wealth of the Cathars was hidden in 1244 and rediscovered in 1891. The hamlet was undoubtedly in an area dense with fervent believers.

Only fourteen miles to the south-east, at St Paul-Fenouillet, a convert told the indignant Catholic Bishop of Alet-le-Bains that 'Everything that exists under the sun and moon is but corruption and chaos' because all physical matter was the work of the Evil One. 'God is perfect. The world is imperfect. Therefore nothing in the world was made by God'.[1]

Closer still to Rennes-le-Château the busy market-centre of Limoux, ten miles to the north, with the river Aude flowing between its higgledy-piggle of streets near the town's arcaded square, was alive with heresy. In 1209 the town had been occupied without resistance by the Catholic crusaders, but the Cathar faith was not eradicated. A hundred years later, in sinister anticipation of the Nazi yellow star for Jews, the Catholic Inquisition compelled no fewer than one hundred and fifty-six believers to wear two large yellow crosses on all their clothes, sewn on the front and the back of their outer clothing to proclaim their heresy.[2]

In 1320, trusting to the town's reputation as a safe place for Cathars to avoid the Inquisition, Béatrice of Planisolles, once the delighted bedfellow of the Catholic priest of Montaillou, fled there to escape torture and death. The priest, Pierre Clergue, obviously regarded his clerical vow of celibacy as no more than an interesting relic of times past.

It was a bad time and it was a good time for women. Marriages of convenience were normal, particularly among the upper classes arranging alliances between families. The women had little choice. Many husbands regarded their enforced wives as the means of producing heirs. Mistresses were for pleasure. And, despite the conventions of courtly love written by the composer-poet troubadours, not all husbands were respected and revered as lords and masters. One of the troubadours, Peire Duran, said so in the 'langue d'oc':

. . . flac cors c'anc non si desnoiri	his flabby body that was never washed, mounted nor held steady; this has robbed me of my mind and memory, my sweet speech, my frolicking, my childish fun; his ill will, too, plus his nasty ways; he's withered my roundness with his sour breath.

A female troubadoure, many of them of the nobler class, said the same thing.

Ia Deus mi.n sal se ia sui amorosa	God save me if I ever love him – I am lovely – I haven't the least wish to love him – I am lovely – in fact, seeing him I feel such shame that I beg death to come and take him soon. – I am lovely.

But there were compensations. Béatrice of Planisolles could find extra-marital pleasures with Pierre Clergue. Another troubadour, Béatrice, Comtessa de Dia, wife of Count Guillaume de Poitiers, reminisced about a knight she had foolishly rejected:

Ben volria mon cavallier . . .

> I'd like to hold my knight
> in my arms one evening, naked,
> for he'd be overjoyed
> were I only serving as his pillow . . .
> [to] lie beside you for an evening,
> and kiss you amorously?
> Be sure I'd feel a strong desire
> to have you in my husband's place.

Béatrice of Planisolles was not alone in her sexual independence.[3] Nor in her belief in the Cathar religion, which had caused her flight to Limoux. She had been to the town fifteen years earlier to make an ostentatious Catholic confession at the church of Notre-Dame-de-Marceille with its famous wooden 'black' Madonna. She discreetly failed to mention that she was a Cathar, hoping that her 'confession' would prove her innocent of heresy. The deceit did not help her. Returning to Limoux in 1320 she was captured at Mas-Saintes-Puelles running away from an inquisitor at Pamiers. She was imprisoned in Carcassonne.

She was released the next year, but made to wear the yellow crosses.[4] They spoiled the elegance of her long gown of fine wool. With her hair braided in a net of silken thread, face framed in a wide linen band from ear to ear and under her chin, her clothes and jewels stated her noble status. Under her gown she wore a smock, similar but of less expensive and plainer material. Underneath the smock she wore nothing.

Towards the end of the long thirteenth-century persecution Limoux became one of the many hiding places of two Cathar 'Good Men', the brothers, Peter and William Autier of Ax-les-Thermes. A Good Man preached to the faithful, known as 'credentes', teaching and explaining the Cathar creed of Dualism, the two Gods of spiritual Good and physical Evil. He dedicated himself to an almost unworldly state of grace, undertaking three years of instruction in a community of Good Men, living a severely restricted life, working manually in crafts such as weaving, eating no meat because flesh was evil. All food from animals was forbidden: eggs, milk, butter, cheese although fish, being cold-blooded and engendering in water, were acceptable.

To devout Catholics such men were sarcastically known as Parfaits, 'the oh-so-perfect ones', perhaps in subconscious resentment of the honesty and asceticism of those preachers in contrast to their own corrupt clergy.

Once ordained a Good Man donated all his goods to the Cathar church and lived in total poverty in contrast to the despised Catholic priests with their self-indulgent, gluttonous and lecherous pleasures. A Good Man lived in chastity, avoiding even the touch of women. He fasted three days a week and was committed to absolute abstinence before Palm Sunday, after Whitsuntide and before Christmas. It was such men who attended the dying, administering the *consolamentum* that prepared the soul for its admission to the joys of the Spirit World of Goodness.

The Autier brothers became symbols of the simplicity and the rigours of a Good Man's life. They gave up everything, wives, children, possessions when they committed themselves to ordination. Peter had been reading St John's Gospel aloud and asked William what he thought of its teaching. 'It seems to me, brother', William replied, 'that we have lost our souls'.[5] And in October, 1296, they left Ax-les-Thermes to go to Italy to be ordained.

It was sacrifice. Peter, about fifty years of age, was a wealthy, well-connected notary with three sons and four daughters by his wife, Azalaïs, and a son and daughter by his mistress, Moneta Rouzy. William, about twenty years younger, well-known for his cheerful laugh and irreproachable manners, had two much-loved sons by his wife, Gaillarda.

The two men left home, family and material comfort. William sold his herd of cattle at the market in Tarascon to pay for the journey through the mountains and, disguised as knife-pedlars, they joined the parties of merchants, shepherds and pilgrims, praying with the others at Catholic shrines, although Peter scoffed at having to make the sign of the Cross, about as useful as flicking away flies, he joked.

South of Turin was the city of Cuneo, a Piedmontese centre of Catharism since 1250, and here the pair undertook three intense years of spiritual tuition and physical preparation for the fasting and the sleepless nights that they were to endure. Late in 1299 they returned to France, moving unobtrusively in the busy streets of Toulouse, shifting from safe house to safe house, resting by day, preaching at night, comforting the dying, teaching, Peter reading aloud, William explaining in the Occitan vernacular about the Fall, about the transmigration of souls, about the way to attain salvation.

Like all Good Men they mocked the Catholic belief in transubstantiation, that the blood and body of Christ could be absorbed by believers through the drinking of sacramental wine and the eating of a wafer. Why, Peter would laugh, if Christ's body had been as big as Mount Bugarach (a 1,219m-high mountain) it would still have been consumed long ago by all those priests' mouths. At her château in Dalou, Béatrice of Planisolles, said much the same thing to the Catholic, Mabille Vacquié, that the body of Christ would have had to be even vaster than the nearby hill of Margail.[6]

In 1257 another Good Man, Bernard Acier, administered the *consolamentum*, a laying-on of hands, to a dying man in Limoux. The ritual was for adults as children were incapable of understanding the sacrament. It was the giving of the last rites whereby a soul entered a state of perfection, ready to depart from the physical world of sin. To receive absolution a believer had to have received and accepted the Cathar teachings throughout his life. It was essential that the dying man or woman was capable of responding to the words to prove that everything had been understood. Only if a person was in extremity could the service be shortened.

Because of this Sibylla, wife of a non-believer, Pierre Pauc of Ax-les-Thermes, suffered a sad death. William Autier was brought quietly into her home while her husband slept in the next room but the dying woman was delirious and unable to make the responses to the Good Man's questions. No *consolamentum* was administered.[7]

Limoux was not the only place near Rennes-le-Château where Catharism flourished. At Coustaussa a few miles to the east the houses of Raymond Faure and Philip d'Aylarac provided a safe haven for Good Men and other believers. A mortally ill woman from the village was taken for the *consolamentum* to Sibylla d'En Baille's home in Ax-les-Thermes, a Cathar well-known for her surreptitious contacts with the Autier brothers. Later, condemned for having sheltered heretics, Sibylla was burnt at the stake in Carcassonne by the Inquisitor, Geoffroi d'Ablis.[8]

After receiving the last rites the woman from Coustaussa lingered for days and nights in a long decline, suffering an *endura* of twelve weeks. The *endura* preserved the pure state of perfection that the *consolamentum* had conferred. 'Nothing could be allowed to corrupt – and thus cancel – the other-worldly grace, bestowed by the *consolamentum*'. Once it had been given believers had to fast, abstaining from all food, taking only water, allowing themselves to decline into death. Cassagnas, yet another mortally ill woman from Coustaussa, underwent a long *endura* at Montaillou and was then buried secretly in a believers' field to avoid the exhumation of her corpse by the Catholic church. The Inquisition would have burned her heretical body.[9]

Ax-les-Thermes was also visited for less worthy activities. The libidinous priest of Montaillou, Pierre Clergue, often stayed there, using the thermal baths as a kind of private brothel for seducing local women. Some arrived without compulsion, anonymously cloaked in pleasurable anticipation, but not all the priest's conquests were volunteers. Many came because refusal could endanger them. 'There was', said a local person, ' no woman, or only a few, whom the rector could not possess when he was there, because of the fear of the Carcassonne Inquisition' – where an accusation from a Catholic priest could mean death. Clergue will return later in the book.

The fine troubadour of the late thirteenth century, Peire Cardenal, whose verses were recited by jongleurs in the courts of noblemen in the Languedoc and the Auvergne, knew of priests like him:

Clergue se fan pastors	Churchmen pass for shepherds
et son aucizedor	But they're murderers.
e par de gran sanctor	Dressed in their robes
qui los vei revestir.	They seem so saintly.

They were wolves in sheep's clothing. Cardenal despised the Catholic priests and preachers. 'Buzzards and vultures and all the scavenging birds are no quicker at smelling out carrion and rotting flesh than priests are at smelling out riches. They befriend the wealthy man but when he sickens in death all his money goes to them with nothing left for his family'.[10]

No sexual scandals such as Clergue's besmirched Rennes-le-Château. Today, centuries after these events, it is a tiny hilltop village overlooking the valley of the Aude. Once it was the fortified capital of the Razés region and a Cathar diocese twenty miles south of the citadel of Carcassonne. From the heights of the village there are fine views of the Pyrenees to the south, the red roofs of Espéraza to the north and the broken outlines of Coustaussa castle to the north-east whose deserted walls were seized by Simon de Montfort in 1210, recaptured by his opponents, besieged and regained by the crusaders in 1211.

Rennes-le-Château is reached by a hillside road, the 'route acrobatique', with more bends in it than a discarded coil of rope. Seemingly as unassuming and undistinguished as its neighbours in reality it has become a place of pilgrimage, myth and credulity. It had a long history. A prehistoric rock-shelter was discovered in its cliffs. During the Iron Age the hill supported a settlement of Gauls, whose word for their four-wheeled chariot, *raeda*, may have been the source of the village's name. It could also have been derived from the name of a Celtic tribe, Rhedonus.

The history of Rennes-le-Château was not only long but disrupted by conquest, destruction and disease. In the fifth century AD it was taken by the Visigoths from the east and then by the Franks from the north. Defences were erected around the crest of the hill but in 1170 the minor citadel was pillaged and destroyed by Alphonse II, King of Aragon, from the south. In 1210 its repaired walls were dismantled by Simon de Montfort during the Albigensian Crusade.

It was rebuilt around 1250 only for the disaster of the Black Death to kill four-fifths of the inhabitants, whose survivors were then subjected in 1362 to the looting and despoliation of the bands of ruffians and rapists known as *écorcheurs* who terrorised whole areas of France during the Hundred Years War. Rennes-le-Château was reduced to mediocrity and centuries of obscurity.

Treasure brought it back to life. In recent years it has been claimed, but never proved, that small fortunes of gold have been found in the area: in 1860, 110 lbs in a field; later, 44 lbs in a wood; in 1928 a half-melted statuette of gold. The remains of tunneled mines and pits are evidence of Roman exploitation of the sources of gold and silver. So are local place-names derived from the Latin *aurum*, 'gold', recording the presence of the metal in the Corbières: the castle of Auriac, the hamlet of l'Auredieu, the Aurio stream. Local folk-tales spoke of a buried treasure protected by the Devil near the castle of Blanchefort.[11]

The resurrection of Rennes-le-Château's village of a few hundred people began at the end of the nineteenth century. In 1885 a new parish priest, the thirty-three year old Abbé François, Bérenger Saunière, was appointed by Arsène-Félix Billard, Bishop of Carcassonne. Saunière was a local man from Montazels a few miles away. Some years later he engaged the eighteen year-old Marie Denarnaud, whose family from Espéraza were lodging with him, to be his housekeeper. She died thirty-six years after Saunière in 1953.

When the Abbé took up his post on 1 June his church, Ste-Marie-Madeleine, on its Visigothic foundations was in disrepair, its roof holed, its windows broken, its fabric decaying. Only three years earlier it had been condemned. Nor was there money for adequate repairs. The priest was compelled to live in near-poverty with a minute stipend of 75 francs a month. In 1890, a year before his controversial 'discovery', his total expenditure for six months on food and bread was just 99 francs. Then, suddenly, six years later the penniless priest began to spend freely.[12]

The ruinous and impoverished church was restored opulently and grotesquely; a semi-fortified library-tower, the Tour Magdala costing 40,000 francs was built in the tiny square; a luxuriously grandiose mansion, the Villa Béthania, was erected for a further 90,000 francs, complete with an expensively elaborate garden, heated tropical greenhouse, orangerie and park with fountains and a menagerie. The Abbé is also believed to have paid for the three-mile twisting road to Couiza. His vulgarised ornamentation of the church was completed in 1897 at an inexplicable cost of three and a half million francs. When Saunière died in 1917 it has been estimated that he had spent over 650,000 gold francs, the equivalent of about four million pounds in today's currency.[13]

On 25 June, 1905, the glorified village was visited by members of the Société d'Études Scientifiques de l'Aude. A year later its pamphlet enthusiastically if tautologically remembered the pleasure. 'We discovered a beautiful crenellated wall, a beautiful villa, a recently constructed tower . . . a beautiful pleasure garden sheltered by a beautiful terrace from which one may enjoy a beautiful panorama; without contradiction, an oasis lost in the middle of a desert . . . All this is the beautiful domain of the Abbé Saunière'. There had clearly been many beauties in the eyes of the beholders although the tower may have felt excluded.[14] Marie Denarnaud never explained where the money came from but did remark that 'with all that Monsieur the curé has left us there is enough to feed the whole of Rennes for a hundred years and more . . . The people who live here are walking on gold without knowing it'. She died, having revealed nothing, on 29 January, 1953.

Explanations for the prodigality all differ and all are suspect. The simplest is that in 1891 during a very modest restoration of the dilapidated eleventh century church, helped by one or two labourers, the impecunious Abbé dismantled the altar-slab that lay upon two ancient Visigothic pillars. One was hollow. In it were four parchments, two of them genealogies, one of 1244 bearing the arms of Queen Blanche of Castile, and a second dated 1644 of the Hautpoul family. There were also two Latin texts written in the 1780s by a former Abbé of Rennes-le-Château, Antoine Bigou. These, it is uncritically speculated, contained coded directions to twelve hiding-places of an unbelievable treasury of gold, silver and jewellery.

It is like stumbling through an overgrown maze on a moonless night to recover any understanding of what had occurred. On 21 September, 1891, Saunière made a tantalising note in his diary: '*lettre de Granès. <u>découvert d'un tombeau</u>. Le soir pluie*'. 'letter from Granès. *discovery of a tomb*. rain in the evening'. The mention of the tomb is underlined. Yet the Abbé appears to have done nothing about the discovery until 14 October when he started restoration again, noticeably with different workers.[15]

Everything is vague. The unspecified tomb may have been in a forgotten crypt below the church, the resting-place both of the deceased and the rich possessions of the powerful fifteenth century family of Hautpoul, Lords of Rennes-le-Château and Blanchefort, reputedly of Visigothic descent. They lived in the château against Ste-Marie-Madeleine. The headstone of one of them, Marie de Négre d'Ablès, Marquise d'Hautpoul de Blanchefort, who died in 1781, is in the cemetery. Some time after 1905 Saunière defaced its seemingly cryptic inscription, from which the name Dagobert has been deduced.

Inevitably the Abbé's sudden wealth and his unadvertised nocturnal activities led to suspicion and accusation. On 12 March, 1895, the mayor of Rennes-le-Château complained to the police that there had been sacrilege in the churchyard: crosses had been displaced, tombstones removed, old graves destroyed, their contents exhumed as though something was being searched for. Saunière explained that he had merely been tidying the graveyard. This was accepted – with prolonged scepticism.[16]

Scepticism became more serious and more dangerous. In 1902 the Bishop of Carcassonne died and his death was followed the next year by that of the easy-going Pope Léon XIII. His successor, Pius X, was sterner and supported the new Bishop of Carcassonne, the suspicious Monseigneur de Beauséjour, who demanded to see Saunière's account books. The Abbé refused to present them and defiantly ignored a transfer to the parish of Coustouge twenty-five miles away.

Subjected to trial by a local tribunal, he was accused of simony, the illegal selling for profit of ecclesiastical pardons and church livings. Other charges were added concerning his disobedience to his bishop as well as the problem of his unexplained expenses. Saunière was deprived of his parochial status and replaced by Abbé Marty. With that drastic change in his affairs his supply of money dwindled and by 1909 valuables were being sold. Then matters changed. In 1914 he appealed to the new Pope, Benedict XV, and was exonerated of all wrongdoing. His spending resumed but in January 1917, he died.[17]

Only Marie Denarnaud knew the truth about the origins of his enormous wealth. She said nothing and with her death only rumours and guesswork remained.

With the publication of provocative and ever-wilder books from the 1960s onwards, Rennes-le-Château became a popular place of pilgrimage and tourism. In 1989 the Museum Bérenger Saunière was opened in the old presbytery alongside the church. The Villa Bethania could be visited, the tower climbed. Souvenir shops and a bookshop flourished.

What had started as a seemingly straightforward mystery, the money that Saunière had apparently found, developed into deductions and delusions of international conspiracies, violent deaths, a search for the 'Holy Grail', whose resting-place was to be revealed through cryptograms and through the unlikelihood of geometrically landscaped castles and churches neatly positioned across miles of countryside. There was even 'proof' of the real burial-place of Christ in a mountain near Rennes-le-Château. Illicit excavations unearthed nothing. The treasure, if there had been one, had a hundred explanations but not one certainty. Truth remained and remains elusive.

Discounting the unlikely and the impossible there are several fairly plausible sources for the 'treasure'. Chronologically they are: AD 70; AD 410; AD 676–679; AD 1156–1169; AD 1250. To the list must be added AD 1244.

If what Saunière chanced upon and spent so prodigally were material riches such as gold and jewellery then their origins may have been as far from Rennes-le-Château as two thousand miles to the east at Jerusalem and as many years before Saunière as the reign of Solomon.

In AD 67 the Romans sent armies to Judaea under Titus to put down a Jewish rebellion. On 7 September, AD 70 Jerusalem was sacked and the third Great Temple, finished just six years before, was demolished leaving only the Wailing Wall standing. The Treasury, which may have contained part of Solomon's fabulous wealth, was plundered. The Jewish historian, Josephus, remembered the event: 'More prominent than all the rest were those captured in the Temple at Jerusalem – a golden table weighing several hundredweight, and a lampstand similarly made of gold but differently constructed from those we normally use. The central shaft was fixed to a base, and from it extended slender branches placed like the prongs of a trident, and with the end of each one forged into a lamp: these numbered seven, signifying the honour paid to that number by the Jews'.

The valuables were astonishing: ivory, ritual trumpets, some twenty-six tons of gold, sixty-five of silver, gems, ornaments, amongst them the Menora, the seven-branched candelabrum described by Josephus which was displayed, carved on the Arch of Titus, being carried in triumph through the streets of Rome.[18] It remained in the city for almost four centuries.

Under the command of Alaric Rome was overrun and ransacked by the Visigoths, the western Goths, in AD 410. The plunder included a lavishly bejewelled golden plate, the Missorium. Gibbon described it and another of the riches, the 'famous *missorium* or great dish for the service of the table, of massy gold of the weight of five hundred pounds' and 'a table of considerable size, of one single piece of solid emerald encircled with three rows of fine pearls, supported by three hundred and sixty-five of gems and massy gold'. He added that the 'far greater part had been the fruits of war and rapine, the spoils of the empire, and perhaps of Rome'.[19]

After Alaric the Visigoths moved westwards, taking the treasure with them, conquering the great part of Spain and by AD 462 had occupied the Narbonnaise region of the Languedoc in south-western France. They established a capital at Toulouse and built fortifications at Carcassonne and Rennes-le-Château. In the desolate fields behind Coustaussa nearby are the remains of substantial drystone walls with others at Rennes-les-Bains.[20]

In AD 507 Franks from the north of Gaul defeated the Visigoths at the battle of Vouillé leaving them with only seven cities in the Languedoc, Carcassonne being one of them. It is believed that what treasure remained was concealed there.

A third theory declared that Saunière's wealth had been partly the same Visigothic treasure inherited by King Dagobert, AD 676–679. whose second wife, Giselle de Razès, had been the daughter of the Count of Razès. Reputedly she married Dagobert at Rhédae, Rennes-le-Château. During his brief reign before being assassinated in AD 679 Dagobert greatly augmented the treasure by ruthless exploitation of his lands. Sixty years later the Franks under Charles Martel attacked the Visigothic kingdom again and overran Carcassonne. Legend has it that the valuables were transferred to the comparative safety of the remaining Visigothic stronghold, Rennes-le-Château and concealed in a dozen secret hiding-places.[21]

Should that story prove to be wrong there is yet another possibility, not very convincing, that Saunière's discovery was that of the accumulated wealth of the Knights Templar concealed in the region around Blanchefort less than three miles east of Rennes-le-Château.

Formed in AD 1119 for the protection of pilgrims on their way to the Holy Land the Templars made themselves rich by lending money for the payment of ransoms, extending the novelty of credit, acting as tax-collectors for popes, emperors and kings, parsimoniously using their own estates for profit, administering them 'primarily with a view to the money revenue which they yielded' rather than the produce itself.

They owned considerable tracts of land in the Languedoc during the twelfth and thirteenth centuries but took little part in the crusades against the Cathars. 'For the majority of the brethren of the Military Orders in Occitan, the events of the Albigensian Crusade unfurled outside their lives and responsibilities'.

It has been proposed that one of their Grand Masters, Bertrand or Bernard de Blanquefort, confusingly either the fourth or the sixth, ordered secret diggings by German miners in the neighbourhood of Blanchefort castle though whether this was to conceal or to discover treasure is unclear. It is also unlikely. Bertrand was Grand Master from 1156 to 1169 and spent most of his time in the Middle East where he was captured by the Saracens.[22]

It has also been claimed that in September 1307 some forty years after Bertrand, Philip le Bel, King of France, ordered the extinction of the Templars so that he might sequestrate their belongings. He acquired some of their lands. But 'when the King's agents visited the Templar treasury immediately after the first arrests, their great treasure had vanished without trace'.[23]

If it had been hidden by James de Molay, Grand Master from 1293 to 1314, among the hills and mountains around Blanchefort, the caches would have been conveniently close to Rennes-le-Château and could explain Saunière's local excavations and, presumably, successful excavations there. Disappointingly for enthusiasts not all fairy-stories have happy endings or even endings at all. There is another explanation. There was no treasure.

Royal inventories made at the time of the persecution show 'that church vestments, livestock and agricultural implements were the only assets of any value. There were no arms, very little money, and the furniture was meagre and poor. Some stores of salted mutton, bacon, salt fish, herrings, stockfish, cheese and a little salt beef were found, but almost no wine'. 'Inventories of Templar moveable property – treasure, cash, gold and silver – show them to have possessed remarkably little at the time of their downfall. The loss of Acre and the subsequent move to Cyprus [in 1291] must have made huge drains on Templar cash supplies, and perhaps the coffers had not been replenished afterwards.[24] This would account for the 'vanishing' of the treasure but it would not account for Saunière's vainglorious building programme.

An equally unlikely hypothesis is that Saunière's discovery was money belonging to the crown, left in the safekeeping of that formidable woman, the queen-mother and regent of France, Blanche of Castile, who travelled to the south of France taking with her ransom money of 800,000 gold bezants. It was for the release of her son, Louis IX, St Louis, captured on the Seventh Crusade in 1250 by Saracens at Damietta in Egypt.

In the absence of the king the queen-regent was surrounded by treachery. 'The barons wanted to regain some of their lost independence.; Blanche had to face a long series of conspiracies and rebellions'. Some believe that when departing for the Languedoc the queen feared that in her absence from Paris the royal Treasury would be broken into and her fortune stolen by avaricious barons. She thwarted them by removing it.[25]

She would have left Paris with the ransom and the royal treasury protected by a strongly-armed retinue on the long and tedious journey through the Cévennes to the marshes of the Camargue in Provence. Her destination was the new town of Aigues-Mortes just south of Nîmes, an inland 'port' with a five-mile canal to the sea. It had been built between 1246 and 1248 on the orders of her son, who needed access to the Mediterranean.

Louis IX was King of France but the title was deceptive. Effectively he was king not of France but merely of the lands around Paris from Compiégne at the north down to Bourges and from Orléans across to Sens in the east. The royal territory was no more than a fifth of modern France. In 1250 England, despite having lost huge areas in the north-west, still occupied the entire south-west of the country, the Holy Roman Empire lined the eastern borders and everywhere there were independently defiant lords with their own armies, petty kings in their domains.

For his crusade, Louis needed an outlet to the sea and the Holy Land. Ports did exist. He dared not use them. Narbonne was held by Spain, Montpellier by the King of Aragon. Marseilles belonged to the Count of Provence. Rather than being humiliated by refusals to admit him or allow his fleet to assemble in their harbours Louis prudently bought land and created a rectangular bastide whose ramparts of 1272 remain the most imposing in the whole of France.

The port did not last. Aigues-Mortes, from the Latin *Aquae Mortuae*, 'dead waters', silted up and the town became a literal backwater. But it did provide a glimpse of medieval severity and decorum. One of its moralistic charters decreed that any of its inhabitants convicted of adultery should be fined or, for the more persistently culpable, made to walk naked through the streets. 'Some experienced clerk added to this provision that adulteresses had to be at least *slightly* clad'.[26]

Blanche of Castile would have had no interest in those immoral near-Godivas. Once the ransom had been despatched she may have travelled to Rennes-les-Bains a hundred miles to the WSW. There, in the town's long green valley of the River Sals were thermal baths established by the Romans, and it is said that she often enjoyed the pleasantly warm mineral waters with their curative powers. The name of the spa is dubiously derived from 'Bains de la Reine' the 'queen's baths' in memory of her visits, the more probable source being the same as for Rennes-le-Château. In support of Blanche being the royal source of Saunière's fortune, it is thought very significant by some investigators that the priest reproduced her seal of a three-towered castle and the fleur-de-lys on the altar of his redecorated church.[27]

It is interesting, but the hidden fortune is unlikely. Had that dominant woman, ferociously loyal to her son and France, taken the royal treasure to Rennes-les-Bains she would not have buried it there. She would have returned it to Paris. Nor could she have taken the ransom with her to the spa if she had sent it on to Egypt. The story is pleasant but no more than whimsy.

By far the most intriguing of the imaginative folk-stories, and just as tenuous as the others, is that Saunière had chanced upon the vast fortune, *pecuniam infinitam*, 'untold wealth' it was termed, amassed by the Cathar church. To avoid its capture it had been smuggled by night down the mountainside of the besieged castle of Montségur in 1244, taken first to caves in the Sabarthés region near Foix and then later concealed in a dozen hiding places around Rennes-le-Château.[28] Whether Saunière had managed to decode messages to their locations is as debatable as all the speculations have been. It can only be added that rumours of Cathar wealth are credible.

Private Cathars like Peter Autier were rich. From them and many others the church had accumulated great funds. At Ax-les-Thermes a shepherd, Peter Maury, said that some of the faithful in Limoux guarded 'the treasure of the heretics' of more than 16,000 gold coins. Even as late as 1323 there were stories of over 100,000 *livres* secreted and well spaced out at Toulouse, at Mirande fifty miles to the west and at Castelsarrasin near Moissac thirty miles to the north. It was all for the preservation of the Cathar church.[29]

There were other benefactors as there had been for the past two hundred years. Always, dying believers were urged to be generous to the church. The hospital at Ax-les-Thermes was used by another credente and minor member of the nobility, Gentille d'Ascou. In September, 1301, seriously weakened and ill, she was taken there to receive the *consolamentum* from the Good Man, William Autier who had danced at the wedding of the sister of Béatrice of Planisolles, another Gentille. In the dark secrecy of night the Good Man was guided through the streets by the fur-coated Raymond Vaissière to the hospital.

Gentille d'Ascou was escorted into a field where Autier waited. He exhorted the woman to repent of her sins, reminded her of the goodness of the Cathar faith, read texts from the Scriptures, always asking whether the dying woman understood his words. She was questioned about her past life, whether she had any debts. As was the custom she willingly made a considerable gift to the church adding to the wealth that the Cathar bishoprics had accumulated over two or more centuries.

Having accepted all the teachings of the Cathars the noblewoman received the Prayer of Absolution. Resting a holy book upon her head and putting his hand upon her as Christ had done to others Autier absolved her of her sins and the Act of Peace was pronounced. So exhausted that standing was a trial, unable to walk, yet her *endura* was to last a further five or six days.[30]

A hundred years earlier than 1301 there would have been no thought of stealth. The noblewoman would have been blessed without secrecy in her own house. Catharism was a faith most easily accepted by the educated and well-born, and with their inherited power they protected their people. At the beginning of the crusade over a third of Good Men were members of the nobility.

Guillaume de Puylaurens writing years after the Crusade had ended condemned the lords and knights for respecting the Good Men, holding them 'in such reverence that they had cemeteries in which those who had been hereticated [consoled] were publicly buried, from whom they received complete beds and clothes'. Guillaume de Tudela confirmed this. 'All his knights and vavasours [vassals] maintained the heretics in their towers and castles, and so they caused their own ruin and shameful deaths'. Guillaume de Puylaurens added, 'Almost all the baronial families of the province . . . gave them hospitality, friendship and protection against God and His Church'.

Once those noblemen with their Cathar sympathies had been defeated the Good Men lost their guardians and became hunted souls. In the early fourteenth century with officers of the Inquisition everywhere, searching for informers who could be frightened or bribed, stealth and subterfuge were vital to the Good Men. It had not always been so. When the first signs of a threat developed in the Languedoc a hundred and fifty years earlier in the middle of the twelfth century few people believed that anything could disturb their peaceful and confident ways.

Maps

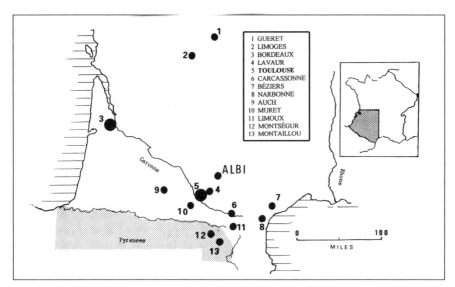

The region of the Occitanian Language, the 'Langue d'Oc'. Places of importance are marked.

1	GUERET
2	LIMOGES
3	BORDEAUX
4	LAVAUR
5	**TOULOUSE**
6	CARCASSONNE
7	BÉZIERS
8	NARBONNE
9	AUCH
10	MURET
11	LIMOUX
12	MONTSÉGUR
13	MONTAILLOU

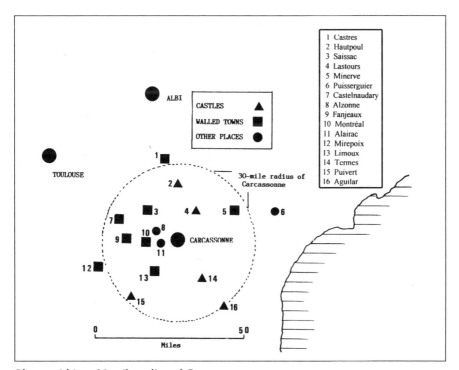

Places within a 30-mile radius of Carcassonne.

1	Castres
2	Hautpoul
3	Saissac
4	Lastours
5	Minerve
6	Puisserguier
7	Castelnaudary
8	Alzonne
9	Fanjeaux
10	Montréal
11	Alairac
12	Mirepoix
13	Limoux
14	Termes
15	Puivert
16	Aguilar

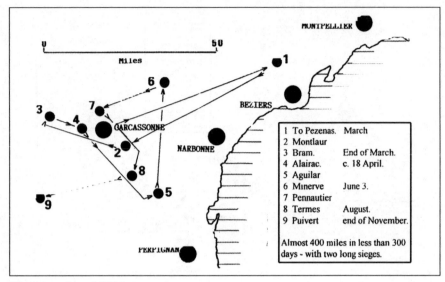

The following text appears within the map:

MONTPELLIER

1	To Pezenas.	March
2	Montlaur	
3	Bram.	End of March.
4	Alairac.	c. 18 April.
5	Aguilar	
6	Minerve	June 3.
7	Pennautier	
8	Termes	August.
9	Puivert	end of November.

Almost 400 miles in less than 300 days - with two long sieges.

BEZIERS
CARCASSONNE
NARBONNE
PERPIGNAN

The campaign of 1210.

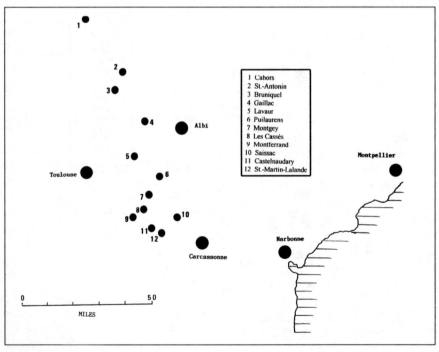

1	Cahors
2	St.-Antonin
3	Bruniquel
4	Gaillac
5	Lavaur
6	Puilaurens
7	Montgey
8	Les Cassès
9	Montferrand
10	Saissac
11	Castelnaudary
12	St.-Martin-Lalande

Albi
Toulouse
Montpellier
Narbonne
Carcassonne

The campaign of 1211.

Maps

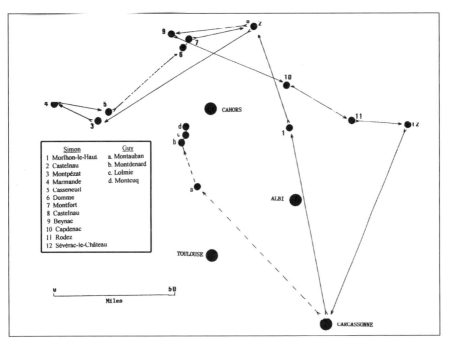

The campaign of 1214.

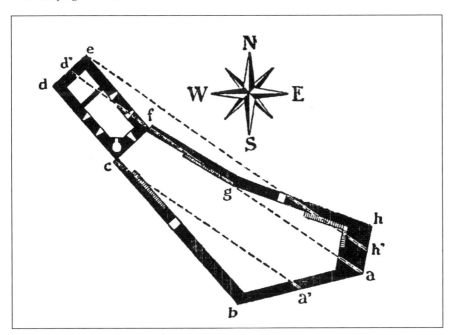

Plan of Montségur showing the imaginary solar alignment.

ONE

To 1208: Catholics and Cathars

In the early twelfth century the Languedoc was a comfortable land of sunshine, civilisation and song. In any society there are discords but in Occitania there was also the distinctive pleasure of chords of lovely music.

'Surely the greatest glory of Occitanian civilisation – that which made it known throughout Europe – was the troubadours. They started writing their lyrics around the time of the First Crusade (1095) and continued even through the catastrophe and decadence until about 1295'.[1]

Society was almost ideal for those poets and musicians. In the Languedoc townsman and countryman mingled, the bourgeoisie, knights, nobles, sharing a taste not only for luxury but also for decorum. There were manuals of courtesy for table manners, conversations and personal cleanliness. Females were not excluded from that way of life. On the contrary, moralists complained that women were laden under the weight of their stoles, capes and fur trimmings; they washed too frequently, took too long over their hair and put so much paint on their faces that none was left for the statues of saints. It was a society moulded by the delicacy and refinement of women. Music was their delight.[2]

The verses and melodies of troubadours and their minstrels were welcome not only in cities like Toulouse, whose count was a regular patron, but in smaller places like Mirepoix, Cabaret and Minerve. The troubadour, Raymond of Miravel, advised a poor colleague to

1

go to the castle of Cabaret, then on to the lord of Saissac 'who is certain to present you with a fine light robe'. At the finest and most generous centre of all, the town of Minerve, it was likely that he would be given a horse and a suit of clothes.

He was not over-optimistic. A late thirteenth century list of payments to minstrels in England supports him. Of players of the vieille, a medieval version of the cello, one received 20 shillings [a pound], another a gold clasp, a blind musician 12 pence and one mark [*c*. 67p]. A tambourinist got 4*s* 8*d* [*c*. 23p] 'for his shoes'. A group of Germans performing on the geige or gigue, a shrill form of violin to accompany dancing, were daily given a shilling and a pennyworth each of bread and wine. A harpist was awarded 6*s* 8*d* [*c*. 34p] for entertaining Queen Isabella. Another had the gift of a fine sorrel riding-horse with £10.00. Even though impossible to translate accurately into today's money these were handsome rewards.[3]

Troubadours and minstrels went everywhere there was patronage: Toulouse, Castile, Barcelona, Normandy, even England. Many were of noble birth, explaining their easy manners in courts; but some of the minstrels or *jongleurs* had bad reputations, 'base, treacherous, debauched, drunken, lying bar-proppers of taverns'.[4]

One of the earliest troubadours, perhaps the first professional, was a Gascon, Marcabru, or Macabrun, a waif discovered on a doorstep and educated by anothe troubadour. He was a moralist, 'one of the first troubadours . . . and he spoke ill of women and love'. From about 1129 until 1250 he wandered in the Languedoc seeking support, raging at the deplorable manners and morals he saw, until he was finally killed by some lords of Guyenne that he had insulted. One of his last verses read:

Lo vers e.l son vueille envier	The words and the tune I wish to send
A.n Jaufre Rudel outra mar.	To Jaufre Rudel across the sea.

Rudel, a minor nobleman of Blaye, who attended the court of Alphonse-Jourdain, Count of Toulouse, was a very different troubadour from Marcabru though not as accomplished. 'He made many poems with good tunes but poor words'. Many of those imperfect lyrics were dedicated to a beautiful woman whom he had never seen, the countess of Tripoli. A dubious history has it that he went to Acre on the Second Crusade of 1147–8 with the Count of Toulouse and others, fell ill there and died in the arms of the lady who had been informed of his adoration and misfortune.[5]

Such men were the precursors of a Golden Age of music in the later twelfth century. Troubadours, such as Peire Vidal, made many references to Raymond V, Count of Toulouse, Raymond of Miravel to Raymond VI. There is a paradox.

Many of their verses survive but of their music there are only whispers. Their instruments are known, the stringed harp, psaltery, lyre, harp; the blown trumpet, cornet, pipe, flute, the cornemuse or early bagpipe, the orgue (organ); the percussive tambourine, cymbal and drum. Modern renditions have been recorded but there are inescapable problems.

Of over two and a half thousand poems fewer than three hundred have known melodies. For over two thousand there is no music. And what does exist in manuscript is too simplified to know whether how or if it was orchestrated, how many instruments were involved, how many players, how many singers there were. It is a loss but it is not a vacuum. The troubadours lived and they brought art and loveliness to the Languedoc, a fact of that society that must constantly be remembered in the story of the religious tragedy of southern France in the Middle Ages.[6]

The history of the Albigensian Crusade, which had little to do with Albi, started long before that crusade began in 1209 and continued for half a century after its end in the 1270s. Around AD 1000 the Languedoc was a land of peace with Cathars and Catholics living harmoniously together, often in the same village. Then, for three hundred years, there was internal dissension, external oppression and a disaster that concluded in the extermination of a faith. It is a tale of bigotry, brutality and bravery with, on one side, a sadistic certainty that Satan was the warlord of the enemy, and, on the other, an equal certainty that their opponents were servants of the Devil.

To explain how harmony became horror it is convenient to open with an episode just after AD 1200. It involved a woman and a castle in decay.

Some two or three years after 1200 there was an unexpected request. A deacon of the Cathar church asked for the ruinous tower of Montségur to be repaired. All over the Languedoc there were defences. Some were huge, like the enormous ramparts of Carcassonne. There were great castles at Puivert, Puylaurens, Quéribus and elsewhere and minor ones such as that at Rennes-le-Château. There were garrisons like Les Cassès and walled villages like Bram. Of all these fortresses, the decaying tower of Montségur was one of the smallest.

It was also one of the most remote. Stranded on a steep-sided, here and there dangerous mountain, 963m high, with treacherous slopes, surrounded by forests and the jagged heights of the Roc de la Mousse, the Massif de Tabes, the Roc de la Gourgues; with only lonely farms and meagre hamlets around it, the nearest village was Bélesta on the Aragon-France border. No city was close and the larger, the farther. Foix was thirteen miles away, Limoux twenty-four, Carcassonne thirty-five and Toulouse, the capital, more than fifty.

Over forty years later in 1244 Raymond of Péreille, son of Dame Fornièra of Péreille and lord of Lavelanet and Montségur a few miles to the south, remembered the deacon's strange demand. Until that time he had been little concerned about his dilapidated, inhospitable and insignificant outpost, the second to have been built on the peak, that was now slowly decaying on its exposed mountaintop. No one lived there, but 'Because of the pressing demands and requests of Raymond Mercier of Mirepoix and of Raymond Belasco and other heretics, I rebuilt the *castrum* of Montségur which up to then was ruinous . . . It was rather more than forty years ago'. At that time there was no foreknowledge of the persecution that was to follow.[7]

Raymond Mercier was a deacon of the Cathar church with its very simple organisation of bishops in the dioceses of Toulouse, Carcassonne, Agen and Albi, one of the earliest. The immediate officers of the bishops were the *filius major* and *filius minor*, 'elder and younger brothers', the elder accepted as the successor to his bishop. Below them were deacons in each of the large towns and cities, administering the spacious 'houses' where Cathar believers could meet. The Cathars had no churches, only domestic meeting-places for believers and visiting Good Men. Such uncomplicated arrangements gave the Cathars easy contacts with their faithful. They were also economical, with no ecclesiastical buildings to administer and maintain.[8]

It has been assumed that the deacon had asked for Montségur to be restored because of the threat of attack from the Catholic church but at the time of his request there was no realisation that a crusade against the Cathar heretics was to be demanded by the Pope. The actual request may have been not the fear of war but the quite different request for the church to provide a secluded 'house' for Good Women, the female equivalents of Good Men.

Dame Fornièra of Péreille and Mirepoix, mother of Raymond, and her female companions already had a well-known Cathar dwelling in the village of Montségur. She wished for a less obvious shelter. When she had decided to became a Good Woman she left her husband, Guillaume de Sault, and retired to a Cathar house in Lavelanet taking her very young daughter, Azalaïs with her. Forty years later, the daughter told the Inquisition how she had been compelled to leave her father's house, and how her mother quickly persuaded her to give herself to God and the angels. But as a young woman, Azalaïs remained an ordained Good Woman for only four years before marrying a knight, Alzeu de Massabrac. Yet she remained a believer and became one of nineteen survivors of the subsequent massacre at Montségur, the 'mountain of safety'.[9]

Fornièra had left all the lordly rights of Péreille, including the castle, to her son, Raymond. She knew that the place was ruinous and it is not impossible to think that the request for repair was to make the building habitable as a 'house' for faithful women.

There were many Good Women in the Languedoc. Witnesses at the severe investigations of the Inquisition between 1245 and 1246 testified to as many as 311 of them, almost the same as the number of Good Men, a ratio very different from that between nuns and monks in the Catholic church. The Cathar women, however, did not duplicate the rôle of the men. They seldom administered the *consolamentum* and very rarely preached. It was reported that, although Good Women had been observed nearly fifteen hundred times, on only twelve of those occasions did one of them preach.

This does not imply inadequacy or a minor importance. Good Women established 'houses' for believers and constantly talked with village women, converting them. Pierre d'Avrigny, a Catholic priest complained that, 'Men may invent heresies but it is women who spread them and make them immortal'. Foulques de Marseilles, a former troubadour who became Bishop of Toulouse in 1205 cursed Dame Esclarmonde of Foix, sister of the Count. 'Through her evil doctrines she succeeded in making a number of conversions'.[10]

Esclarmonde is perhaps the most famous of the Good Women. Widowed, mother of six children, she was consoled and ordained in Fanjeaux by Guilhabert of Castres in 1204. It was a coruscating court scene of satins and jewellery with fifty-six nobles and other notables attending the ceremony, 'much as a great Parisienne of the seventeenth century might vie with her contemporaries for the most fashionable confessor of the day'.[11]

Esclarmonde formed a house for women in Pamiers and, when a prestigious debate between Cathar and Catholic clergy took place there in 1207, being both educated and eloquent, she spoke. Aghast at such intrusion by a presumptuous female a Cistercian monk, Frère Étienne de Minsèricorde, rudely rebuked her. 'Go back to your distaff and spinning, Madame, it is not proper for you to speak in a debate of this nature'. It was boorish and, as Costen thought, 'Probably what she had to say made the Catholic clerics uncomfortable'. By 1215 the unperturbed woman was in charge of the 'house' instituted by Fornièra at Montségur.[12]

She also became a legend. In his late nineteenth century, fanciful rewriting of Cathar history, Napoléon Peyrat, curé of St Germain-en-Laye in Paris, transformed her from a real woman into a blend of Joan of Arc, a prestigious priestess, a protectress of the Cathar treasure, both persuasive and beautiful and a martyr in the flames of the Montségur massacre, from which she emerged as a dove. In the twentieth century, deeming this too mundane, a German student and later SS officer, Otto Rahn, made her the Guardian of the Holy Grail.[13]

Life was less romantic. Not every Good Man or Good Woman walked hand in hand with the angels. They could be cruel. To some, their loathing of the body was so rancid that they denounced Cathar wives who became pregnant, blaming them for bringing more corruption into the corrupt world. It was a dark side of Catharism, especially among the jealous and the ignorant. Some more biased Good Men could advise expectant mothers to liberate themselves of their unborn devil. Others were warned that if they died in pregnancy they could be offered no *consolamentum*.

The results could be unexpected and fatal. In 1222 when a young wife, Ermessinde Viguier of Cambiac, a small village east of Toulouse, attended a Cathar meeting she was jeered at by other wives because she was carrying a child. Mockingly they told her that she had a demon in her belly. She was bearing wickedness. The infant would have horns and a tail. She never forgot. She abandoned the church and refused to rejoin it even when thrashed with a stick by her husband, William, in an attempt to 're-convert' her.

She not only remembered the insults of the women but became active against all Cathars. She spied on Good Men and informed the priest, Martin d'Auriac, of their whereabouts. Carefully searching the surrounding woods she found a sack with fresh eels in it, permissible food for a Good Man. There was also a shirt, onions, a bowl of chickpeas, a loaf and flasks of wine hidden there for the man. In the same forest was a shed where two Good Women, mother and daughter of Raymond Rasaire, lived in secret. A friend of Ermessinde, Raymonde Olmier, sometimes went there to pray with them. Other Good Men worked openly in the fields of Cambiac like ordinary peasants. The priest learned everything.

By 1245 the Inquisition was everywhere. The alarmed inhabitants of Cambiac confronted Ermessinde as she walked through the village hand in hand with her son. In desperation, they imprisoned the woman in a wine vat to keep her silent, saying, 'Boy, do you want to help this hag who wants to destroy us all?'

The years were so fearful that everywhere silence and deception became the custom. Entire villages hoped to confuse inquisitors by assuming false names but the ruse was unrealistic. In an entire village it needed only one informant like Ermessinde for the entire village to be condemned. Cambiac was.[14] Heretics were betrayed to Inquisition.

The 'shaming' of Ermessinde explains the contrast between the almost identical numbers of Good Women and Good Men, and the large difference between female to male credentes. Hardly a quarter of ordinary women were believers. Maternal instincts were too strong for many to accept the Cathar disgust of procreation.[15]

Yet that horror of the physical world was the basis of the Cathar faith. The Catholic Eucharist, the doctrine of transubstantiation whereby the body of Christ could be passed to believers, was an illusion. Material was evil. The perfect spirit of Christ could never have been flesh and blood. Descending to the world he had merely metamorphosed into a human body. He could not have been physically crucified for our sins nor eaten the Last Supper. Lacking a genuine body he could not have been resurrected.[16] Neither could there be redemption for sins. Sin was inevitable. Only the *consolamentum* could save a person's soul. The Catholic Mass was a contradiction. So was Heaven, Earth and Hell. The Earth itself was Hell.

Such a belief in dualism, the conflict between Good and Evil, had an ancestry many centuries old. Zoroaster, an Iranian prophet in the sixth century BC, divided existence into Truth and Lie. Truth or the Holy Spirit and the People of Righteousness whose God was Ahura Mazdah, were opposed by the People of the Lie led by the Fiendish Spirit, Ahriman. For his unorthodox and destructive creed Zoroaster was supposedly murdered, aged 70, when at prayer.

The cult of dualism flourished but it also generated divisions. Mani, *c.* AD 216–76, a Persian born near Baghdad, was expelled by the Zoroastrians as a heretic because of his preaching that there was a Spirit or Light struggling against Matter or Dark. He taught that each individual body held an almost unconscious spark of divine light and by abstinence and prayer a person would gradually become aware of the light. The awareness might require several reincarnations but souls would be rescued by messengers like Jesus. Mani termed himself the 'Apostle of Jesus Christ'.

The teachers of Manichaeism, like the Good Men long after them, accepted an existence of extreme poverty, preaching to their followers, the 'Hearers'. For his blasphemies Mani was flayed to death by Zoroastrian fanatics in AD 276 but his sect spread rapidly westwards into the Byzantine empire and Bulgaria.

There in the tenth century a Macedonian village priest, Theophilis, 'Beloved of God', translated into Bulgarian as 'Bogomil', claimed that God's eldest son, Satan, had rebelled and created the material world and mankind. God endowed the human beings with a soul but Satan enslaved them until God's second son, Jesus Christ, came to earth in an assumed body and redeemed them. Much of this faith was to be adopted and adapted by the Cathars of the Languedoc.[17]

By an historical irony, 'Cathar', from the Greek *katharos*, 'pure', was a word never used by Cathars. It was a sneer at the self-appointed 'pure ones', by a German monk, Ekbert von Schönau. Fearful that his Catholic congregation might be tainted by the founding of a 'Cathar' church at Cologne, he preached sermons against the dualists and presided over the burning of heretics in the city in 1163.

Preposterous accusations of devil-worship, blasphemy and foul practices such as sodomy and sexual perversion were made against the disbelievers. 'The Albigensians were . . . the most detestable of heretics – licentious and seditious; they propagated their execrable tenets by fire and sword, rapine and plunder; they burned the crosses, destroyed the altars and churches, and desecrated the latter by converting them into brothels'.

In 1198 Alain de Lille mocked that 'Cathar' came from *cat* in whose form Satan appeared to them. The bestial heretics filthily kissed its backside. The medieval German 'Ketzer', or 'heretic', de Lille claimed, also meant 'cat'.[18] It was bad philology. The true word was Katze. There was little forbearance and no acceptance. Disagreement became persecution. Around 1114, decades before

Ekbert, two peasants of Bucy-le-Long near Soissons to the north-east of Paris were arrested because of a superstitious belief that they had prepared and eaten a devilish meal from the ashes of a dead child. The monkish historian, Guibert de Nogent, said that there were many other heretics like them in the district.

The Bishop of Soissons who examined the men was taken aback by their obviously sincere Christian answers. Baffled and worried he left the city for a synod at Beauvais. 'Fearing clerical leniency' a mob stormed the ecclesiastical prison, dragged the heretics out and burnt them. There were similar violent murders elsewhere, including one at Vezélay in 1167. Wherever the Catholic church was strong enough there was persecution. Even in the more relaxed and easy-going lands of Occitania there were occasional executions. Around 1120 some Cathars were burned at the stake in Toulouse.

In England, in 1159, thirty refugees from Germany were tried in Oxford, whipped, branded on the foreheads, turned out as heretical vagrants and left to die of cold. Four years later, after a preaching tour by that remarkable woman, Hildegard, abbess of Bingen near Frankfurt, two Cathars being questioned in Cologne were seized by an impatient mob incited by her words. The men were burned.

Hildegard, musician, mystic, writer of a medical treatise and a book of apocalyptic visions, was not unworldly. For an avowed and undoubted virgin she had an unexpected understanding of physical sex, describing erection, ejaculation, insemination and the act itself in which the man 'races swiftly to the woman and she to him – she like a threshing floor pounded by his many strokes and brought to heat when the grains are threshed inside her'.

She had an affinity with a modern Sister cycling through Protestant Belfast. A boy shouted 'fucking nun' at her. She turned back to contradict him. 'One or the other but never both'. Hildegard would surely have approved.

Dying at the great age of eighty-one in 1179 despite her numerous virtues she was never canonised yet is often considered a saint and has her own feast-day of 17 September. She loathed the Cathars as a force of corruption and visualised their emergence when the Devil escaped from his bottomless pit, releasing the four angels of the winds that blew spiritual destruction to every corner of the world.[19]

Pure Catholic that Hildegard was, it is a paradox that one of the attractions of Catharism was its obvious superiority over the corrupt Catholic church. The Catholic clergy were despised, even by the popes. Innocent III criticised the Bishop of Narbonne and his priests. '. . . blind men, dumb dogs who can no longer bark . . . men who will do anything for money . . . They give church offices to illiterate boys whose behaviour is often scandalous. Hence the insolence of the heretics . . . Clergy acted as lawyers, judges, went hunting, gambled, fornicated as Pierre Clergue was to do at Montaillou. 'Monks had left their cloisters and lived openly with women, some of whom had been enticed away from their husbands'. They may even have contracted venereal disease. Long before the return of Columbus from the New World at the end of the fifteenth century evidence of unsuspected non-American syphilis has been detected in the skeletons of fourteenth century Augustinian friars in a priory at Hull in England. There is no reason to assume continence and celibacy in their profligate counterparts in France.[20]

Nevertheless there was active dislike of the Cathars amongst the Catholics as the words of the female troubadour, Gormonda de Montpellier show:

Greu m'es a durar . . .	It's hard to bear it
	When I hear such false belief
	spoken and spread around . . .
Dieus auja mos precz . . .	May God hear my plea;
	Let those, young and old,
	Who cackle viciously
	Against the law of Rome
	Fall from its scales.

It is believed that Gormonda, associated with a Dominican community, may have been a lapsed Cathar. It could explain her vehemence.

Clerical laxity was commonplace in Occitania, the land where the *langue d'oc* was spoken. It was a countryside of an educated society, cultured, hedonistic, famous for its troubadours with their jongleurs to speak and sing their verses in the tapestry-hung halls of the nobility. 'In general a jongleur was considered inferior to a troubadour because he did not compose the songs he performed'. But he did sing and play excellently.[21]

It was a countryside rich from the sale of wine and woad centuries before the introduction of indigo from India. In civic matters the Languedoc was very different from the feudal societies of northern France. Its cities had noble counts and viscounts but they also had consuls: rich merchants, prosperous landowners, lawyers, Jews, all of whom participated in and were responsible for the affairs of the city. It was a form of democracy that bewildered and offended autocratic northern knights.

The Middle Ages would not only have bewildered but also disgusted any visitor of today. Tales of Robin Hood, Friar Tuck and Maid Marion under the greenwood tree are appealing to the modern mind but the realities of life would repel the modern nose. Medieval men and women lived in a world of smells, few of them fragrant. Even in cities and towns streets never lost the stench and filth of horses, cattle and dogs. There were middens reeking of rotting meat and vegetables and human ordure dredged from domestic *garde-robes*, lavatories, in which furs were hung durinjg summer months. Villages and farms reeked like abattoirs and needed breezes and winds to clear the contaminated air.

Humans added their own scents. The nobles and the wealthy washed in the cold water of troughs in their courtyards, bathed, changed clothes, bought delightful perfumes. Shopkeepers, craftsmen, artisans moved in the ambience of their body-odours. Peasants stank. Nobody noticed.

Languedoc should have been a powerful society. It was not. In reality it resembled an archipelago of large and small islands cut off from each other by the fierce currents of fears, suspicions, envies and vendettas.

There were the extensive domains of powerful men: the King of Aragon; the Count of Toulouse; the Count of Foix; the Viscount of Béziers and Carcassonne. There were dozens, even hundreds of smaller estates, many lords and knights sharing their properties with others: thirty-six landowners at both Montréal and Mirepoix, no fewer than fifty at Lombez west of Toulouse. The massive walls of Carcassonne had sixteen towers, each belonging to a separate noble family.[22] Socially the Languedoc was weak. But Catharism was becoming stronger.

The Catholic church had become its own enemy. For centuries it had spread the Word, done good, but in those years it also acquired lands, power, wealth and they became its poison. Abuses, degeneracy, ostentatiously-robed bishops, overweight, gluttonous, ignorant clergy, became figures of ridicule.

Acceptance of Catharism was made easier by the growing anti-clericism of society. Preachers fulminated against the Catholic church. Early in the twelfth century a village priest, Peter of Bruis, went from town to hamlet criticising and condemning the useless conventions of the church. There should be no baptism of uncomprehending infants, no celebration of the feast days of saints, no prayers for the dead, no worship of the cross.

To his preaching he added practice. Throughout Provence in the 1130s Peter and his adherents burned crucifixes, destroyed altars, physically attacked priests and monks until the iconoclastic campaign ended at St.- Gilles on a tributary of the Rhône. The town and its Romanesque abbey will be mentioned many times in these chapters. On Good Friday in 1139 Peter had intended to burn the church's altar. Instead, a lynch mob hurled him on to his own bonfire.[23]

That the actions of the militant priest had been condoned for so many years is an indication of the contempt so many people had for Catholicism. A companion of Peter's, a northern monk named Henry of Lausanne, tall, lean with cropped hair and long beard, continued the struggle, less violently. Preaching in Le Mans, Poitiers, Bordeaux he was arrested in 1135 and taken to Pisa where he recanted to escape death for heresy. Once pardoned he returned to Toulouse and his rabble-rousing.

With such an anti-Catholic background it is understandable that the honesty and obvious austerity of Cathar preachers attracted the disenchanted. It is also understandable that in the summer of 1145

Pope Eugenius III, alarmed at the decline in influence of his Church in south-eastern France, appointed the finest preacher of the time, Bernard of Clairvaux, founder of the Cistercian Order, together with two abbots, to go to Languedoc on a mission of reform to restore heretics to the true faith.

Bernard had just been preceded by Alberic, Bishop of Ostia, but he had been a failure. 'At Albi he was receive with a kind of *charivari*, the townsmen coming out to meet him mounted on asses, and beating kettle-drums in derision of his pretensions; and when he celebrated Mass in the Church, and expected to have all the inhabitants assemble to meet him, barely thirty people attended'. Bernard replaced him.

Saint he was to become but tolerance and gentleness were not Bernard's outstanding characteristics. Only six years earlier he had been raging against the Cistercian monk, Abelard, whose nominal-istic teaching that there were no universals, only individual things, was both unorthodox and heretical to the Church. Calling him 'a thorough hypocrite, having nothing of the monk about him but the name and the habit' whose words stank of Arius, Pelagius and Nestorius, those vile, impious apostates, Bernard was almost hysterical in his denunciations. Twenty years before the quarrel Abelard had been castrated for his affair with the lovely Heloïse whose letters are regarded as classical expressions of love. Bernard would have considered them repugnant. He reacted similarly to Catharism.

His mission of reform was moderately successful in Toulouse where the eloquence of Bernard persuaded many in the city to return to the Church, and it was triumphant in Albi. A papal legate had been humiliated there a few years earlier but Bernard's addresses and sermons brought crowds from their homes, filled churches whose bells rang and pealed their joy. There might have been less popular acclaim had not Henry and other abominators of Catholicism left the town.

Bernard achieved some satisfaction in the cities. He failed in the conservative countryside. When he began his words of denunciation at Verfeil east of Toulouse the congregation walked out of the church. When he tried to speak outside, mounted knights clanged and clashed on their armour and inside their homes villagers beat loudly on their closed doors. Nothing but the din could be heard.

Furious, the abbot kicked the dust. It was to be an omen. All would become dust. 'May God wither you, Verfeil', he cursed, grimly making a pun of the name, '*verte feuille*', green leaf. The Languedoc was, he realised, 'a land of many heretics'. It was the first general threat. Until that time individuals had been caught, examined, punished. Now a whole population was endangered.

A mission of two brief months with too few missionaries to accomplish a general conversion was little more than a venture into the impossible. Bernard knew it. An over-optimistic correspondent assured him that 'the wolves have been tracked down'. On the contrary, they roved in packs. There were Cathar dualists everywhere, increasing daily. The Pope's hoped-for reform was being overwhelmed by the surge of determined heresy.[24]

In 1163 a Council of Tours denounced the advance. It continued. Two years later, apprehensive because there were so many suspected Cathars in the countryside south of Albi, the Catholic church decided to challenge and accuse the leaders of the heretics in a 'debate' ten miles south of the city at the small town of Lombers. Organised by Giraud, Bishop of Albi, it was after this meeting that the term, 'Albigensian' became applied to all Cathars even though the majority lived a long way from Albi, including the villagers of Montaillou eighty hilly miles to the south. Many years later the crusade was named after it and it became the title of the book, *Historia Albigensis* of 1212–18 by the monk, Pierre des Vaux-de-Cernay.

The Lombers confrontation was a nervous, rather half-hearted affair. With so many opponents all around Albi the Catholics were unlikely to condemn anyone to death. Nevertheless, the meeting attracted an astonishing audience of five bishops, seven abbots, and Constance, wife of Raymond, Count of Toulouse, and sister of the king of France. The chair was taken by the seemingly impartial Raymond-Trencavel, Viscount of Béziers and Carcassonne.

Appearing before this awesome gathering was a group calling themselves not Cathars, a word hardly known at that time, but

Good Men. They were led by a man called Oliver. Caution was vital. In O'Shea's sardonic words, 'Everybody . . . on that day knew that there was dry wood in the vicinity'. Despite this the men were confident enough to deny much of the Old Testament, deplore the baptism of infants, and stated that the swearing of oaths was a sin. It was sufficient for them to be pronounced guilty of heresy.

Instead of retreating or pleading innocence they accused the assembled bishops and abbots of being mercenaries, hypocrites, seducers, 'false prophets and wolves in the midst of the Lord's flock' and 'lovers of this world's honours and goods'. They were anathematised, excommunicated from the Church and deprived of its protection. As they had already rejected most of its teachings the condemnation meant little to them. They went free.[25]

In 1167 at a black-robed synod at St.-Félix-de-Caraman, today's St.-Félix-Lauragais, in the heartland of Catholicism between Toulouse and Castres, the Cathars became an organised church. Under the supervision of Nicétas, a Bulgarian and Bishop of Constantinople, and Marcus, Bishop of Lombardy, the first Cathar bishops were nominated: Bernard Raymond, Toulouse; Guiraud Mercier, Carcassonne; an anonymous man for Agen; and Sicard Cellerion, Bishop of Albi.[26]

Under their instructions Good Men were sent out to teach the way to salvation. Humbly dressed, dependent on believers for sustenance, quiet but persuasive they converted scores, hundreds of men and women already disenchanted by the excesses and insincerity of the Catholic church.

That church ordered the Languedoc nobility to suppress the Cathars. Some would not because they were Cathars themselves. Others pleaded inability. Even Raymond V, Count of Toulouse and of the populous lands around it, claimed that he was powerless. Instead, of him helping the church he wrote, it was the church that should come to his assistance.

He asked the general Chapter of Citeaux for help against the 'alarming development' of heresy. 'I have to recognise that my strength is not sufficient to overcome so widespread and difficult a problem, because the most important nobles of my land are ravaged by this disease, drawing away after them a very great multitude of men who apostatise from the faith; so that I neither dare nor can undertake anything'.[27]

It has been suggested that the letter was a forgery but it was probably the truth. Inheriting the county of Toulouse in 1148 when only fourteen years of age he swiftly became surrounded by enemies. Taking advantage of Raymond's youth and inexperience the Count of Barcelona, Raymond-Bérenger, began encroaching upon the fertile lands to the south of Toulouse. Raymond-Trencavel, Viscount of Béziers and Carcassonne, a traditional rival to Toulouse, coveted a region as far west as Lavaur not far from Toulouse itself. There was sporadic fighting. Mercenary armies marauded through the lands, retreated in winter and returned to raiding in the Spring. The acquisitive Count of Foix, Raymond-Roger, also greedily took up arms against Toulouse. The struggles continued intermittently with alliances constantly in change as opportunities developed into territorial possibilities and the land became 'a vast, desolate emptiness left behind by mercenary troops, the image of death and the smoke of fire hanging over every town'.

With no allies and with enemies to the east, west and south the Count of Toulouse was suddenly faced by an even greater crisis. Henry II, King of England, acquired vast territories to the north and west of the Languedoc when he married Eleanor, Duchess of Aquitaine, in 1152. Despairing of military success Raymond accepted Henry as his liege lord in 1173.[28]

Threatened politically on all sides the Count had little time for ecclesiastical problems. Certainly his court did not discriminate between faiths. In it, among the Cathars and eminent Jews, was the Catholic troubadour, Alamanda de Castelnau-d'Aude, who later became a canoness of St Étienne in Toulouse.[29]

The Languedoc was a world of privilege and poverty. It was a world of contrasts in geography, in religion and in society. It was also a tolerant world. Castle, town and village mingled in a social fluidity that amazed the contemptuous crusaders. As late as the fourteenth century Béatrice of Planisolles, noblewoman, would gossip and exchange confidences with women of lower classes, peasant wives, maids. Indiscreetly she even had a servant, Sybille Teisseire, keep watch at the open door while her mistress 'mingled her body with that of the priest' in the cellar below. At the other end of the social scale and a hundred years earlier Raymond-Roger Trencavel, Viscount of Béziers, employed a Jew, Simon, as his representative in the city.[30] Conditions of life, however, were very different.

In cold, bleak castles near-armies of servants served noblemen and their wives. The handsomely-clad lord had an equally finely-robed wife, wimple falling in folds around her head, embroidered dresses, jewelled hands. They ate well. Light breakfasts and suppers and a full main meal in the Great Hall around eleven o'clock in the morning, fish on Wednesdays, Fridays and Saturdays, otherwise courses of boiled meat: beef, pork, mutton, poultry, some-times venison, everything flavoured with pungent sauces of herbs and expensive spices like pepper and ginger, served with dried beans, peas, onions, always accompanied by the finest wines of the region. 'No knight fought well on an empty stomach'. Very few had to.

The lord ruled everything. Below him were counsellors, his chamberlain, his treasury officials who in turn commanded a group of well-born young men, esquires that oversaw the minions of the castle, the valets, cooks and huntsmen.

Even amongst that class there were distinctions down to the scullions of the kitchens and the peasants on the lord's estates. Lodging for months, sometimes years, among these courts were the artists, craftsmen and, above all, the troubadours and their itinerant jongleurs with rebecks, tambourines and flutes.

It was an existence of dank chambers, straw bedding for everyone except the lord and his wife, but it was also a magical world of tapestries, large allegorical paintings, and of a lavish table with sumptuous food, excellent wine and brilliant conversation between the lord and his guests.

Around the castles were the cities and towns whose merchants traded across the Mediterranean to North Africa, Egypt and the Holy Land. There were imports of spices, sugar, alum, silks, carpets, perfumes and dyes. Some goods were sold to the north. Others were profitably taken to the great fairs of St.-Gilles, Moissac and Nîmes, famous for its cloth then, famous for its 'de-nim[es]' today.

There were tradesmen, weavers, leather-workers, shoe-, hat-, dress-makers, tailors. Leatherware and cloths were exported. Masons and carpenters thrived as churches and houses were built. Pedlars took trinkets, ribbons and flummery to the poor and gullible villages.

The Jews were an integral part of society. Lords relied upon them for the collection of taxes, the administration of toll-gates, salt-pans. Jews enriched themselves by the lending of money and they acquired estates in the Languedoc at a time when the possession of land by non-Christians was a crime in northern France. In England there was persecution. At the coronation of Richard I in 1189 some Jews attended the coronation. The mob was incensed. The resentful cry of 'down with the usurers' incited a murderous attack in London's Jewry quarter. Neither age nor sex was spared. Houses were pillaged and burnt. The following year there was butchery in York encouraged by complacent churchmen. No one was punished.

In the late twelfth century the Languedoc was different. In Béziers and a dozen other towns there were unmolested synagogues. Narbonne and St.- Gilles alone had three hundred or more Jewish families comprising a population of over a thousand men, women and children.[31]

Outside the busy and prosperous towns on the lowlands of central Languedoc peasants toiled through the year at what the sixteenth century artist, Brueghel the Elder, called 'Labours of the Month': hunting in January, gathering wood in February, haymaking, harvesting, returning cattle to their stalls in November, plodding through the drudgery of ploughing, harrowing, milling, culling, flaying.[32]

Everywhere, on all kinds of soil, there were vineyards: on the outskirts of towns; on the terraces of the Minervois in the north; on the dry, rocky slopes of the Corbières in the Aude; on the red earths of Roussillon in the foothills of the Pyrenees whose splendidly scarlet wine of Pamiers, pressed from the Carignan grape of Aragon, was prized as far north as the royal court of Paris. In the same foothills wandering shepherds and their flocks retired in the winter to the shelter of hamlets like Montaillou with their houses of a cramped, hearth-warmed room, a loft for silage and a cellar for the animals.[33]

Whether Lord, merchant or peasant, Cathar, Catholic or Jew, people in the Languedoc lived in harmony together. It was not to last. In contrast to such tolerance the Catholic church was becoming angrily impatient, although it remained locally ineffective. Reforming preachers visiting Toulouse were greeted with hoots and catcalls. Desperately attempting to gain respect and re-establish authority the bishop summoned two Good Men, Raymond de Baimiac and Bernard Raymond, to answer the charge of heresy. Inevitably they were condemned and just as predictably they were allowed to return to Lavaur, the notorious haven of Cathars and the 'capital' of anti-Catholicism in a heretical region of over six hundred square miles of disbelievers in the Lauragais.[34] Henry de Marsiac, Catholic abbot of Clairvaux, visiting Toulouse, noticed how Catharism continued to spread.

In 1181 in response to the Pope's pleas Henry, now Cardinal Pietro d'Albano, raised an army and besieged Lavaur. With no relief offered from Toulouse or Foix to a possession of the hated Trencavels, and with a promise of leniency from the cardinal, the walled town quickly surrendered. By the rules of war resistance could have resulted in slaughter. But despite taking the town the attackers achieved little. After all the exhortations of Catholic preachers that the unbelievers should abandon their false creed, only two Cathars recanted.[35]

Like granite inexorably eroded by the splashing of a tiny stream, a more serious force slowly but persistently intervened. In Rome the third Lateran Council called by Pope Alexander III announced stronger measures. An anathema was proclaimed against heresy that was known to exist in the districts of Carcassonne, Toulouse and Albi. All Christians were to arm against heretics.[36] When Philippe-Auguste became king of France in 1180 the Pope urged him to lead a military crusade against the heretics. He did nothing. He was too busy with the unending attempt to recover French lands from the

English. Since 1173 Eleanor of Aquitaine had been inciting Henry II's two surviving sons, Richard and John, and his grandson, Arthur, to rebel against her husband and reclaim French lands in Normandy. Philippe-Auguste persistently encouraged the tensions, gave assistance, offered men, concentrating on politics, ignoring the irrelevant concerns of the church.

In December 1194, Raymond V died at Nîmes and his son, Raymond VI, became the new Count of Toulouse. Cathar by inclination he was Catholic by baptism. Perhaps because of this contradiction he was indecisive in religious matters, admired by his people but always unreliable, a procrastinator. To him the Cathars were never a threat, either religious, political or military. Although they were to prove the cause of disaster they were still his people under his protection.

His reluctance to hunt out Cathars was understandable. They were his countrymen, neighbours, friends, kinsmen. Foulques de Marseilles, former troubadour, who became Bishop of Toulouse in 1205, once asked a Catholic knight, Pons Adhémar of Rodeille, why he had not expelled heretics from his lands. 'We cannot. We have grown up amongst them. We have relatives among them, and we see them living good, decent lives of perfection'.[37]

Raymond VI had reacted similarly. As Laurence Olivier observed of Hamlet, 'This is the story of a man who could not make up his mind'. Raymond, a Catholic but also lord of his people, many of whom were Cathars, may, like Béatrice of Planisolles at Limoux, have hoped that an outward show of fidelity would divert attention from his actual inertia. During his lifetime he made numerous promises of action but always temporised, infuriating the Pope and his impotent bishops.

His actions were unquestionably affected by a determination to protect his domains against secular enemies even if that had to be at the expense of the Catholic church. He needed defences in strategic places. Without permission he had a castle built on the lands of the Bishop of St.-Gilles. The Pope threatened excommunication. Raymond ignored him. He took possession of the fortified cathedral of Rodez far north of Albi. He commandeered two castles belonging to the abbot of Carpentras. For their resistance he expelled the Bishop of Agen, imprisoned the Bishop of Vaison and the abbot of Montauban. Unsurprisingly, in 1196 he was excommunicated. It was the first but not the last time, either for him or for his son.

Elderly pope after pope died, all too old and tired to be concerned with anything outside Rome except the recovery of Jerusalem, the Holy City, from the Saracens. The death of Alexander III, about seventy-six years old, in 1181 was followed by Lucius III in 1885, then both Urban III and Gregory VIII in 1887, Clement III in 1191 and finally by the ninety-two year old Pope Celestine III on 8 January, 1198.

A sterner, more implacable man took his place. Innocent III, thirty-seven years old, rough-tongued, clever, capable, was fair-minded but implacably opposed to heresy.[38] For ten years he tried ways of converting the Cathars without threat of violence. And in 1202 a minor French baron, Simon de Montfort, and his brother Guy, both serving on the fourth Crusade, refused to participate in the disgrace of the siege of Zara, now Zadar on the Adriatic coast of Yugoslavia many miles north of Dubrovnik.

Zara was a fortified Christian trading port. The crusaders needed ships and provisions to carry them to the Holy Land. Enrico Dandolo, the calculating Doge of Venice, agreed to supply them but as the Crusaders were unable to meet his exorbitant charges he offered the ships as a bribe in exchange for the capture of Zara whose cargoes would bring him personal enrichment and power. The Abbot of Vaux forbade the attack, 'for those within it are Christians, and you are pilgrims'. Cynically the Christian crusaders pillaged the Christian city, looting, raping and killing the inhabitants. The honourable and scrupulous de Montforts took no part.[39] Nor were they present when the Venetians persuaded the crusaders to storm Constantinople in 1204.

In 1203 two papal legates, Cistercians Pierre de Castelnau and Raoul de Fontfroide, were sent to the Languedoc by Innocent III on a mission of conversion. As befitted Catholic dignitaries they moved in great state, richly-robed, with a mounted cavalcade of priests, bodyguards and servants and a train of pack-animals and equipment. It was ostentatious. To the already prejudiced Cathars accustomed to the asceticism of Good Men the prelates appeared ridiculous and hypocritical. Apparelled in such pomp they looked ludicrously pompous.

Compounding their ignorance of the resentment caused by their appearance their preaching was stiff, pedantic, academic and unsuccessful.[40] Delivered in Latin to audiences most of whom spoke only colloquial Occitan their words were incomprehensible. To those who did understand them they were inconsequential. They achieved nothing. A year later, learning of their failure, the Pope sent a third super-legate, Arnaud Amaury, Abbot of Citeaux, to support them. There was no military assistance from the king.

After the death of Henry II of England in 1189 and the departure of his heir, Richard I, on a crusade to the Holy Land, there had been a struggle for power between Henry's youngest son, Prince John, and the followers of the king's adolescent grandson, Arthur. Keen to exacerbate friction Philippe-Auguste supported Arthur's claim. John retaliated by imprisoning the youngster, who died at Rouen in 1203. Being suspected of murder John, a vassal of Philippe-Auguste, was summoned to appear before him. John refused, giving the French king the excuse to invade Normandy in 1204 and recapture it and the lands to its south: Anjou, Maine and Touraine. John did nothing.

These were years when civil law hardly extended beyond the cities. Once out of bowshot a fugitive was free of the law and bolder outlaws such as Robin Hood of Yorkshire created their own petty kingdoms in forests and on moors where no man travelled alone but only in a strongly-armed group. It was true in Britain. It was true in France. Philippe-Auguste was content with the retaking of a large part of France. The affairs of a few bandits or a church conflict four hundred miles south of Paris were minor concerns to him.[41]

Despite this royal indifference, in the Languedoc the Catholics did begin to make progress. It was the achievement of one man. In March, 1206, Dominic Guzman, born a Spanish grandee but later a sincerely pious Catholic canon, and ultimately the revered St Dominic, returning from negotiations in Denmark, met the three disenchanted legates quite by accident in Montpellier.[42]

Listening to their complaints he told the legates that their methods were wrong. They had unwittingly thrown firewood onto a bonfire. The Cathars would not be browbeaten. Nor would they be overawed by expensive vestments. Catholics should argue against the Good Men and their followers in imitation of their ways, not in opposition to them.

'It is the pretence of poverty which has won the heretics their victories'. Catholic preachers should be as obviously austere, going barefoot, penniless, asking for food, not travelling in grandeur with a multitude of horsemen 'but along the footpaths, from castle to castle, walking with bare feet, to the disputations arranged'. Between 1206–8, to the astonishment of the people, the preachers limped painfully from city to town to village, 'cicuibant per castella' it was recorded.[43]

Debates were held. Pedro, King of Aragon, Catholic but friend of Raymond VI, arranged some. At Dominic's instructions they were not confrontations but serious arguments. Nor were they brief afternoon affairs. Some lasted for days on single topics, written statements submitted, taken away, considered, rebutted, eight days at Verfeil on the human nature of Christ, fifteen at Montréal on the nature of the Catholic church, another at Pamiers in 1207 against distinguished Cathars such as Guilhabert of Castres, and more at Servian and Carcassonne, eight days each, and Béziers for fifteen.[44]

There was considerable resistance, and scepticism. In the summer of 1207 Carcassonne expelled its Catholic bishop. Elsewhere, Dominic was informed by Arnold Oth that the Roman church 'was espoused of the Devil and its doctrine diabolical. It was that Babylon which St John called the mother of fornication and abomination, drunk with the blood of the Saints and of Christ's martyrs . . . Christ and his Apostles never ordained or laid down the Canon of the Mass as it now existed'.[45]

That year Arnaud Amaury returned with thirty more Cistercian preachers. Territories were organised with rest-points and provisions. Conversions were made, but few. Dominic is claimed to have gained between a dozen and one hundred and fifty. There were too many cities, scores of towns, a wilderness of villages.

There were disagreements between the leaders. Pierre de Castelnau developed into an overbearing and arrogant bully, imprisoning anyone who dared to argue with him. In the end he had to be barred from the disputations and his place was taken by Foulques de Marseilles, Bishop of Toulouse. Internal dissension increased. Wearied preachers became discouraged, gave up. By 1208 after the vigorous but frustrating years the mission waned into oblivion.

Dominic did not surrender. He had settled in Fanjeaux to the west of Carcassonne and Montréal, a hilltop town ravaged during the civil war between Toulouse and the Trencavels. His bedchamber in the saddlery of the now-destroyed castle was consecrated as a chapel in 1948. And from Fanjeaux he had his one lasting success.

Given permission by Foulques, Bishop of Toulouse, between 1206 and 1207 he founded a hospice-cum-nunnery in the half-derelict church of Ste.-Marie in Prouille, a village in the valley below Fanjeaux. In many ways the foundation was 'an alternative to the houses of Perfects [Good Women] where penniless knights tended to leave daughters whom they could not afford to endow'. The women, none under the age of eleven, were a mixture, some the unendowed daughters, others converted Cathars.[46]

There was an apparent miracle. Nine reformed ladies from Fanjeaux were shown what they had escaped. Before their eyes on 17 April, 1207, the Devil appeared in the form of a cat, 'whose eyes, as large as those of an ox, seemed to be burning flames; its tongue protruding to the length of half a foot, seemed to be of fire; it had a tail of half an arm's length, and was easily the size of a dog'. Dominic banished it through a hole in the belfry.[47]

The foundation prospered. At the beginning of the crusade in 1209 when Simon de Montfort reached it Fanjeaux was a ghost town. The houses of its Good Women were empty. 'In the valley below, at Prouille, Dominic's young women worked hard in their new convent, but their heretical kin had vanished'.[48]

Unlike the Catholic mission Dominic himself had never been a failure. His obvious sincerity impressed the Cathars. On one occasion he met some peasants in the fields who asked why they should not kill such an enemy of theirs. His reply was famous. 'I should beg you not to kill me at one blow, but tear me limb from limb, that thus my martyrdom might be prolonged; I would like to be a mere limbless trunk, with eyes gouged out, wallowing in my own blood, that I might thereby win a worthier martyr's crown'. He was not harmed. He was also human. Of women, he much preferred the company of the young.[49]

It may have been in 1207 that he encountered his potential killers. It was an eventful year for other reasons, a year which brought misfortune and massacre closer and when apprehension developed into justified fear. Provocatively, the arrogant Pierre de Castelnau organised a league of barons to suppress heresy in Provence, but without the use of mercenaries. Predictably, Raymond VI refused to lead it. Instantly, probably by premeditation, he was accused of protecting heretics, hiring foreign mercenaries, violating feast-days, employing Jews, and turning churches into fortresses.

Angrily, Innocent III sent him a ferocious letter of condemnation. 'Are you not ashamed of breaking the oath by which you swore to eradicate heresy from your dominions . . . Are you so mad that you think yourself wiser than all the faithful of the universal Church?' On 29 May, by Innocent III's order, the legate excommunicated Raymond VI, Count of Toulouse, as 'a protector of heretics'. 'He who dispossesses you will be accounted virtuous, he who strikes you dead will earn a blessing'. In response Raymond gave his customary glib promises. In August he was reprieved. The promises were not kept.[50]

On 12 November that year, in another extraordinarily intemperate letter, Innocent III asked Philippe-Auguste to order a crusade against the Cathar heresy which 'gives birth continually to a monstrous brood, by means of which its corruption is vigorously renewed, after that offspring has passed on to others the canker of its own madness and a detestable succession of criminals emerges . . . Eliminate such harmful filth. Let the strength of the crown and the misery of war bring them back to the truth'. He was supported by the testimony of Dominic, who stated that he had preached, begged, failed. Now the rod must be used. 'The force of the stick will prevail, where sweetness and blessing have been able to achieve nothing . . .' The heretics would all be reduced to servitude.[51]

Alarmed at the likelihood of an invasion, Raymond VI once again promised to obey the Church and, at the end of December, he invited Pierre de Castelnau and the Bishop of Couserans to visit him and discuss means of suppressing Catharism. On 13 January, 1208, the three met at St.-Gilles, now a dull town ten miles west of Arles, just north of the Camargue. Its fine Romanesque abbey, begun in 1116, was almost destroyed in the seventeenth century Wars of Religion. Only the harmoniously decorated west front with its three portals survived the damage. The remainder is drab.

The meeting was one more failure. Discussion became argument and argument became quarrel. For the first time there are the words of contemporaries to report what happened. Pierre des Vaux-de-Cernay, thirteenth century monk but prejudiced reporter, wrote that, with no progress being made, the irritated legate and his party decided to abandon the useless talk and leave St.-Gilles. 'Thereupon', wrote the chronicler, 'the Count publicly threatened them with death, vowing to keep a close watch on their departure whether they went by land or by water'. Without proof, let alone probability, he added, Raymond had treacherously prepared an ambush. Pierre's party left St.-Gilles that evening with the abbot's bodyguard.[52]

A direct journey from St.-Gilles to the banks of the Rhône opposite Arles was no more than nine miles. In the Middle Ages it was possible only for birds. Outside St.-Gilles the Petit-Rhône flowed northwards in a long arc that added at least three miles for the plodding animals as the clerics and their baggage-train trailed through the dark midwinter night. It was late when they reached the banks of the Rhône near modern village of Fourques. While Pierre de Castelnau and his priests slept in their tents the soldiers of the consuls of St.-Gilles kept watch.

Next morning, 14 January, before dawn the clerics celebrated communion in the dim twilight. Then while servants dismantled the camp, folded bedding and loaded the pack-animals, Pierre de Castelnau sat apart on his mule waiting for the ferry.

Suddenly, shockingly, a rider appeared, galloping, lance levelled, that pierced savagely into the back of the legate between his ribs, hurling him to the ground. It was done in seconds. The assassin raced away. Pierre de Castelnau lay dying, his deep wound drenching his robes with blood.

Even in his agony he asked forgiveness for his murderer. 'Yet the legate raised his hands to heaven before he died and in the sight of all those present asked God to forgive this wicked man . . . Then he died, just as day was dawning'.[53]

Two months later, on 10 March, he was canonised and interred in the crypt of St.-Gilles alongside the saint's shrine. It was a considerable honour. Gilles, or Aegidius, one of the most popular saints in western Europe, had been an early eighth-century hermit near Nîmes. He became the patron saint of cripples and his church at St.-Gilles developed into a centre for pilgrims on their way to the shrine of St James of Compostela, now Santiago in western Spain, and the Holy Land. For Pierre de Castelnau to have a tomb against such a venerated figure was remarkable.[54]

His killing shocked Christendom almost as much as that of Thomas à Becket in England almost forty years earlier. 'Will no one rid me of this turbulent priest?' Henry II had shouted in 1170 and four knights, hoping for reward, had hacked the archbishop down in his cathedral at Canterbury.

The Pope accused Raymond VI of having plotted a similar crime. The Count could not, asserted Pierre des Vaux-de-Cernay, 'hold back the hatred he conceived against Peter'. The assassin was never named. 'A number of men in Peter's [Pierre] identified the murderer as a member of Raymond's entourage at the abbey'. Guillaume de Tudela, another contemporary chronicler, misreported the killing but was slightly more specific. 'An evil-hearted squire, hoping to win the count's approval, stepped like a traitor behind the legate, drove his sharp sword into his spine and killed him. The man fled at once on his fast horse to his home town of Beaucaire where he had kinsmen'. His motive may have been as self-seeking as those of Thomas à Becket's killers. The Count of Toulouse probably had no part in the matter.[55]

Innocent III, however, had no doubts. Raymond VI was guilty and must be punished. 'For if pestiferous men of this sort, are trying not only to ravage our possessions but also annihilate us ourselves they are not only sharpening their tongues to crush our souls but they are also in reality stretching out their hands to kill our bodies: the perverters of our souls have also become the destroyers of our flesh'. Once more, he excommunicated the count.[56]

Raymond could be hasty, could delay, but he was rarely known to be stupid. For him to plot the death of a papal legate on his own metaphorical doorstep would have been an act of lunacy. He protested his innocence for eighteen months. In the winter of 1209 he even sent an ambassador to Rome but made entirely the worst choice. Raymond of Rabastans, former Bishop of Toulouse, was despised and loathed by Innocent III. In the years around 1200 the bishop had mortgaged every one of his episcopal estates to fund a private war against a personal enemy. He bankrupted the bishopric and it had taken the Pope five tedious years to replace him with Foulques.[57]

Significantly, on the very same day as Pierre de Castelnau's canonisation, 10 March, Innocent III entreated the king yet again to order a crusade, an army of 'Soldiers of God' to suppress the Cathars. In conference earlier with Arnaud Amaury, Bishop of Citeaux, Milo, curial notary, and twelve cardinals, it had been decided that the heretics should be annihilated; a decision 'that left so many men dead with their guts spilled out and so many great ladies and pretty girls naked and cold, stripped of gown and cloak'. From Montpellier to Bordeaux the Cathars were to be destroyed.[58]

Arnaud Amaury and Foulques of Toulouse went from city to city exhorting the nobility to join the holy war. Injudiciously the Pope offered any volunteer part of the estates in the conquered lands. Stiffly, the king reminded the prelate that the fiefs were royal possessions and did not belong to the papacy. Innocent III had no right to dispose of territories belonging to the kingdom of France.

Philippe-Auguste had his own difficulties. John, now King of England, had raised a rebellion in Poitou. Count Otto IV of Germany was threatening to support him. They were, the French king informed the Pope, 'two great lions worrying his flanks'. Reluctantly, he agreed to allow the Crusade but imposed restrictions. The twenty-two year old Dauphin, Prince Louis, would not take part. There would be only a limited number of lords led by two prominent nobles, Eudes, Duke of Burgundy and Hervé, Count of Nevers, both of whose lands were close to Occitania. On 28 March Arnaud Amaury was appointed the spiritual leader of the Crusade.

Among lesser figures were Pierre de Courtenay, Count of Auxerre, and petty barons like Simon de Montfort but there were to be no more than five hundred knights, all from Burgundy. Despite this restriction, the crusade grew into an enormous collection of knightly families not only from south-eastern France but from Germany, Gascony, Poitou, 'the biggest ever to assemble in the Christian world'. There were feudal levies of thousands of common soldiers, many of them peasants, but there was one enormous handicap. Service on the Crusade was limited to forty days for the lord and lowborn alike, a vestigial relic of the 'free' time between planting and harvesting. Unless departing crusaders were continually replaced by new arrivals the holy war might dwindle into a few ineffective bands.[59]

While the host was assembling at Lyons, Raymond VI was hoping to have his excommunication annulled. On 18 June at St.-Gilles he agreed to atone for 'his grievous sins' by taking a solemn oath to obey all the edicts of the Catholic Church – as long as they were not pronounced by Arnaud Amaury. The reservation did not help. The terms were imposed by Milo, now a papal legate, and they were humiliating territorially, mentally and physically.

The Count of Toulouse was to renounce all rights to religious foundations; to restore fortified churches to an unfortified state; to accept all stipulations of the Church; to apologise to the prelates he had offended including the Abbot of Carpentras and the Bishop of Vaison; to surrender seven castles in Provence: Opéde; Mornas, Beaumes de Venise, Roquemaure, Fourques, Montferrand, Largentière; prosecute heretics; dismiss all Jews and mercenaries, the banditry that had caused such destruction in the Languedoc.

Mercenaries, '*routiers*' or men of the road as they were nicknamed, were professional soldiers who did nothing for which they were not paid. They were godless and callously merciless, giving no quarter to man, woman or child, expecting none. They were said to be emblems of hell on earth. Contemptuous of death, living for the pleasurable moment, they were ideal shock-troops, attacking, slaughtering, bloodthirsty, skilful fighters, feared by everyone, even those who paid them.[60]

Raymond, Count of Toulouse, agreed to everything; but the abasement was not done. Naked to the waist, barefooted, he was led to the crowded square in front of the abbey of St.-Gilles. An altar laden with relics had been placed there. Before a disbelieving public and faced by the archbishops of Arles, Auch, Aix-en-Provence, and nineteen bishops a halter was put around his neck and he was ritually scourged by the legate, Milo. Penitent and punished, his excommunication was lifted.

His ordeal was still not finished. The throng of onlookers was so dense that the churchmen were unable to leave the square. Instead they entered the church where Raymond was taken down to the crypt and the tomb of the martyr. There he stood 'naked by the tomb of the blessed martyr . . . whose death he had caused. How just a judgement of God! The Count was compelled to show reverence to the dead body of the man he had used so spitefully whilst he lived'.[61]

The tomb no longer exists. On the wall alongside its shelved recess in the dark crypt there is a slab commemorating the martyr. Opposite on the far wall are the pilgrims' steps by which Raymond VI left the church.

Four days later on 22 June the Count, as always calculating, became a member of the crusading army. He accepted the Cross in St.-Gilles and then rode eighty miles northwards to Valence where he waited the arrival of the army. It was astute and in character. By becoming a crusader his lands were safe. The Church would safeguard them. After his recent degradation he could look forward to attacking his enemies, the Trencavels of Béziers and Carcassonne.

31

TWO

1209: Béziers and Carcassonne

By 24 June, St John's Day, a chaotic army of barons, knights, foot-soldiers, mercenaries, bishops, priests and a mob of hangers-on had assembled at Lyons. It was, claimed the chronicler, 'the greatest Christian army ever mustered'. The King of France, Philippe-Auguste, had refused to lead the Crusade in person but had allowed a number of vassals to participate. Raimond de Cahors, a banker from Montpellier, had underwritten the enterprise. The unforgiving prelate, Arnaud Amaury, Abbot of Citeaux, had been given the task of raising the army whose crusaders were to wear silk crosses on their chests. He has been given a confusion of names: Arnaud, Arnald, Arnold followed by Amaury, Aumary, Aimery and Amalric, often hyphenated. Here the detached pair of French Christian name and surname has been preferred.

Some years before the Crusade the polynomial but inflexibly arrogant prelate had been preaching to the Cathars. They 'laughed at him and scorned him as a fool'. He never forgot. He was fanatical in his persecution of the unbelievers, a spiritually ruthless forerunner of the Inquisition.

To help him in military matters he had the equivocal assistance of two powerful magnates, Eudes III, Duke of Burgundy and Hervé de Donzy, Count of Nevers, two powerful magnates who detested each other.[1]

The Pope offered almost incredible terms to those who volunteered to join the holy war, the first occasion when the term 'crusade' had been used against fellow-Christians. Innocent III promised each crusader remission not only for his past and present sins but also those of the future. All debts were to be suspended and those to Jewish money-lenders annulled. While away from his home a crusader's possessions would be protected by papal edict. To these spiritual attractions was added the very physical likelihood of plunder. Greed as much as piety ensured the size of the Crusade, perhaps gathering in as many ten thousand combatants with a comparable number of camp-followers.[2]

The venture possessed the advantages of a crusade to the Holy Land with the benefit of being much closer. The Languedoc was little more than two hundred miles from Lyons and that rich countryside promised abundant plunder.

It was a vast host that straggled down the valley of the Rhône, an army of lords with feudal levies summoned from their fiefs for the obligatory forty days of military service. The assembly stretched for miles, an untidy crowd of horsemen, clerics, foot-soldiers, crossbowmen, archers, mercenaries, servants, carpenters, sponging drifters intermingling with carts of food and wine in the sweltering heat of a summer in the south of France. It was a line so long that it would have taken a day to walk from the front to the rear. It was a swirl of coughing dust, and a stench of sweating clothes and horses, an odour growing staler and thicker the farther back a person was among the wives, traders, pedlars, pickpockets and prostitutes.

Not all were militant pilgrims. Many were part of an 'ignorant and fanatical multitude which followed each preacher, armed with scythes and clubs, and promised to themselves that if they were not in condition to combat the knights of the Languedoc, they might, at least, be able to murder the women and children of the heretics'. Béziers was to suffer them.[3]

At the dust-free head of the column were the great lords and their squires, the lords on their horses. There were horses everywhere. Even a poor knight had a palfrey for everyday riding and a heavier, short-legged war-horse. A rich nobleman like the Count of Toulouse had a stableful of mounts, at least two palfreys for him on a long day's travel and a rouncey or riding-horse for his squire. There were horses for his mounted men-at-arms, a mule, and hackneys as baggage animals to carry his weapons, armour, tents and food. Above all there was his powerful destrier, a war-horse whose reins were held in the right hand, dexter, of his squire.

It was a valuable animal that had undergone a long training to charge without swerving, never shying or rearing in battle as swords and axes slashed the air around it. A nobleman could pay up to a hundred *livres*, £100, for a good horse. Raymond-Roger Trencavel rode into Béziers on 'his thousand-shilling [£50] horse'. Armour for the horses was becoming fashionable. It was claimed that a knight with an armoured horse was worth two knights without, or eight foot-soldiers.

Palfreys or rounceys were a tenth the price of a destrier and a hackney could be bought for a few sols, shillings, at any local fair. The attractive but lighter jennet from Spain was for ladies. By today's standard none of the steeds was large, bigger than ponies but smaller than a full-grown stallion. They are best compared with the sturdy Suffolk Punch or cob. Destriers walked but seldom galloped. The custom was to bear down on the enemy at a steady canter much as pilgrims on their way to the shrine of Thomas à Becket are said to have ridden comfortably at a 'Canterbury pace'.[4]

The knights were medieval killing machines, trained in weaponry from childhood in exercise, joust and tournament, murderous in their use of dagger, double-edged sword, lance, short-handled battle-axe for a horseman, ball-and-chain, almost invincible in their chain-mail and flat-topped 'pot' helmets over a padded coif or hood. On the Crusade to the Languedoc they advanced righteously and confidently, gonfalon banners aloft streaming with their colours.

With the knights were their sergeants, sometimes squires, always mounted but less well armoured, socially a grade lower and with no more than half the amount of land of a knight. Foot-soldiers and followers trailed behind them under the sun, along the rough tracks, through the dust.

Trotting, trudging, creaking wheels rolling, moving at an ox-plod pace, crossing and recrossing the Rhône, an arsenal of barges drifting along the nearby river with their freight of weapons, dismantled siege-towers, scaling-ladders, battering-rams, the monstrous slings and catapults of trebuchets and mangonels. Keeping pace with the vessels the army not so much advanced as crawled down the old, worn, weathered Roman roads. It was dirty, tiring, no more than eight miles a day for almost two hundred and fifty miles from Lyons to Béziers.

Behind the nobility with their private armies came the mercenaries '*routiers*', mounted brigands and foot-soldiers, and behind them came the *ribauds*, an unwashed riff-raff with no scruples but with an elected king who decreed which of the ruffians should rob corpses, which could be trusted to pay the whores. If mounted knights were the cream of the army, these were the curdlings.

Mercenaries, or routiers, of course, had to be paid and often the wages were the results of scutage or 'shield-money'. A knight's fee demanded his military attendance but if he were old or sick or his fee had been inherited by a woman or a child it was possible to pay for his absence. Often it benefited a lord. The possibly reluctant 'forty-day' man could be replaced by a skilled, unscrupulous fighter who would remain for as long as there was money. Mercenaries, for all their disadvantages, were invaluable in battle. 'And when we rode forth the country trembled before us', one boasted.[5]

From Lyons on 2 July they came to Valence where Raymond VI, having ridden eighty miles from St.-Gilles, had been waiting since 22 June to join them. With him was his squire and his men-at-arms, their upper bodies protected by the cheap equivalent of armour, *cuir bouilli*, toughened leather moulded to shape. With them was a standard-bearer, and a gathering of servants: ostlers, armourers, cooks, scullions, a miniature army in itself. The Count joined the head of the column.

Eight days later, fifty miles farther, Montélimar surrendered. Then onwards from Montélimar to Orange, veering away from the Rhône until at Nîmes the river was fourteen miles to the east. Barges were unloaded. Carts followed the army.

At Montpellier, a town protected by the Pope, and only fifty miles north of Béziers, the young Raymond-Roger Trencavel, Viscount of Béziers, twenty-four years old, asked to be allowed to join the crusade. Arnaud Amaury refused. The Viscount pleaded that his lands contained many Cathars but he had never favoured them. Like any other nobleman he was powerless to suppress the heretics. Innocent III remained unaware of that genuine predicament but Arnaud Amaury understood it and resolutely ignored it. He was determined to eradicate the Cathars and their weak-willed lords by force. He informed Trencavel that the Viscount should defend himself as much as was in his power for the Church would show him no mercy.

Rejected, Trencavel went back to Béziers, ordered its citizens to defend the bridge across the river Orb and delay the army while he would go on to Carcassonne and if possible return with help. He took the city's Jews with him. It was a desperate time. From Montpellier to Béziers was barely six days of travel for the crusading army, less for mounted knights. The citizens would have to depend upon their strong walls.

It has already been noted how disunited the Languedoc was. Externally it was surrounded by enemies, the King of France to the north, the Counts of Provence to the east, the lands of the King of Aragon all along the southern border. To the west there were the English. Even after the loss of Normandy the King of England remained stronger than Philippe-Auguste. From south to north immediately west of the Languedoc the whole of Aquitaine was English and England's claim to the city of Toulouse itself was only relinquished when the sister of Richard I, Joan, was married to Raymond VI.

Internally the Languedoc was fragmented. At its south-eastern corner from Montpellier to Carcassonne the lands of the Trencavels, Viscounts of Béziers and Carcassonne, prodded like a buckled triangle up to its north-western point at Albi, over two thousand square miles that intruded deeply into the heart of Toulousian territory. At the south-west corner of that territory were the smaller but just as independent holdings of the Count of Foix. Around these upstarts like a huge hand grasping and crushing them was the county of Toulouse, from that great city up to Cahors and eastwards to St.-Gilles and Nîmes.

On a map Toulouse appeared dominant. It was an illusion. Never having adopted the principle of primogeniture whereby the eldest son inherited the possessions of his father, every son in that part of France was left a diminishing share. A papal legate observed that there were at least five hundred fiefs in the county of Toulouse that owed no enforceable allegiance to the Count, and that three hundred and fifty of five hundred castles in Trencavel lands gave no service to the viscount.

The geographical situation was made even more complicated by the presence of two powerful orders of Knights with considerable possessions in Languedoc: the Knights Hospitallers, the Order of St John of Jerusalem founded around 1070 to tend sick pilgrims in the Holy City; and the Knights Templars, Knights of Christ and the Temple of Solomon of about 1120, to protect pilgrims on their way to the Holy Land.

Both orders held castles in south-eastern France including St.-Gilles. Mas-Dieu, in Roussillon was one of the most important Templar strongholds not far from Villerouge-Termenès, the scene of the execution of one of the last Good Men, Remoulins was another. Despite their strength, however, neither Templars nor Hospitallers took much part in the coming crusade. It could be said that the Hospitallers tended to side with Toulouse although less for religious reasons than for the generous contributions of land and money that they received. If anything the Templars supported the crusaders. In practice both orders remained neutral and uninvolved in the coming war.[6] But when in 1212 to pay for the costs of the Crusade the Pope imposed a Hearth Tax of three pence across the Languedoc it was the Templars who collected it.

External threats, internal disruption, outside orders, everything splintered the countryside creating distrust, petty feuds among minor knights agitating beneath the much larger disputes between counts and viscounts. Because of the disagreements and quarrels there was to be no concerted resistance to the crusading army as it reached Béziers. With its many troubadours the Languedoc was called a land of song. It was to become a *'terre de sang'*, a land of blood.

At Béziers the mood was calm. The Viscount had gone but reinforcements would be sent, the walls were thick and high, provisions were plentiful and, as everyone knew, the crusade was effectively limited to forty days of service, less than six weeks. The city could resist a siege for much longer than that. The citizens deepened the city's defensive ditches, closed the gates and waited.

On 21 July, arriving with the army, the aged Bishop of Béziers, Reginald de Montpeyroux, entered the city and advised the consuls to surrender. They should give up the city's heretics and save their own lives. The majority refused, thinking 'no more of his advice than of a peeled apple . . . They would rather be drowned in the salt sea . . . the crusaders should not get so much as a pennyworth of their possessions'. It was obvious that the invading host was far too big to endure 'for it stretched out for a full league long and could barely be contained on the roads and pathways' . . . Even after a month's siege Béziers could not be stormed. . . . Rather than commit the baseness demanded of us we would eat our own children'. The Bishop left, taking with him a list of the known Cathars in Béziers.[7]

He knew very well that the citizens could be rough. Four years earlier his own predecessor, Guillaume de Roquessels, had been murdered by them. They had, wrote Pierre des Vaux-de-Cernay, even killed their own lord, Raymond-Roger's grandfather, for infringing upon their liberties, 'and broke the teeth of their Bishop' when he tried to defend the man. They were heathens and ruffians. 'One night just at daybreak a priest of the city was going to his church to celebrate the divine mysteries, carrying a chalice. Some of the citizens laid an ambush, seized him and beat him violently, breaking his arm and seriously wounding him. They took the chalice, disrobed him and urinated on him to show contempt for the body and blood of Christ'.[8]

Back in the camp, Reginald de Montpeyroux gave the list of heretics to Arnaud Amaury. It contained some two hundred names, presumably those of the heads of Cathar families in a city of well over ten thousand inhabitants. The social status of the heretics was very varied, a baron, four doctors, and a medley of craftsmen: hosiers, blacksmiths, cobblers, a carpenter, weaver, saddler, corn-merchant, cutler, tailor, taverner, baker, money-lender. Weavers had traditionally been closely associated with Catharism. Significantly, the list contained at least ten artisans involved in the textile industry.[9]

Outside Béziers in their encampment the crusaders were anxious. The besieged city was strongly fortified. The bishop had informed them that food was plentiful, and there were only forty days to starve the people out. Arguments about tactics continued between the hostile leaders, one demanding an assault, the other more cautiously advocating a siege. Amid the indecision the mercenaries, notoriously unreliable, might wander off for plunder where it was easier to obtain.

Meanwhile, farther to the west, about a hundred miles from Bordeaux, in the heartlands of Catharism, a minor crusade under Guy, Count of Clermont and Auvergne and the Archbishop of Bordeaux accompanied by the bishops of Limoges, Bazas, Cahors and Agen, was preparing to attack the heretical towns. Near Cahors the army was joined by a second detachment under the guidance of the Bishop of Le Puy-en-Velay. With little opposition the crusaders rapidly took Caussade, St.-Antonin and the unresisting bastide of Puylaroque.

Farther to the west at Tonneins the bishops condemned several Cathars to be burnt at the stake to destroy their evil bodies and save their souls. It was the first of many executions. 'The crusaders regarded their capture as the object and recompense of their enterprise. Men and women were all precipitated into the flames, amid the acclamations of their ferocious conquerors; all the wealth found in the castle was afterwards given up to pillage'. Neighbouring villages were sacked.[10]

Casseneuil on the River Lot was only fifteen miles away but it defied the invaders. With rivers on three sides and with a steep ditch at the south-east it was a redoubtable stronghold and one that was vigorously defended by its knights and Gascon mercenaries brought there by Casseneuil's lord, Seguin de Balenx.

The Gascons used two fearful weapons. The crossbow had a very limited range and was clumsy to reload but its bolts were deadly when fired from high walls down into a crowd of jostling attackers. So murderous was the bow that in 1139 the Church forbade its use against Christians.

When the besiegers retreated in defeat from the killing ramparts they were assailed by the mercenaries hurling 'dards', thin, shortened spears that could be thrown accurately from some distance and penetrate even chain mail. Only *dardasiers* could have such an effect upon armoured foes. Under his body-length mail a knight wore a thick quilted underjacket lined with heavy leather almost impenetrable by ordinary missiles.

Confronted by a possible disaster the Count of Auvergne, always a reluctant combatant against his own people, insisted on making terms with the defenders. Guillaume de Tudela understood why. The crusaders, he wrote, 'would have taken the place if Count Guy had not prevented it. He had much property there, and so he quarrelled with the Archbishop on this score'. The Archbishop accused him of betraying the Church but the western crusade was petering out.[11]

There was a last flicker of panic. Sixty miles to the south-east, the appalled inhabitants of Villemur-sur-Tarn were told on Sunday, 21 June 1209 that the army had left Casseneuil and was advancing towards them. Without waiting for confirmation of the false report 'They set fire to their own stronghold on the Monday evening and burned it down and then fled away by moonlight'.[12]

The day before, the main army of the Crusade had reached Béziers. To the attackers the city was dismayingly forbidding, high on its steep escarpment, its walls tall with stark towers climbing above them. Some of the defences are still visible. Water was plentiful. The River Orb flowed close to the west gate where a bridge led onto the Narbonne and Carcassonne road. A siege would be long. Lives would be lost. Inside the city Bernard of Servian was organising the defences.

The crusaders camped on the sandy plain at the south-west of the citadel. At a distance far enough away to be safe from a surprise attack they set up the tents of the knights and the luxurious pavilions of the nobles. Nearer the river were the makeshift shanties of the mercenaries and the ragged pole-propped shelters of the *ribauds*.

The onset of the assault was planned for the following day. Carpenters assembled the machines that would hurl heavy rocks against the walls and gates, the catapults of mangonels and the heavier trebuchet, ponderous and inaccurate but capable of flinging massive boulders to smash at the ramparts. There were siege-towers, battering-rams, scaling ladders, 'cats', those mobile hide-covered shelters that 'crept like cats' up the walls, protecting their occupants from the stones and arrows of the defenders. 'The cat which Simon de Montfort produced at Toulouse in 1218 was particularly large, holding 400 knights, and 150 archers; it was made of wood, iron and steel, with a platform, a door, and a roof'.[13]

Squires examined the armour of their lord. Knights had swords sharpened. Foot-soldiers checked their halberds, axes and pikes. It was noisy, methodical and merciless. 'The lords from France and Paris, laymen and clergy, great nobles and marquises, all agreed that at every castle the army approached, a garrison that refused to surrender should be slaughtered wholesale, once the castle had been taken by storm'. If there was unconditional surrender then only the mercenaries would be killed. It was a rule of war that applied to men. Women and children were always excluded from the slaughter.[14] Béziers was to be an exception.

Amid the bustle of arms and armour the church was not forgotten. Bishops went from tent to tent blessing the crusaders. Groups of monks sang the *Te Deum* and chanted holy verses.

> White was his naked breast,
> And red with blood his side,
> Blood on his tragic face,
> His wounds deep and wide.
>
> Stiff with death his arms,
> On the cross wide spread,
> From five gashes in his side
> The sacred blood flowed red.

Dawn came early on Monday, 22 July. It was the Feast Day of Ste Marie Magdeleine, a woman that Cathars mocked as the concubine of Christ. Some authors of modern books about Rennes-le-Château argue that Mary Magdalene had married Jesus and went with him to the Languedoc where they were buried together in a mountain near Arques a few miles east of the ancient Visigothic capital.[15] It is likely that neither Cathars nor today's revisionists knew the truth. Devout Catholics in Béziers simply worshipped in her church, Ste.-Marie-Magdeleine.

In that city and in the camp of the besiegers most people still slept. But that dawn was about to become the turning-point of the war. There was an incident, almost a frivolity, but it was fatal.

History is filled with the words, 'If only . . .'. If only Marshal Ney had obeyed Napoleon in 1815 and made Quatre-Bras his headquarters he could have prevented the British and Prussian armies uniting and the French might have won the battle of Waterloo. If only there had not been an irresponsible sally from the gates of Béziers the ambitious Crusade might have dwindled into little more than a scorched-earth campaign of trampled crops and vines, burnt-out villages, corpses of suspected heretics dangling from trees. The great cities would have been left untouched, unaffected by assault. But there was a sally.

Perhaps contemptuous of the filthy ragamuffins lurking under their city walls and knowing that the real army of knights and soldiers was too far away to be a threat a band of young men rushed out of the gates, shouting, shrieking, waving untidy flags of white cloth. Catching one of the *ribauds* on the bridge, they stabbed him and threw the corpse into the river.

Awakened by the noise and seeing the murder of one of his men, the 'king' of the *ribauds* ordered an immediate attack on the city. Seizing clubs, tent-poles, anything to hand the ruffians in torn shirts and trousers raced barefoot across the river and up to the walls. They stormed the gate. They clambered up ladders. Taken by surprise, awakening from sleep, the disorganised defenders were helpless and within less than an hour the city had been overpowered by a riff-raff whose only weapons were knives and cudgels.

There were hundreds, perhaps thousands of them and they were murderous. They stabbed, cut, slew anyone they met, bursting into houses for victims and plunder, out into the streets again, encountering defenceless men, hysterical women and shrieking children as the citizens fled to the protection of the churches.

There was no protection. Catholic clergy in their vestments tolled the bells as though for a funeral, people huddled by the altars, but the invaders broke in: into the cathedral of St.-Nazaire, into the churches of St.-Aphrodise, St.-Jacques, St.-Jude, Ste.-Marie-Magdeleine. Whomever they found, they killed. There were no survivors, wrote the chronicler. 'No cross or altar or crucifix could save them. And these raving, beggarly lads, they killed the clergy too, and the women and the children. I doubt if one person came out alive'.[16]

Aroused by the racket of clamorous bells and distant screams, realising with astonishment that the impregnable city was theirs, the knights prepared themselves. Armed and mounted they had one question. How were they to distinguish between Catholic and Cathar? According to legend it was Arnaud Amaury, Abbot of Citeaux, who gave them the infamous command, 'Caedite eos. Novit enim Dominus qui sunt eis', 'Kill them all. God will know his own'. Legend may be truth. It was a learned answer based on a deep knowledge of both Testaments: 'The Lord knoweth those that are His'; from Timothy in the New, and 'The Lord will show who are his, and who are holy' from Numbers in the Old. It was the response of an educated churchman, an order from his holy lips that absolved the knights from any wrongdoing. Only Amaury could have given such an order. A few years later the Cistercian monk, Caesarius of Heisterbach, confirmed that he had given it.[17]

It also suggests that Amaury and the bishops, all of them mocked and insulted by heretics in the past, had already decided that Béziers should be a warning of what any resistance would incur. Catharism was to be eliminated even if the innocent had to suffer. It was genocide for the benefit of Christianity.

What ruffians had begun the knights finished. At least a thousand of their prey, although not the impossible seven thousand of popular belief, were slaughtered in the church of Ste.-Marie-Magdeleine. 'A jumble of bones, the victims of the massacre, was discovered under the floor of the church during renovations in 1840'. The Cistercian monk, Pierre des Vaux-de-Cernay thought the carnage justified. 'It was right that these shameless dogs should be captured and destroyed on the feast day of the woman they had insulted and whose church they had defiled with the blood of their lord, the Viscount, and their bishop'.[18] The massacre was over before noon, just three hours of pitiless bloodshed. What Raymond VI, Count of Toulouse, did during this assault on his enemy's city is unrecorded.

As so often in the confusion of battle there was an ironical aftermath. The *ribauds* had overrun the city on their own, doing the knights' work for them, and for their enterprise they had rifled and looted and made themselves rich beyond their limited imaginations. The highborn knights were furious. By the accepted rules of warfare all booty belonged to them alone and this infringement of the courtesies of chivalry enraged them. They clubbed and beat the scoundrels and recovered the wealth. In revenge the deprived riff-raff set fire to the timber dwellings of the city, and fetching 'huge flaming brands as if for a funeral pyre set the town alight. Panic spread and the town blazed from end to end'. The roof of Ste.-Marie-Magdeleine fell in.[19] The flames of the pyre could be seen for miles across an appalled countryside.

In a letter to Innocent III Arnaud Amaury exulted at the bloodshed. 'Neither age, nor sex, nor status had been spared'. There was no compunction, no sympathy for the innocent. Catholics in the city could have given up the Cathars. They were equally guilty.

How many had died is unknown. It was a multitude. The city may have had a population of about ten thousand inhabitants but that number must have been swollen by crowds of refugees from the villages. 'The abbot of Citeaux, feeling some shame for the butchery which he had ordered, in his letter to Innocent III reduced it to fifteen thousand, others make it amount to sixty'. One can only state that the deaths must have extended into the thousands.[20]

The Catholic troubadour, Gormonda, made an oblique apology for a massacre that had occurred on the actual Feast Day of the saint.

Greu m'es a durar' . . .   It's hard to bear it
                                  When I hear such false belief . . .

Roma.l Glorios . . .   Rome, may the Glorious One
                                  who pardoned Mary Magdalen . . .
                                  kill the rabid fool
                                  who sows so much false speech,
                                  he and his treasure and his evil heart;
                                  and when he dies may he die
                                  in the torments suffered by heretics.

Guiraut Riquier of Narbonne, one of the last of the troubadours, born around 1230 over twenty years after the tragedy, a man who lamented the passing of Languedoc's courtly, artistic life, 'Evil's so proud they've put Good up for sale', composed a canso about the sack of Béziers. Of his one hundred and one surviving poems the melodies of forty-eight are still known. The tune for this one is lost. The bitterness remains.

> Béziers has fallen. They're dead.
> Clerks, women, children. No quarter.
> They killed Christians too.
> I rode out. I couldn't see or hear
> A living creature.
> I saw Simon de Montfort.
> His beard glistened in the sun.
> They killed seven thousand people,
> Seven thousand souls who sought sanctuary
> In Ste.-Madeleine.
> The steps of the altar
> Were wet with blood.
> The church echoed with their cries.
> Afterwards they slaughtered the monks
> Who tolled the bells.
> They used the silver cross
> As a chopping-block to behead them.[21]

A psychological obstacle to an understanding of the reasons for medieval brutality is the conditioning of the modern mind. In the thirteenth century death was a daily, even hourly happening.

Existence today is sanitised. A relative dies in a hospital bed. Disasters are reported in newspapers but few readers will have witnessed the killing of an animal, let alone a fatal accident to a human being. The countryside is a pleasant region to visit on holiday and livestock in fields are unfamiliar objects of interest. They die unseen. Pre-packaged food arrives in refrigerated lorries. Centuries ago life was different.

Death was a commonplace. So was pain. In the farms and villages cattle, sheep, poultry were slaughtered in the open air as the occasion required, flayed, disembowelled, blood sluiced away, guts and offal dumped in middens of reeking, rotting flesh and splintered bone. It was ordinary.

Nor was death camouflaged from cities. There were no closed delivery vans. In the Middle Ages herds were driven through undrained streets that stank of their dung. Within the walls the beasts were taken to the butchers' 'shambles', slaughtered and cut up for sale. Unplucked, gutted birds hung outside poulterers' shutters. At the gates and on hills there were gallows. Death was a commonplace.

People were not indifferent to suffering but accustomed to it. And to what the eyes were used to, the mind added another dimension. The Crusade was not a contest between Christian and Christian. The bellowing of a terrified cow or the screaming of a follower of Satan were accepted as events ordained by God. It was not Christian against Christian but Christian against sub-humans who denied Christ, the Cross and Communion. Death was justified. Béziers was on nobody's conscience.

Three days of rest for the crusaders followed as the fires of the holocaust diminished. On the fourth, leaving the burnt-out wreckage of the city behind them, the Crusade rode out into a countryside of ghost towns, their welcome granaries untouched, abandoned by Cathar and Catholic alike. The horrified citizens of Narbonne instantly capitulated. The army moved on towards Carcassonne, passing just a few miles north of the lovely Cistercian abbey of Fontfroide where Pierre de Castelnau had been a monk, where Arnaud Amaury was to die.

On 28 July the first crusaders rode up to Carcassonne. By the first of August the main body of the army arrived and the siege began. The defences were even more daunting than those of Béziers, today the largest medieval fortress city in Europe, rampart within rampart, towers, barbicans, a turreted castle, 'the wonderful city . . . the sight of which still seems to transport the visitor into the Middle Ages'. When the invading English army of the Black Prince saw it in November 1355 they quickly burnt the lower town whose inhabitants 'fled to the old city, which was a very strong castle', the prince wrote to the Bishop of Winchester. He did not besiege it.[22]

What is seen today is not the citadel of 1209. The outer wall with its seventeen towers was the handiwork of Louis IX in the mid-thirteenth century when, in 1247, he also had the chequerboard pattern of streets of the lower town laid out on the scorched remains of the earlier settlement. To provide it with water he had the River Aude diverted. Thirty years later Philip III, the Bold, further strengthened the defences of the town, which became known as the Maid of Languedoc.

But Carcassonne was to become a backwater. With the Treaty of Roussillon in 1659 the boundary of France was extended over a hundred miles to the south and the huge fortification was neglected. The walls were used as quarries. Towers decayed. It was only the intervention in 1835 of Prosper Merimée, French novelist and Inspector-General of Historical Remains, dismayed at the deterioration, that led the government to appoint the architect and archaeologist, Eugéne Viollet-le-Duc, to begin the work of restoration in 1844.

The results are contentious: gun-emplacements removed, roofs and turrets redesigned, too much imaginative romanticism although the work did preserve the military magnificence. The writer, Henry James, was impressed but sceptical about the reconstruction, 'moving but almost too perfect – as if it were an enormous model, placed on a big green table at a museum'.

Today Carcassonne is for tourists. There is a sense of newness. Souvenir shops, a miniature railway, guided tours, cardboard cut-out models, Carcassonne sweat-shirts and badges, cafés, they are all there but it still possible to stroll along the walks between the walls with towers rising high above, still possible to tramp up the steep ramp to the Aude gateway just as people did in 1209.[23]

Even then it was ancient, a sixth century Visigothic citadel on a Roman site. In the twelfth century the old walls were reinforced by an ancestor of Raymond-Roger, Viscount of Béziers and Carcassonne, who added a great castle. Raymond-Roger himself had timber hoardings constructed to overhang the battlements from which defenders could hurl murderous stones and boiling oil on to attackers.[24]

It was strong but there was a weakness. The position was well-chosen on a high and steep spur of the Corbières but it had been a compromise. The city was almost a quarter of a mile east of the Aude and the crusaders immediately took control of the Pont Vieux that crossed the river. Carcassonne was dependent on its own internal wells in the middle of a long, hot summer.

On 3 August the army attacked the outskirts of the city. With monks intoning, '*Veni Sancte Spiritus*', 'Come, Holy Spirit, fill the hearts of Thy faithful', which was to be the anthem of the Crusade, the walls of the north suburb, the Bourg, were overrun in two short hours. The southern outpost, the Castellar, was more obstinate. For four days sappers under the protection of their 'cats' undermined and breached the walls. Catapults bombarded the houses. The inhabitants fled to the citadel leaving their homes burning behind them.[25]

Stalemate followed. The approaches to the citadel were steep and wide and even the gigantic trebuchets could not project their missiles so far. The lighter mangonels and petraries were used but to little effect. Assaults were driven back by the crossbows. There was no impetuous sally from the gates. Under the sun the crusaders waited in frustration.

It was during that impasse that Pedro II, King of Aragon arrived with a token retinue of a hundred knights. Monarch since 1196, brother-in-law of Raymond VI, dedicated Catholic and even more dedicated womaniser, he was concerned that the lands of his vassal and liege, the Viscount of Béziers and Carcassonne, should not become the property of some petty baron from northern France.

Those lands held the overland routes to Provence and the Mediterranean. The king was militarily too weak to oppose the crusaders but he could negotiate on Raymond-Roger's behalf and perhaps achieve some form of truce.

Resting for a while in the comfort of Raymond VI's tent in a meadow by the river he then went with three companions into Carcassonne. The city was packed and stifling. He told the young Viscount that the crusaders were prepared to allow him and eleven of his men to leave the city under safe conduct taking what they could with them. Everyone else would be killed. The city would be spared as those crusaders who remained in the Languedoc would need a well-protected base.

The terms were not only harsh, imposed by the grim mind of Arnaud Amaury, but they were not to be trusted. Even Pedro doubted them. 'When donkeys fly we shall see that happen', he is reported to have said about the so-called safe-conduct. Raymond-Roger refused to abandon his subjects whom the prelate had cursed as a nest of heretics. 'I would suffer myself to be flayed alive. He shall not have the least of my company at his mercy, for it is on my account that they are in danger'.[26]

The siege was resumed. Another attack was ordered. Bundles of wood were dumped in the ditches to allow men to reach the walls but cascades of boiling water and oil, stones and arrow-bolts repelled the soldiers. They retreated.

It was a critical time for both sides. For many of the knights and their feudal levies the forty days of service were reaching an end. The siege would have to be abandoned with as much dignity as possible. Inside Carcassonne there were quite different misgivings. The wells and cisterns were supposedly failing in the sultry weather. There were, it is said, too many mouths to quench. There is a contradiction that is seldom mentioned but will shortly be discussed. Whatever the truth, the besieged garrison did have problems. There were mosquitoes. Meat was rotting in the unceasing heat and attracting swarms of black meat-flies. A parley was arranged.

On 14 August under the promise of safe-conduct Raymond-Roger and nine others were allowed to enter the crusaders' camp to the tent of the Count of Nevers where the conditions under which the occupants of Carcassonne would be allowed to go free were to be decided. It would be in the minimum of clothing and with no possessions. Reluctantly the terms were accepted in the presence of Arnaud Amaury.

As anticipated, treachery followed. In spite of all the promises of good faith Raymond-Roger was clamped in chains and imprisoned in one of his own chillingly damp and maladorous dungeons. To the closed mind of Arnaud Amaury it was not betrayal but a justified punishment for a known protector of heretics, a man who had dared to oppose the army of Christ.

Next day the inhabitants of Carcassonne left 'bearing nothing but their sins', applauded Pierre des Vaux-de-Cernay. Guillaume de Tudela noted that they were 'quite unprotected, they rushed out pell-mell in their shirts and breeches, nothing else, not even the value of a button were they allowed to take with them'. Inexplicably, not one Cathar of that cesspit of heresy was arrested. Others also got away without penalty. Peter-Roger, a fierce warrior who was to bedevil the crusaders, escaped to his castle of Cabaret at Lastours, rumour having it that he and his men had used a subterranean passage out of Carcassonne.[27] The citadel became the headquarters of the Crusade.

The affair is a mystery. It is stated that Carcassonne capitulated because its wells were dry and there was no water. Yet when the crusaders entered they found not only riches but also 'many mules and horses', all of which would have had to be fed. Water must have been plentiful.

To mystery must be added perplexity. This was a crusade against Catharism and it was to be merciless. In his letter to the Catholics of Narbonne and elsewhere Innocent III was explicit. 'You must try in whatever ways God has revealed to you to wipe out the treachery of heresy and its followers by attacking the heretics with a strong hand and an outstretched arm'. But no one was wiped out. Men, women, children, Catholic and Cathar, all went free except Raymond-Roger, the Viscount.

It is arguable that military necessity outdid religious zeal. The army needed the safeguard of a secure fortress and Carcassonne was ideally placed, thirty miles from Narbonne to the east, thirty-six to Ax-les-Termes at the south, forty-five to Albi and Toulouse to north and west respectively. The citizens were unharmed and so was the city, left not so much to its conquerors as to its secretive negotiators. Arnaud Amaury had the one consolation of the imprisoned Viscount.[28]

The contented crusaders pillaged the city, piling everything valuable into one enormous heap. Arnaud Amaury refused to allow them to keep it. All the booty was to be given to the leader chosen to continue the Church's crusade against the heretics of the Languedoc. There was reluctant and not entirely unanimous consent. Knights were elected to watch over the riches of gold and silver, fabrics and weapons. Three months later some of them were excommunicated for having purloined goods to the sum of five thousand *livres*, a *livre* being the medieval equivalent of a pound's weight of silver.[29]

With the forty days' service coming to an end the Crusade needed a leader who would continue the struggle. The three most powerful nobles, the Duke of Burgundy, the Count of Nevers and the Count of St.-Pol all refused for a variety of reasons, some of them honest. They had plenty of land already. They considered it dishonourable to accept another person's inheritance. To acquire vast estates in the south of France would establish a very dangerous precedent against the king who would not want over-powerful barons in such a distant part of his realm.

There were other considerations. Captured land could be recaptured. As well as apprehension there was terror. In that superstitious age men feared that there was a curse on the Trencavel lands. The three cautious noblemen, moreover, were aware that of the many castles and strongholds in the Languedoc only two had yet been overcome. Conquering the others would demand a long and bitter campaign. They would rather go home.[30]

At the end of August a committee of Arnaud Amaury, two bishops and four minor lords elected a little-known knight, Simon de Montfort IV, as the new leader. His credentials were impressive. Born of an ancient aristocratic family he was Lord of Montfort-

52

l'Amaury with lands in the Rambouillet forest of the Ile de France near Paris. The second son of Anglo-Norman parents he was the titular Count of Leicester in England but those estates had been sequestered by King John who would not allow a loyal vassal of France to occupy an English fief. De Montfort has an additional place in history. He was the father of the famous English Simon de Montfort who was to defeat Henry III at the Battle of Lewis in 1264 only to be defeated and killed by the king's son, Prince Edward, at Evesham in the following year.

The knight had no qualms in accepting his nomination although he did have reservations about his status. Unlike the great noblemen who had refused the honour he possessed little land in northern France so had no fear of the French king confiscating it. He was already a distinguished warrior who had fought against Richard I.

His was an uncomplicated character, straightforward, religious, devoutly Catholic. 'My work is the work of Christ . . .', he stated. He sincerely hated all forms of heresy. Monogamous, he was as faithful and loyal to his wife, Alice de Montmorency, the daughter of the Constable of France, as she was to him. She bore him seven children. Pierre des Vaux-de-Cernay greatly admired her for her piety, wisdom and compassion.

To these considerable virtues she added determination. During the campaigns that followed she brought reinforcements to her husband at the siege of Termes. There she pleaded with men not to desert their leader. She travelled hundred of miles to Paris to intercede on his behalf with the king. She assisted over-burdened soldiers as they struggled through the hills. Pierre des Vaux-de-Cernay who was with her remembered how she gave her horse to two exhausted men and walked along the rough, sun-burning trails. Trapped inside a castle at Toulouse she successfully resisted attacks.

Her reputation was so high that without being inconvenienced by any need for proof or credibility, Maurice Maugre, twentieth century Cathar apologist, maligned her as 'a creature with rotting teeth, sallow skin the colour of Sicilian lemons and a big nose'.[31] It was unpleasant and unjustified. There is no contemporary description of the countess.

She was not untypical of her times. The popular impression of downtrodden, physically abused wives of the Middle Ages, spinning and weaving, meekly obeying every command of their husbands, is misleading. There were many strong-willed women. One thinks of the Cathar noblewomen, Esclarmonde and Fornière, of the dominant queens, Eleanor of Aquitaine and Blanche of Castile, of troubadour women like Gormonda. So far from being the acquiescent playthings of men there is even a hint of lesbianism in a canso addressed to a lady, Mary, by the female troubadoure Biétris de Roman:

Qui mi donetz, bella dompna, si tu platz . . .   so you will grant me, lovely lady,
        please,
        what I most hope to enjoy,
        for in you lie my heart and my
        desire.

Even Béatrice of Planisolles chose her own, although more conventional, pleasures. Long before Joan of Arc there were many French women of character. Alice, Countess of Montfort, wife of Simon, was one of them.[32]

For a soldier in the Middle Ages de Montfort was old, in his forties. In appearance he was tall, long-haired, firmly built, of endless stamina and valour. At Carcassonne, accompanied by only one squire, he jumped into the ditch under an avalanche of stones and arrows to rescue a wounded foot-soldier. To these formidable but ordinary qualities he possessed a virtue that would affect the course of the crusade. He was a military genius, with an unusual understanding of tactics and strategy, a great leader who inspired loyalty in everyone at all times. He was also unyielding and singlemindedly ruthless, using terror as a weapon. 'He prayed, took Communion and killed as easily as drawing breath'.[33] At first he refused to accept the leadership but finally consented as long as he was given Raymond's titles of Viscount of Béziers and Carcassonne.

In the Autumn of 1209 the Crusade was abandoned and De Montfort was left with little more than a token force of about thirty knights and some five hundred soldiers, 'falcons'. Even though safe in Carcassonne he had understandable anxieties. 'Very few of his friends decided to stay with him; most of them preferred to go back to the neighbourhood of Paris. The mountains were wild and the passes dangerous and none of them wanted to be killed in that country. However, some nine or ten of the greatest lords did stay'.[34] With that travesty of a military force he had to man a dozen captured castles and maintain an army in the field.

On the tenth of November, almost three months after his arrest, the Viscount, Raymond-Roger Trencavel, died in his cell. Immediately there were accusations of murder. It is unlikely. Locked deep in the pits of the castle, incapable of escape or rescue, malnourished in his unsanitary cell, dysentery was the probable cause. No one benefited from his death. Simon de Montfort had the body cleaned and dressed and buried it in state in the cathedral of St.-Nazaire. In exchange for an annual pension of three thousand *livres*, and twenty-five thousand *sols melgoriens* in cash the Viscount's widow, Agnès of Montpellier, surrendered all rights to her dowry including the pair of adjacent fortified towns of Pézenas and Tourbes just north of Béziers.[35]

The motto of the young Viscount had been '*J'offre une ville . . .*' 'I offer a town, a roof, a shelter, bread and my sword to all the persecuted people who will soon be wandering in Provence without a town, or roof, or place of refuge, or bread'. It was sadly prophetic.

The Viscount's tomb has been destroyed, as has that of Simon de Montfort, but the church does contain a curious relic of the Albigensian crusade. Once worn-down by the feet of worshippers but now safe from damage, attached to the wall by the north transept, is a large slab of white and pink marble whose fourteenth century inscription is of Sans Morlane who died in 1311. He had been an archdeacon of Ste.-Marie-de-la-Bourg-Neuf, a church destroyed in the mid-eighteenth century for a covered market in the lower town. Morlane had not been a Good Man but he did attend many Cathar meetings and during the time of the Inquisition he plotted to steal and destroy some leather bags containing lists of suspected heretics. Discovered and denounced to the Pope by an Inquisitor, Jean Galand, the pontiff simply condemned the Inquisitor's own actions as illegal.

The epitaph of Sans Morlane is the only one known of a Cathar.[36]

THREE

1209–1210. Towns and Castles

In their hundreds and thousands the host left Carcassonne, barons, lords, knights, foot-soldiers, feudal levies, mercenaries who saw no likelihood of pay, the cheated and penniless hooligans, almost everyone departed in the summer of 1209. Only Simon de Montfort, Viscount of Béziers and Carcassonne, a score or more of knights, nicknamed 'falcons', with their men and a few mercenaries who demanded double pay, remained, a remnant of the multitude that had engulfed the Languedoc.

A defeatist would have no thought of staying. It was almost September. Winter was coming. There were no supply lines. There were fewer, very many fewer than a thousand men to dominate almost ten thousand square miles of a region to which they were strangers, an unknown land of hostile southerners, innumerable castles and defensive towers, fortified towns, a landscaped bewilderment of rivers, marshes, hills hidden behind mountains, a wilderness of ravines and gorges ideal for ambushes.

De Montfort was not a defeatist but he was an experienced soldier and he decisively imposed himself upon the Languedoc. Regions had to be taken and governed by his lieutenants. Bouchard de Marly with his followers was put in charge of the castle of Saissac twelve miles north-west of Carcassonne. Guillaume de Contres was sent back to Béziers to protect the Biterrois countryside to the east. Lambert de Crécy was ordered to strengthen the walls of Limoux near Rennes-le-Château, the town that a hundred years later Béatrice of Planisolles hoped would conceal her from the Inquisition.[1]

De Montfort himself planned his own short autumn campaign. He went to the pleasantly wooded and hilly countryside of the Lauragais just west and north of Carcassonne where every town and village was occupied by Cathars, the reason why Dominic had gone there and settled in Fanjeaux a few years earlier. The area was not a hotbed of heresy, it was an inferno.

Within thirty miles of Castelnaudary, a resort famous today for its cassoulet, that savouringly thick stew of haricot beans, sausage, port, goose and red garlic,[2] but eight centuries ago the heartland of anti-Catholicism, there were places that were to become notorious: Labécède-Lauragais whose crusader garrison would be slaughtered; Les Cassès where there was to be a mass execution of Cathars; Saissac in whose forests de Marly was captured; Avignonet where monks were brutally massacred and whose priest was a secret sympathiser of the Cathars, as were the priests of Sorèze and St.-Félix-Lauragais.

It was a region to be suppressed. With hardly more than a troop de Montfort rode out and with that troop he triumphed. To defenceless country people his soldiers were a commandingly fearsome danger with their tunics of the red cross, knights on their war-horses, men in chain-mail with swords and shields, veterans of Béziers marching with crossbows and pikes and long-handled axes, these were terrible invaders. Added to that physical threat there was a greater dread. Days before the arrival of the war-band there came, like a mist drifting before them, the frightening possibility that there could be a second Béziers.

Everyone had heard of that pitiless bloodshed. Everyone had surrendered. There were no leaders. Trencavel was in prison. Raymond VI had joined the Crusade. Raymond-Roger, Count of Foix, had no army capable of opposing even so few crusaders.

Montréal just west of Carcassonne was taken. With no men to spare and as the town was so close to the citadel and its protection, de Montfort left Montréal in the charge of its Catholic priest. Some miles farther to the west was Prouille where Dominic had founded his hospice-cum-convent. On the hill above it were the narrow streets of Fanjeaux, a small town silhouetted on its upland like a basking whale.

On its outskirts today is a bridge on which stands a circular stone cross considered by some to be a relic of the Cathars left behind by Good Men when they quitted the town. It is not. It is a Greek or Toulousian cross with four lobates. Cathars, with their rejection of the physical crucifixion of Christ, abhorred the symbol of the cross as a corruption of Christianity.[3]

Fanjeaux was an established Cathar stronghold. There had been a women's community there for years and the grand-daughter of the noblewoman, Guillelme of Tonneins, remembered visiting it and being given bread, wine, nuts and fruit. There was a weavers' workshop. Apprenticed in it Peter of Gramazie became a convert. The town had been the home of many Good Men such as William of Carlipa, Peter Belhomme and Arnold Clavel. Some of them went to the safety of Montségur on the approach of the crusaders. There was also ambiguity. Na Cavaëre, *la dame chevalier*, was a devout Cathar but made donations to the Catholic convent in Prouille and, in her old age, became a nun there.[4]

When Simon de Montfort arrived Fanjeaux, despite its tall walls and deep moats, was deserted. Its frightened inhabitants had fled, taking what they could with them, leaving a town of abandoned houses and empty streets. There was silence. Yet only five years earlier townspeople had gazed in awed respect at the opulence of the assembled aristocracy of the Languedoc, the men in ankle-length, fur-lined tunics over bright shirts, heads covered in coifs like skull-caps but ingeniously exposing the neatly-trimmed beards and moustaches, the ladies in embroidered kirtles with their skirts trailing behind them. It was a dazzling group and it included the Count of Foix who had come to see his sister, Esclarmonde, ordained as a Good Woman by the Cathar Bishop of Toulouse, Guilhabert of Castres. Now there was no one. Even the castle of the Cathar lord, William of Durfort, was vacant. De Montfort made it his headquarters.

Early in September he embarked on 'a series of raids spreading out in all directions like the points of a star which enabled him to install his followers in the country around'.[5] Towns as far away as Albi became his. So did Bram, Bellegarde, Gontaud, Mirepoix to the west, Preixan to the south whose lord, Raymond-Roger of Foix, left his son there as a hostage to prove his good faith.[6]

Late in September Castres, a town thirty miles north of Castelnaudary, sent a deputation offering submission to the crusaders. It was the major town in the vicinity of Albi which today is a busy city of a hundred exits, most of them unsignposted.

While de Montfort was inspecting the defences of Castres two suspected Cathars were tried in his presence.[7] Both were condemned. One, a Good Man, said nothing. The other, a believer, recanted, forswearing his beliefs, begging to be restored to the Catholic church. There was argument between the clergymen. Some wanted clemency, others shrugged. The man was a hypocrite. His 'conversion' was not a true rediscovery of faith. It was cowardice and the fear of a painful death.

The court compromised. The man should still be burned because if he were sincerely contrite then the fire would expiate his sins. If he had lied then his punishment was justified. The men were taken to the stake. Heavy chains were bound around their legs, their middles and their necks. Their hands were manacled behind their backs and the dried straw, tinder and bundles of faggots were ignited. It was the first public execution of Cathars on the Crusade but, wrote Pierre des Vaux-de-Cernay there was a miracle. The Good Man died 'but the other quickly broke the strong chains that bound him and escaped from the fires so unharmed that he showed no sign of injury from the flames except that the tips of his fingers were slightly scorched'.

Superstition and credulity were hallmarks of the medieval mind. The monk had not witnessed the event. It was not until March 1212 that his uncle Guy, Bishop of Carcassonne, first took him to the Languedoc where, on and off, he stayed until 1218, often travelling with the crusaders. What really happened at Castres is unrecorded.[8]

With so many almost instantaneous conquests the Lauragais appeared to be lost. An anonymous troubadour sang its death:

Carcassona fo preza, si co	Carcassonne was taken, as I told you,
avetz auzit . . .	Across the entire region everyone fled,
	Montréal and Fanjeaux taken by the French,
	No one stayed whether large or small.[9]

Fanjeaux, Castres, the others had been gifts. The siege of the almost impregnable castle of Cabaret and its two companions at Lastours was not. Defended by Peter-Roger, the elderly warlord who had got away from Carcassonne, the castle stood high on an almost sheer, rocky crag, surrounded on three sides by steep cliffs and the fast-flowing River Orbiel. Except for individuals it was virtually unapproachable.

Today there are four castles on the height, to be viewed spectacularly across the valley of the Grésillon. It is a jaggedly bleak landscape but of a lovely golden stone that glows in the afternoon sunshine, and one can tramp and scramble up the slopes first to the tower and walls of Quertinheux on its separate pinnacle; then to the highest of the fortresses, the sub-rectangular Surdespine or Fleur Épine; on to the latest, the round Tour Régine of about 1260; and finally to the barbican, ramparts, keep and tower of Cabaret itself.

The approach was precipitous and forbidding. Today most of it is eased by steep steps and slopes although the final third is almost 'every man for himself', not dangerous but needing care. That anything of cumbrous stone could be built on such sharp heights makes one aware of the obligations of feudal serfdom and also of the skills of medieval masons.

Stone had to be quarried from the outcrops on the mountain, rough blocks dragged and scrambled to the peak, shaped, scaffolding from the valleys pulled and shouldered up the slopes, erected, foundations set out on the laboriously levelled site and the building begun. In 1210 there were three castles at Lastours alone. But there were even greater monsters elsewhere: Peyrepertuse, Puylaurens, Quéribus, Termes, hundred of smaller fortlets on their hills and crags.[10]

The results were masterpieces of strategic positioning and fortification. Defensively awesome they were but they were not places of comfort. The 'Great Hall' of Cabaret is a cramped rectangle, no more than 7m by 14m, with a raised dais at its southern end for the lord and his lady. Even with just one long table below for the closely seated garrison the chamber would have been crowded with twenty people in it. Yet troubadours had been welcomed there.

Early in the thirteenth century Raymond of Miravel advised his jongleur or minstrel to look for patronage at Lastours. It had been partly owned by one of its co-seigneurs, lord of the nearby Pennautier, whose beautiful wife, Auda, was also known fancifully as Na Loba or '*Louve*', she-wolf.

The accomplished troubadour, Peire Vidal of Toulouse, who dressed in black and shaved his head at the death of Raymond V in 1194, is reputed to have loved her.

Et ab joi li er mos treus . . .	I go to her with joy
	Though wind and snow and sleet.
	The She-Wolf says I am hers
	And, by God, she's right:
	I belong to her
	More than to any other, even to myself.

Vidal's biographer termed him 'the most foolish man in the world' who fell in love with every woman he met. A legend in his lifetime, in *Les Vidas*, a medieval compilation of fantasies about the troubadours, Vidal is reported to have disguised himself in a wolf's hide to lure the lady to him but, instead, was hunted and attacked by a peasant and his hunting-dog. Badly wounded he was carried to Lastours where he was nursed by his lady, '*n'en doutons pas, courtoisement*', with every courtesy. But like so many love stories the ending is sad. The lovely but emotionally peripatetic Na Loba, an early Béatrice of Planisolles, turned her polite affections to that other troubadour, Raymond of Miravel and then to two or three noblemen.[11]

A few years later, in 1210, matters also became worse for Simon de Montfort. The winter was freezingly cold and wet and with so small a force it as impossible to maintain the siege of the three mocking castles. It was his first failure after so many easy successes and it must have been with an unwelcome sense of frustration that he left Lastours behind him. But worse was to come from the place.

Marching away he left orders to commanders in nearby castles that the defenders of Lastours should be harried often and hard. Raiding parties should be sent out. Early in November Bouchard de Marly with fifty of his men left the stronghold at Saissac and advanced upon that 'fountain of heresy' only to be ambushed by a bigger force under the command of Peter-Roger of Cabaret, 'an old man rich in years of wrong-doing'. In the fighting that followed many men died. Gaubert d'Essigny, a knight from Paris, refused to surrender and was cut down. Bouchard de Marly, a Montmorency and cousin of Alice, Countess of Montfort, was captured and taken for ransom. He would be chained in a cell at Cabaret for sixteen months.

The loss and imprisonment of one of his closest and most loyal followers enraged de Montfort. When reinforcements arrived he would besiege the three castles once more. They, and especially the home of Peter-Roger, Cabaret, had become a symbol of defiance that had to be terrified and destroyed.[12]

But he was powerless. As Count of Béziers and Carcassonne he was by law the vassal of the King of Aragon and at Montpellier he offered to do homage to the king, hoping to gain his support. Pedro II refused to accept him. He had no wish to create any form of legality to an intruder from the north of France. To the contrary he informed several of the Languedoc lords that he would help them if they resisted the invaders. They did. A set battle was not feasible. Guerilla warfare was.

It began with murder. To conclude some legal transactions the Count of Foix asked the abbot of a Cistercian house between Foix and Toulouse to go to St.-Gilles on his behalf. Returning, having passed through Carcassonne, the weaponless abbot, Stephen of Eaunes, with two monks and a lay brother, was assaulted by the brother of the Bishop of Carcassonne. 'This most cruel man inflicted thirty-six wounds on the Abbot and twenty-four on the lay brother. He left one of the monks half-dead with sixteen wounds. The other monk escaped alive, because he was known to the tyrant's companions'. The tyrant himself, William of Roquefort, went on to Foix where the Count welcomed him with warmth.[13]

The failure of the siege at Lastours, the ambush of crusaders, the murders outside Carcassonne were the beginnings of misfortune for de Montfort. Even private quarrels brought disaster and vengeance. One of the Count's companions, a highborn Frenchman, killed one of the few southerners with the Crusade. Learning of the incident, determined to be just, de Montfort ordered the accepted punishment in the Languedoc for such a crime. He had the Frenchman buried alive.

Honour should have been satisfied but the southerner had been the uncle of Gerald of Pépieux who also had joined the Crusade. For this de Montfort had entrusted him with the control of some castles and fortlets near Minerve. Hearing of his uncle's death and unsatisfied with the execution he avenged the killing of his relation by capturing the garrison of the castle of Puisserguier west of Béziers. De Montfort surrounded it but without siege-weapons could not take it and departed.

Next night de Pépieux set fire to the keep and had its fifty soldiers thrown into the moat. Stones were hurled onto them until all were dead. Their two commanders, both knights, were chained and taken to Minerve.

Béziers was a massacre. Minerve was an atrocity.

The knights were stripped. Their eyes were gouged out. Their noses, ears, upper lips were cut off. Already mutilated beyond Christian belief they were ejected naked into the winter night. One, it is said, died stumbling into a dung-pit. The other was found by a peasant and guided to the care of his companions in Carcassonne.[14]

It must have been with a shuddering horror that those soldiers watched the mangled thing that had been a man stumble into the citadel and to their compassion was added the ugly need for revenge. 'Vengeance is mine; I will repay, saith the Lord' but His was a form of repayment that the crusaders rejected. 'Recompense no man evil for evil', the Bible ordered, 'live peaceably with all men'. But there was no charity in the men's hearts and souls as they took the disfigured knight to shelter. It was retribution that they wanted.[15]

Their chance for reprisals seemed no more than a hope. By the end of 1209 Simon de Montfort had lost nearly everything that he had won. Rumours of the death of Raymond-Roger Trencavel, suspicions of his murder, spread from Carcassonne into an already disaffected countryside. Resentment of presumptuous strangers from foreign parts grew into hatred and revolt. Towns like Lombers rebelled. 'Almost all the local people became affected by the same ill-will and deserted our Count'. Raymond-Roger, Count of Foix, recaptured Preixan and released his son. The Catholic priest and surrogate commander handed Montréal back to Aimery, its rightful seigneur. De Montfort was left with eight scattered towns. More than forty castles had turned against him.[16]

Amid this turmoil of military successes and setbacks the original cause of the struggles, religion, was not forgotten. In Toulouse Arnaud Amaury made zealous enquiries and, announcing the names of suspected heretics, he demanded that they be brought to him for interrogation. The independently-minded consuls and burghers refused. Typically arrogant and thoughtless of the consequences, stubbornly determined to impose his will, Amaury placed an interdict on the city. It was stupid. The ban worried not one Cathar but deprived the Catholics of their devotions.

Then the Count of Toulouse, Raymond VI, was summoned to Avignon to explain to the Lateran Council why he had not done as he had promised, to close all the toll-gates in his domains, expel mercenaries and Jews and search out heretics. The Count replied that those promises were barely three months old and he had been with the Crusade. He had not had sufficient time. Arnaud Amaury was unimpressed. Six more weeks were allowed, but no longer. Raymond VI, as always, practised quiet inertia and on the first of November was excommunicated once again by the Council.

Protest and counter-protest followed. Sending two ambassadors to Rome the Count appealed to the Pope that the sentence was both unfair and illegal. The Legates sent their own representatives. In January, 1210, Innocent III lifted the excommunication.[17]

It had been a perplexing six months for the Crusade. The army had occupied great cities: Béziers, Narbonne, Albi, Carcassonne, Toulouse. It had taken towns and castles and overrun an entire countryside. It had been the greatest host Christendom had known, an invincible partnership between Church and military, a multitude of bishops and barons, monks and mercenaries descending on the Languedoc in obedience to the Pope's wish that heresy should be eradicated.

Innocent III loathed the Cathars. 'A monstrous breed', he called them in his letter to Philippe-Auguste, a disease that had to be obliterated 'making their memory perish with the trumpet's blast. . . . You must eliminate such filth'.[18] Addressing the crusaders themselves Arnaud Amaury and the bishops urged that the vast battalion of ten thousand or more men should hunt the heretics relentlessly in every city, town and village.

Yet for all the exhortations the enterprise had been a failure. Toulouse had defied Arnaud Amaury and given him no Cathars. At Tonneins several were burned but so few that Pierre des Vaux-de-Cernay did not record the event and Guillaume de Tudela merely mentioned the taking of the town. The so-called 'massacre' appears only in the unreliable history of Sismondi (1773–1842). At Castres just two heretics had been condemned and one of them may have been reprieved. 1209 had seen six months of military conquest without spiritual achievement.[19]

1210 was better for both Catholic and crusader. A religious struggle was developing in Toulouse, the city of Raymond VI and a place where Cathar and Catholic, nobleman and churchman had lived at peace together. More than fifty miles west of Carcassonne and Simon de Montfort it was a place too important to be ignored. Situated at the crossroads between Bordeaux to the west and Narbonne to the east, between Limoges to the north and Andorra to the south it was a city of two halves and two factions. In it was the old ramparted citadel, the Cité, guarded to the west by the vast bend of the River Garonne. On the far bank was the suburb of St.-Cyprien. Attached to the Cité at the north was the more recent twelfth century borough or Bourg with its own walls and towers and with the fine church of St.-Sernin in its north-eastern corner. Around it the mansions were a fairy tale of golden stone.

Within the Cité Foulques de Marseilles, Bishop of Toulouse, was organising the Catholics into a militant body. Catholicism was strong among the craftsmen and their families in their narrow streets and crowded houses. Life was different in the Bourg. There were few huddled shops and hovels there. It was mainly a residential settlement of the rich, of nobility rather than merchants, and the inhabitants with their aristocratic traditions were Cathar by custom and conviction.

Foulques, ex-troubadour who had abandoned his wife and children in 1195 to become a Cistercian monk, stern but fair-minded, encouraged the faithful to enlist in his White Brotherhood, a so-called 'pious institution', in reality a mob of thugs and rowdies, an armed militia wearing a white cross on their dark robes who rampaged on torchlit marches, breaking into the houses of Jews and Cathars, smashing, plundering and burning. 'Arson became respectable, almost sacramental.'

In defence the Cathars founded a Black Brotherhood to resist the destruction. Until then both faiths had worked and lived together. Now there was civil war and oppression. 'Daily', wrote Guillaume de Puylaurens years after the mayhem, 'the two parties would clash, banners flying, bristling with weapons, even with cavalry in evidence. Through the agency of His servant the Bishop [Foulques], Our Lord had come to bring them, not a bad peace but a good war'. Foulques did more. From the White Brotherhood he created a band of five hundred trained fighting-men who would join Simon de Montfort at the siege of Lavaur in 1211.

In March Arnaud Amaury came to Toulouse and instantly caused disruption, demanding once again that the city consuls deliver the known heretics to him and pay the Catholic church a thousand *livres* in compensation for their previous defiance.

As always he asked too much. Most of the money would have come from the wealthy citizens of the Bourg. With their Catharist inclinations they gave little. Arnaud Amaury was offered five hundred *livres*. Predictably he announced an interdict. Foulques, realising that his good work would be destroyed if his Catholics turned against such an unjust imposition, intervened. Reluctantly Amaury repealed the interdict and the uneasy semi-truce continued.[20]

In Carcassonne Simon de Montfort waited for reinforcements. With winter passing he was anxious to get out of the city and stamp out the petty rebellions that had been reported to him. The ubiquitous Arnaud Amaury reminded the crusaders of their mutilated comrade. 'The Lord revengeth and is furious', he told them, 'the Lord will take vengeance on his adversaries, and he reserveth wrath for his enemies'.[21] The men had not forgotten. They waited. 'Revenge is a dish that is best eaten cold', the proverb says, The massacre at Béziers had been a hot-blooded madness. Retribution in 1210 would be callous and unyielding. Simon de Montfort thought of Bouchard de Marly suffering in neglected gloom and dirt at Cabaret. The lord of the castle, Peter-Roger, would be reminded that nemesis awaited him. And Puisserguier was in every man's memory.

On the third of March there was a message that Alice de Montmorency was waiting seventy miles away at Pézénas with a contingent of several hundred knights. De Montfort rode out to meet his wife. It was the beginning of a year's odyssey, a campaign of nearly four hundred miles travelling along tracks, over hills, across rivers, through forests, to towns and castles, a merciless journey of gallows, savagery, massacre and capitulation, the fading of a crusade and the onset of a war of conquest.

What had been de Montfort's was to be his again but this time taken with brutally instant punishment. Fear would ensure that there would be no more local uprisings by peasants. A rebellion at Montlaur was the first to be suppressed.

It was another seventy slow miles past the burnt ruins of Béziers, through Narbonne and along the valley of the Orbieu, keeping the wilderness of the Montagne d'Alairac to the north, twisting bend after bend through the hills and they came at last to the keep of Montlaur. A small garrison had been left there and in the discontent of the previous winter villagers had surrounded it, barricading the defenders. On the news of the approaching crusaders most of the besiegers fled. Those that stayed were hanged without trial.

By the end of March, after more dragging miles westwards through Carcassonne, then Alzonne the crusaders came to Bram. The Languedoc was a pin-cushion of defences, citadels, almost seventy castles, 'new' towns of bastides like Mirepoix and Montauban with their neat grid system of streets and central square, walled towns like Bram whose circle of walls surrounded radiating streets and ring within ring of houses like an architectural darts-board. There were defences everywhere. But none of them, not even Carcassonne, could withstand a determined siege in good weather. Bram was no different.

After three days of suicidal resistance the gates were broken and the town taken by direct assault leaving its occupants the victims of the severe rules of medieval warfare. The treacherous priest of Montréal, honoured with its gift by Simon de Montfort, had returned the town to its original lord. At the arrival of the crusaders he had slunk to the supposed safety of Bram three miles away. He was recognised. Deprived by the Bishop of Carcassonne of clerical status and immunity from physical pain he was tied to a horse's tail, dragged in flesh-tearing agony to the city walls and hanged.

Puisserguier had been atrocity. Bram was horror. Its hundred defenders were violated. Their eyes were gouged out, their noses, ears, upper lips sliced off, just one man left with one eye to lead the living carcases out of Bram.

Guillaume de Tudela said nothing about the barbarity. Pierre des Vaux-de-Cernay excused it. 'The Count had this punishment carried out not because such mutilation gave him any pleasure but because his opponents had been the first to indulge in atrocities and, cruel executioners that they were, were given to butchering any of our men that they might capture by dismembering them'.

He was half correct. Bram was Puisserguier writ large. What the monk did not explain was that Simon de Montfort, medieval prac-titioner of psychological warfare, did not casually turn the deformed creatures out of Bram. He used them ruthlessly. The blinded men were to be guided to Lastours more than fifteen sightless miles to the north-east where their ghastly fate would be a forewarning of what awaited Peter-Roger and his supporters at Cabaret.[22]

It was probably this warning and the sudden realisation of the danger they were in, how defenceless they were individually, that explains the unexpected supplication of three lords to the king of Aragon. Peter-Roger of Cabaret, Raymond of Termes and Aimery of Montréal offered their homage to Pedro II, a monarch whose army would surely be a match for Simon de Montfort. The four men met at Montréal.

The king accepted their offer but on the onerous condition that, should he ever have need of their castles, they should immediately be rendered to him. The lords refused. It was the invariable tragedy of the Languedoc that there was no consistency. Had the great nobles, the Count of Toulouse, the Count of Foix acted together, had the lesser lords with their powerful castles put aside their feuds, they might, united, have defeated the crusaders. But whenever there was a possibility of co-operation the tentative alliances always disintegrated.[23]

A difficulty in writing a history of the Albigensian Crusade is the unreliability of its chroniclers. Guillaume de Tudela is sketchy. Pierre des Vaux-de-Cernay is biased. Guillaume de Puylaurens wrote of events that he could not have seen. This does not impugn their honesty. It does question their objectivity and knowledge. The modern writer is, to paraphrase Casey, at the mercy of incompetent historians who handed out their lack of knowledge and prejudices like tarnished coins.[24] Happily, this disadvantage is largely overcome by the researches of later historians and of the existence today of the towns and castles in which the events occurred.

Obvious examples of such advances are the works of Ladurie and Weis with their detailed studies of the men and women of Montaillou whose long-forgotten statements to the Inquisition were stored in the Vatican and elsewhere. Archaeology has helped as well. Excavations, at Montaillou, have clarified the development of the castle there and the structure and domestic layout of houses in the village. More excavations have been undertaken at Lastours and other castles. It all enhances the history of the Crusade and the imperfect records of the first chroniclers.

The fragmentary remains of the castle of Alairac on its long, snow-covered range of mountains, is an example of what can still be seen, its dark history sensed. The Visigoths erected a fortress on the site but the present ruins date only from the eleventh century. In a screaming, soaking gale de Montfort besieged it in April. In the torrential weather the siege endured for fifteen days by which time, realising that they were doomed, many defenders began creeping away at night. Some escaped. Most were caught and they and the garrison were slaughtered.

The crusaders were relentless. Wherever there was resistance they went. It was a deliberate display of intimidation, a parade of power as they trailed through the hills past villages and hamlets, an awesome mile of several hundred nobles and knights on horseback, thousands of soldiers marching, a train of baggage-carts. They went past a procession of castles in an unspoken but unmistakable threat. Where there had been rumours now there was military reality.

From Alairac they moved south-eastwards to Limoux, past Rennes-le-Château on its hilltop, past the feeble castle of Coustaussa whose winding road is a wriggle of hairpins, past the honey-coloured keep of Arques later rebuilt for more comfort, into the uplands, announcing their presence, past Albières and Auriac with its castle and abandoned Roman gold-mines, past the mountainous strongholds of Peyrepertuse and Quéribus, too formidable and remote to be attacked that year, and up to the six high arrow-slitted towers, ramparts and rectangular donjon of Aguilar on its gigantic dome of rock. In an arid landscape it is a wreck today with fragrant lavender growing inside the roofless keep and with vineyards spreading at the foot of the height but in 1210 the defences and the defenders were strong enough to repel the besiegers who departed for the heretical stronghold of Minerve thirty miles to the north.

Unharmed and never again threatened Aguilar became the fourth of the five 'Sons of Carcassonne', the massive castles that protected the frontier of France until the border was moved southwards in

1659, the others being Peyrepertuse, Puylaurens, Quéribus and Termes. And for decades in the thirteenth century Aguilar also became the last refuge of *'faidits'*, knights of Languedoc who had been dispossessed of their lands.

Aguilar was a minor setback. Turning northwards the army passed the castle and fortified village of Durban. With his host of some seven thousand men Simon de Montfort ignored it and marched towards Minerve, a town doubly notorious as a sanctuary for Cathars and the place where Gerald of Pépieux had mutilated the two knights of Puisserguier. Religion and revenge merged in the minds of the crusaders.

After miles of pleasant countryside and villages lovely with bougainvillaea and oleander the land becomes wilder as one comes to the *causses* north of a line between Carcassonne and Narbonne, river-eroded bare limestone sheets and undulating tree-thick ridges that become even more bleak in the vicinity of Minerve, a name perhaps deriving from *men-herba*, 'the rock of refuge'.

The town was indeed a natural defence, a near-island on its high cliffs the height of three steepled churches, with just one cramped neck of land joining it to the outside world at the north but cut off from it at east, south and west by the gorges gouged out by the rivers of the Briant and Cesse. The cramped approach across the isthmus was guarded by a castle beyond which the ramparted streets and houses of the town swelled out like a tear-drop from the eye of the castle. The symbolism is apt.

This is Minervois country, a land of vineyards whose traditions reach back to Roman times around 125 BC when the first vines of the deep crimson wine were planted around Narbonne. Rabelais had Pantagruel speak longingly of the wine of Mirevaux, perhaps Mireval-Lauragais, miles west of Minerve.[25]

Minerve's was an ancient landscape. In the cave of the Grotte s'Aldène, discovered since the war, are Palaeolithic paintings and the footprints trodden into the mud by Aurignacian hunters thirty thousand years ago. Casts can be seen in the town's museum. On the *causses* are stone-built tombs, the regional variations of chambered *allées-couvertes*, that seem almost modern with an antiquity of a mere four or five thousand years. One of them, the Dolmen des Fades, is close to Pépieux whose seigneur 's name remained bitterly in the minds of the advancing host.

Minerve is quiet today. Out of season hardly seventy people live there. It is a place of narrow streets. Visitors leave their cars outside and walk across the bridge over the Cesse which becomes subterranean at that point. The cobbled main street rises slowly past the souvenir shop of the private Musée Hurepel in one of the town's oldest houses with its evocative hand-crafted exhibition of dioramas of peasant life, of Raymond-Roger Trencavel in his cell, of crusader fighting. Farther on is the eleventh century Romanesque church of St.-Étienne, then the museum and, finally, the castle of which only an etiolated pencil of the tower survives.

Probably unnoticed but close to the bridge on the right hand side of the street is the now-roofless Maison des Templiers with its eight-pointed Maltese cross carved at the head of the arched gateway. Locally it is believed that it had been the house of the Good Men.[26]

Minerve is quiet today. Once it was formidable. There was, wrote Guillaume de Tudela, 'No stronger fortress on this side of the Spanish passes, except Cabaret and Termes' The cliffs were 90m high making the town inaccessible to siege-towers and scaling-ladders. The isthmus was only 30m wide and suicidal to storm. Overlooking it was the castle with its garrison of two hundred men. Its two gates were defended by artificial moats, one of which separated it from the town.

Minerve was a besieger's worst thought but it had one failing, water. Being so high above the rivers no well had been dug through the solid limestone bedrock inside the town. There were cisterns in the houses but the only well was outside in a spring at the cliff-bottom. Being vulnerable to attack, a thick three-sided stone bastion protected it at front and sides. From the south-east corner of the town an alley way still leads to a serpentine descent of once-covered steps and gentle ramps down to the Puits St Rustique that today is open to the sky.

The siege began at the beginning of June in fine, hot weather. The leader of Minerve, Gerald, had led many raids against the invaders during the winter and was an experienced soldier. Although his garrison was small he had defences that were almost impregnable. Against him but outside those barriers of rivers, cliffs and heavy ramparts was Simon de Montfort. His co-leader, Arnaud of Narbonne, an enemy of Gerald, had a vast, mixed army, mainly French from Champagne, Maine, Anjou, Brittany, Lorraine, Gascons under the Bishop of Auch. There were also Frisians and Germans. It was an invasion.

De Montfort followed custom and set up camps to surround Minerve, his own on the east beyond the Briant, with the Gascons on the far side of the town to the west of the Cesse. Arnaud of Narbonne camped to the north outside the castle.

For a siege to be successful it was usual to follow a pattern, first to encircle the enemy to starve them out, to prevent them escaping and to stop assistance reaching them. Attack would follow. Long-range weaponry bombarded the walls and gates. There were ballistas like enormous crossbows. There were stone-throwing machines, mangonels and trebuchets, to shatter walls. After some days sappers under the cover of 'cats' would try to fill in ditches and moats and undermine the defences. Then came the ultimate stage when battering-rams pounded at the gates, and siege-towers and scaling-ladders were pushed up to the walls for men to scramble up to the battlements while archers and crossbowmen fired at the defenders. That was conventional warfare but at Minerve only bombardment was possible. The town itself was virtually unapproachable.

De Montfort was a good tactician. He assaulted the town. He also assaulted the well. To the west of Minerve Gascons bombarded the town with their mangonel, a catapult standing on a heavy, wheeled base that supported a frame of two ponderous wooden posts and a crossbar. An arm like a gigantic spoon passed under the crossbar and was tautly windlassed down by twisted ropes onto a roller at the rear of the mangonel. A stone or heavy lump of lead was lifted into the cup. The ropes were freed, the arm shot up, jolted against the padded crossbar and hurled its missile with shattering velocity. With stones smashing into the town from west, south and north buildings were wrecked, people were killed. Fearing infection in the blazing weather men dropped the corpses into the ravines.

Mangonels were effective but trebuchets were heavier and even more powerful. The crusaders had three, two at south and north to bombard the defences, the third at the east to demolish the well.

From the Old French *trebucher*, 'to overthrow', for that is exactly what they did, they flung destructive missiles from a long wooden arm that acted like a see-saw or ducking-stool. Assembled on site by a team of experienced engineers who were paid as much as twenty-one *livres* a day for their expertise a trebuchet, covered with hides to protect it from fire-arrows, consisted of a sturdy upright oak frame over whose top the arm of lighter wood was pivoted. At one end was a counterweight of a box filled with a ton or more of sand and stone. It was ingenious medieval craftsmanship. To prevent its contents spilling out and having to be refilled each time the trebuchet was fired the box was hinged so that it swung backwards and forwards when the arm was released. A rigid container suddenly stopping would have ejected everything.

At the other end of the arm was a bolted sling to hold a projectile, often a stone. Weighing up to five hundred pounds, ideally it was a smooth stone ball to improve the accuracy of its flight. Stone was often available locally. But it had to be hard. When Raymond VI besieged Castelnaudary in 1211 he had a trebuchet 'but neither on road or path could they find stones which would not shatter on impact'. In frustration they had to bring three from some miles away.

When the necessary calculations for directions and distance were settled the arm with its sling was winched down lifting the counterweight high in the air. The ropes were released, the counterweight dropped, the sling flew up hurling the stone towards its objective as far as two hundred metres away. There was more ingenuity. The trebuchet was mounted on a wheeled base that stabilised the machine by 'damping' the movement, preventing any jerk as the heavy box jolted down.[27]

Trebuchets were deadly. At the siege of Castelnaudary one of the good balls smashed down a tower, a second a building, and a third broke on impact killing the people around it. They were reliable and accurate. Guillaume de Tudela admired the manner in which they were able 'to hit the mark at an incredible distance'. Pierre des Vaux-de-Cernay was awed by de Montfort's trebuchet, 'a huge and most effective petrary'.[28]

It was the biggest of the three catapults and it was mockingly nicknamed *Malevoisine*, 'bad neighbour', just as fifteenth century gunners would affectionately call their gigantic cannons Long Meg, Mad Meg, Foul-mouthed Meg. The function of de Montfort's 'bad neighbour' was to demolish the defences of the well and covered passage. It was an easy target. Exactly where the Puits St Rustique was would be familiar to outsiders. Almost equidistant between Béziers and Narbonne, Minerve was continually visited by merchants to haggle over the price of the year's vintage. They and all other callers would know the position of the well.

It was strongly protected, concealed behind its tall bastion. That was its strength. Its weakness was that it was no more than 55m from the eastern bank of the Briant with the trebuchet at the cliff-edge high above it. Day after day and into weeks stones crashed down, gradually but inexorably smashing down the front of the wall and battering its sides. It is a modern irony that small notices reading *Défense de lancer des pierres*, 'it is forbidden to throw stones', line the path down to the well.

Inside Minerve the inhabitants were beginning to despair as week after week the bombardments continued. Food became scarce. Cisterns emptied and dried in the hot weather. With sections of the covered way broken it was increasingly dangerous to go to the well. On Sunday 18 July, in the seventh week of the siege it was agreed that *Malevoisine* had to be destroyed.

Evading sentries in the darkness, cautiously wading across the almost dry bed of the Briant, scaling the cliff, the band of saboteurs with baskets of oakum, straw, wood and animal fat reached the deserted trebuchet near the sleeping camp. The baskets were attached to the trebuchet, set on fire and soon the timbers were deeply burning. It was daring and it was doomed. One of the engineers had left his tent to relieve himself and seeing the fire shouted a warning. He was stabbed and badly wounded but the alarm was enough. The flames were quickly extinguished, 'no longer than the time taken to fire two shots', perhaps twenty to thirty minutes, vividly revealing the rate at which a trebuchet could operate.[29]

It was the critical incident. On 22 July, after a prolonged siege of seven weeks, with provisions almost gone and the well near obliteration, Gerald of Minerve asked for acceptable terms that would end the struggle. He was justified. The town had not been taken. But while Simon de Montfort and he were negotiating Arnaud Amaury, Bishop of Citeaux, with other bishops arrived.

The possibility that all the inhabitants of Minerve, heretics included, should be released unharmed agonised the bishop. 'He wanted the enemies of Christ to die but as a monk and priest he did not dare condemn them to death'. He advised de Montfort that both sides should set down their terms in writing. They did so but Minerve's demands were not acceptable to the crusaders. Undismayed, Gerald replied that he would accept whatever de Montfort demanded as long as it was consonant with the rules of warfare. This still meant that the people of Minerve, all of them, would be spared.

A highborn French nobleman, Robert of Mauvoisin, staunch Catholic, objected. He had come to destroy heresy. Clemency was intolerable. Arnaud Amaury calmed him. The years of humiliation with Dominic while those Catholic priests were preaching conversion to the unconvertible convinced him that Cathars would never renounce their faith. All that was needed was that the crusaders' conditions should stipulate that everyone would be spared who agreed to be reconciled with the Catholic church. Not one of the heretics would recant, he assured Mauvoisin.

The terms were accepted. Marching past the undefended castle, singing the *Te Deum Laudamus*, the crusaders entered the town holding high a large crucifix and the battle standards of Simon de Montfort. In person the Count spoke to the assembled Cathars, first the men, then the women, urging them to abjure their false beliefs. Amaury followed, speaking of the glory of God and of the merciful

Pope who was His representative on earth. Uncompromisingly he added a warning. 'Be converted to the Catholic faith or ascend this pyre'. As he expected he was defied. 'Why do you preach to us? We will have nothing of your faith. We renounce the Roman faith. You labour in vain. Neither death nor life can separate us from the beliefs we hold'. Not one man, Good Man or believer, was moved by the bishop's appeal. The women were even more obdurate.

Out of the town they were led, one hundred and forty of them, to a clearing where a huge pyre of stakes surrounded by kindling had been prepared. It was set on fire. There was no resistance. Men and women went willingly to their deaths. 'There was no need for our soldiers to throw them on, since they were so hardened in their wickedness that they rushed into the fire of their own accord. Three women only were rescued, whom the noble lady [Matilde de Garlande] the mother of Bouchard de Marly snatched from the flames and reconciled to the Holy Church'. 'Not the value of a chestnut was left to them. Afterwards their bodies were thrown out and mud shovelled over them so that no stench from these foul things should annoy our foreign forces'. It was the first large-scale burning of the crusade.[30]

De Montfort left a garrison in Minerve and with his triumphant army rode to join his wife, Alice, at Pennautier. Gerald had lost Minerve but became a vassal of Simon de Montfort and was granted lands near Béziers where he joined the Knights Hospitaller. He later renounced them in favour of the *faidits*, those landless knights, who fought against the crusaders. He was severely injured at the siege of Beaucaire in 1216.

Minerve's castle was abandoned at the end of the Crusade and for many years became a useful retreat for footpads and thieves until in exasperation the indignant locals complained to the king, Louis XIII, who had the fortress destroyed in 1637.

There is another memento of the siege of the town. By the church of St.-Étienne alongside the town wall there is a stone slab through which the sculptor Jean-Luc Séverac carved the shape of a dove in commemoration of the massacre. From their houses the Cathars would have been escorted along the main street, past the castle to the open countryside and the fires of persecution. Eight hundred years later the street is still called the rue des Martyrs.

De Montfort was not finished with the year. There were two more castles to be assaulted, the first almost a military impossibility. From Minerve he went miles south to the mountainous fortress of Termes whose minor road climbs, twists and tunnels through the living rock of the Gorges de l'Orbieu. The quietly pretty village of Termes is a gentle thing literally lying in the shadow of the immense fortification high above it on a towering pinnacle of rock, steep and cut off from below by deep and rough ravines.

De Montfort arrived in August, 1210. Today the castle is a colossal, shapeless wreck. All the great strongholds of the Languedoc are ruinous, slighted by foes, remodelled in more peaceful times, neglected and eroded by weather. They are romantic relics but they remain recognisable as castles. It is a strange coincidence that the two fortifications of 1210, Minerve and Termes, are beyond comprehension and for the same reason. Robbery.

Like Minerve, Termes became the base for outlaws who raided and pillaged the surrounding countryside. Just as the wastes and forests of Sherwood and Barnesdale sheltered men like Robin Hood so the hills, valleys and caves of the Languedoc concealed bands of criminals who preyed on the weakness of unguarded villages. Termes had to be destroyed and in 1653 it was exploded into devastation by Louis XIV, the 'Sun King', at the precise cost of 14,922 *livres* and ten *sols*.

Once, the castle had spread over four acres of mountainside, double-walled battlements, castle and keep, an outer borough with a church and an isolated tower where the approach was least difficult. Tudela praised Termes. 'This is a wonderful castle, and before it falls many souls will quit their bodies, dying unconfessed, and the siege will cost many a mark . . .'.[31]

The defences were awesome in themselves but made almost invincible by the terrain. What would be a pleasant outing for mountain goats is thirty breathless minutes' hard walking for today's visitors, starting from the car-park halfway up the mountainside. For men in the valley below with armour and weapons it was physically exhausting. And that was just to reach the outer walls.

The place was defended by Raymond de Termes, hardened warrior and determined heretic with many estates as a vassal of the Trencavels. With him in 1210 were his sons, Oliver of Termes, some ten years old, already skilled in the arts of combat, and the younger Bernard.[32]

De Montfort had planned his campaign. For Termes siege-machines could be used and at the end of July a caravan of ox-carts with weapons and catapults had been prepared outside Carcassonne. Believing them to be weakly guarded that dedicated enemy of the crusaders, Peter-Roger of Cabaret, with Peter Mir of Fanjeaux, other knights and three hundred mounted men were all 'galloping full tilt for Carcassonne' from Lastours. They were seen and driven off but returned at dawn and a minor battle developed on the banks of the Aude. Guillaume de Contres, leader of the crusaders, fought valiantly. 'He encountered one of Mir's men and struck him so hard on his flowered shield that his hauberk was no more use to him than a rotten apple; down into the water he went'. The men from Cabaret retreated, Peter-Roger escaping in the confusion of battle by shouting 'Montfort, Montfort' as though he were a crusader.[33]

August was the beginning of a four-month siege. In the sheltered gorge of the Sou valley de Montfort set up a camp of 'tents of rich silk and fine pavilions, many silk tunics and rich brocades'. With him was the most skilled siege engineer in France, Guillaume, a man expert in judging how best to undermine a wall, a man who designed siege-towers and more effective catapults yet who was, rather unexpectedly, the archdeacon of Paris. Presumably in the wrong profession he was so dedicated to his craft that in 1212 he refused the bishopric of Béziers in order to stay with the Crusade.[34]

Both sides had mangonels, trebuchets, ballistae but behind the concentric ramparts of Termes there was little apprehension. Roger 'who feared not God nor regarded man . . . counted them not a button for no one saw a stronger castle than his'. He had mercenaries from Spain and his own soldiers. Termes was well supplied with food and wine. The siege went on with sorties by the defenders, sallies to the gate by reckless crusaders. 'Reinforcements trickled through slowly, and left promptly when their forty days were done, sometimes even earlier. Raiding parties from Cabaret swept the roads north of Termes, picking off small groups of crusaders and sending them on to Simon's camp with pierced eyes and severed lips and noses'.[35]

The expenses of the siege left de Montfort almost penniless and he 'very often was even short of bread, and had nothing to eat'. At the end of August, Bretons came with siege-machines. Early in September an army from the Ile-de-France arrived under the unenthusiastic command of the bishops of Chartres and Beauvais, and the counts of Dreux and Ponthieu. For the first time the crusaders had enough men to surround Termes. It made life more dangerous for both sides.

A trebuchet of the crusaders was attacked but saved by the extraordinary courage of a knight, Guillaume de Ecureuil, who single-handed repelled several assaults. The defenders also had mangonels and the lethally accurate ballistae, gigantic crossbows that fired savagely long bolts. One of them almost killed de Montfort as he heard Mass in his tent, toppling a soldier behind him. Another day, out in the open, a boulder from a mangonel crushed a soldier to whom de Montfort was talking.[36]

Through the cloudless, hot days the siege continued its deadly stalemate. Termes was battered but, outwardly, to little effect. Inside, matters were different. It suffered the usual weakness of a besieged castle, water. Cisterns were almost empty and as Guillaume de Tudela observed, 'they had wine for another two or three months but I do not think anyone can live without water'.

Urged on by his mercenaries who knew that there would be no mercy for them if the castle fell Raymond of Termes offered to negotiate as long as conditions were in his favour. To the crusaders he appeared to argue from strength. He would permit de Montfort to possess the castle for the winter but it was to be returned to him at Easter, 1211. In the meantime he would retain all his lands.

De Montfort had to consent. Ignorant of the shortage of water he did know that the combined forces of the Bishop of Beauvais and the Counts of Dreux and Ponthieu were departing in twenty-four hours and that the Bishop of Chartres had very reluctantly promised to stay for only a short while longer. It was agreed that the crusaders would enter Termes next day when the entire garrison would be allowed to leave unmolested.

It was a brief capitulation. When the crusaders approached next morning they were treacherously met with unanticipated showers of arrows and stones and left with many casualties. After the long, dry months of the summer and autumn there had been a heavy and prolonged storm overnight and the cisterns had been refilled. Only two knights of Termes honourably observed the agreement. They refused to remain. Everyone else stayed. The siege was renewed.

The Bishop of Chartres left. German reinforcements from Lorraine replaced him. There was more rain. Trebuchets were dragged closer and began to damage the walls seriously. The rain turned to snow. October lengthened. Then sentries on watch around the castle noticed that men were beginning to sneak away from the inviolable fortress. They were escaping disease. Rain had refilled dried cisterns that were polluted, causing an outbreak of dysentery so severe 'that the sufferers could not tell where they were'. Those who were fit enough took the ladies to the safety of the keep and prepared to escape. Many did.[37]

Raymond and his sons got through the lines; but then the father decided to return for something, and was discovered in the woods by a poor soldier from Chartres. The lord was imprisoned in Carcassonne where he died three years later.

His castle had been an heretical place. Pierre des Vaux-de-Cernay, Cistercian monk, was aghast to learn that 'thirty years and more had now passed . . . during which the Holy Sacraments were never celebrated in the church at Termes', a chapel of which only a cross-shaped window survives. Another monk, Guillaume de Tudela, more concerned with courtesy than Catharism, recorded how chivalrous the crusaders had been. They 'behaved very well and took nothing from the ladies, 'not even the value of a penny coin or a Le Puy farthing'.[38]

Termes was given to Alain de Roucy, a famous jouster, who later was to fight at the siege of Beaucaire and the sieges of Toulouse in 1216, 1217 and 1218 before being killed in Montréal castle in the winter of 1221.

News of the capture of Termes reached Cabaret, whose garrison was already beginning to desert. Alarmed, Peter-Roger offered Bouchard de Marly his freedom if he promised to ask de Montfort for generous treatment. The code of chivalry was respected. Bouchard agreed to speak on Peter-Roger's behalf. His chains were removed. His verminous rags were stripped. He was given a scented bath, a haircut, rich robes, a fine pacing palfrey and three squires to escort him to Carcassonne where the crusaders celebrated his safe return. De Montfort was equally chivalrous to a man who had caused him so much harm and gave Peter-Roger some lands well away from regions where he might cause further mischief.[39]

The conquest in the same year of two seemingly unassailable strongholds astonished and terrified the occupants of other castles as they learned of the calamities. If the unreachable 'island' of Minerve could be breached, if the impregnable barricades of Termes could be broken then no defence was secure. Castle after castle was abandoned.

De Montfort marched on to the next fortress to be attacked, retracing his way past Arques and the deserted walls of Coustaussa, ignoring the harmless fort of Rennes-le-Château, advancing westwards towards the 'green mountain' of Puivert, the most accessible of all the great castles of the Languedoc. It fell. Within three days at the end of November the disheartened garrison had surrendered.[40]

Several miles west of the dull town of Quillan with the decaying shell of its overgrown castle, Puivert is surrounded by forests to north, south and west where Belista is the largest expanse of woodland in the whole of the Pyrenees. Despite this, Puivert stands in the pleasantly open and green valley of the Blau. Unlike the mountaintop fortresses of the Languedoc it rests on an easy hill, partly protected by natural cliffs.

In plan it resembles a merchant ship with squared stern and pointed bow – but a merchant ship in wartime, stern torpedoed on the port side, bows dive-bombed and buckled into untidy wreckage. It is a castle of two sections, its ruined western bows being the remains of the castle taken by the crusaders. Behind it is the fourteenth century extension of an elegantly rectangular tower and spacious courtyard.

The first castle had long been well-known for its Cathar sympathies and for the welcome it gave to troubadours. There had been a famous meeting of them there in 1170. The lord, Bernard of Congost, welcomed them. So did his wife, Alpaïs. Showing how closely interconnected some of those noble Cathar families were she was the sister of Raymond of Péreille who had undertaken the renovation of Montségur in 1204. The cousins of Alpaïs were to be savagely involved in the murder of monks at Avignonet in 1242.

Puivert had its own Cathar deacon, very similar to the role of a castle chaplain, and it was he who administered the *consolamentum* to Alpaïs when she became mortally ill in 1208.[41]

With the castle's surrender two years later it was a Catholic crusader, Lambert de Thury, who became its new lord. A few decades more, and it was acquired by Pons of Bruyères. It was his family who built the enlarged castle of today. It is of particular interest because of its keep and its music, an important and cheerful part of life in the Languedoc and worth including here as a reminder that there was poetry, song and melody as well as massacre at the time of the Albigensian Crusade.

The songs were not always about love. There was humour. At Puivert Peire d'Auvergne, some known as d'Alvernha, even d'Alverne, well-read, handsome and composer of 'the finest melodies ever written' announced to his audience that

> I'll sing of those troubadours
> Who sing in a myriad styles . . .

and described his comrade, Guiraut de Bornhelh as 'like an oyster dried out in the sun', then Bernart de Ventadorn as even 'shorter than Bornelh' and whose minstrel from Limousin sang 'like some sick pilgrim'. En Raimbaut was 'much too proud of his own verse'. These were not insults. They were jests. D'Auvergne mocked himself:

> Peire d'Auvergne's voice
> Is like a frog singing in a well,
> Yet he compliments himself in front
> Of everyone, for he's master of them all;
> But it's a pity his meaning isn't clearer,
> For almost no one understands him.
>
> This poem was made for bagpipe players
> At Puivert in sport and laughter.[42]

Puivert's tall keep, standing high above the walls of the castle, has a cellar basement, a ground-floor guardroom, then a chapel over which is the 'Salle des Musiciens' beneath the battlements. It is a spacious room with a vaulted ceiling from whose central keystone eight ribs splay out to the walls, each terminating in a head-high sculpted stone as a base for a lamp. The sculptures, all different, are of jongleurs, those talented musicians who sang and played the compositions of troubadours.

They were proficient, skilled in the performance of many instruments. 'I can play the flute, the trumpet, the guitar, the harp', bragged one, 'the flageolet [a small pipe], the tambourine, the violin, the set of bells, the organistrum [hurdy-gurdy], the bagpipe, the psaltery, the tabor, the lute, the sackbut, the rebeck, the trumpet marine and the chirping gigue [a tiny violin]'.[43]

Eight of these instruments can be seen at Puivert. One jongleur plays a *cornemuse*, an early form of bagpipes whose bag was often designed as the body of a tortoise with the lower end of the pipe as its head. There is a flautist, a drummer with his *tambourin*, a violinist holding his *vieile à archet*, used when the jongleur was singing without any accompanying players, another with a *cittern* and plectrum. A sixth has the enchanting three-stringed *rebeck* and its bow. The next *cul à lampe* has a psalterist plucking the long strings of his instrument, and finally comes a jongleur with his *orgue portatif*, a hand-organ somewhat like a guitar but with keys that tapped the strings by the turning of a wheel. The carvings are difficult to see in the castle itself but there is a fine set of reproductions and an exhibition of musical instruments in the handsome Musée Quercorb in the village.

Music was one delight. Water was another. A later châtelaine of Puivert, Blanche of Aragon, liked to walk and muse along the shores of a nearby lake where at the water's edge there was a rock weathered into the shape of a couch. In 1279, finding that the lakeside was often submerged after rain, she ordered an engineer, Jean de Bruyères, to lower the water-level. A miscalculation flooded the countryside, overwhelming Chalabre five miles away, even reaching Mirepoix fourteen miles to the north, and reducing the lake to today's small reservoir.

'*Le trône de pierre bascule* . . .', 'the natural throne see-sawed, rocked and broke, the waters poured into the valley: land, boulders, princess, labourers, all were swallowed up, carried away by the flood'. [44]

FOUR

1211. From Crusade to Conquest

They were years when the clear-cut intention to suppress heresy was corrupted by a decision to oppress a population. Towns were taken and sacked, castles seized, the smoke of pyres darkened the air and the wrath of God poured like a thunderstorm across the Languedoc as far away as Cahors ninety miles north of Carcassonne. It was the north that was to suffer.

In his city to the south Raymond VI, Count of Toulouse and token crusader, lived in gentle disregard. Like some young man in debt but hoping that his money-lenders would forget, he did nothing. Money-lenders seldom forget. Arnaud Amaury certainly did not.

In May of 1210 Raymond had given the bishop the fortified palace of the Château Narbonnaise by the south gate of Toulouse as a gesture of his good faith. He gained no benefit from the present. To churchmen his inactivity was sinful. Guillaume de Puylaurens blamed him for the persistence of heresy 'through whose negligence and failure the evil increased in these parts . . . I have crossed the field of the slothful man, and lo, nettles have completely filled it'.[1]

In June the count was summoned to a meeting at St.-Gilles by Milo, the papal legate who planned to incite the count into disobedience, having taken the precaution of warning the Pope to 'mistrust his plausible tongue, which is skilled in the distillation of lies and all moral obliquity'. Arnaud Amaury was equally determined 'to find some lawful means by which the Count could be prevented from demonstrating his innocence'.

Raymond was informed that he had not obeyed the instructions of the legates, had not searched for heretics, had not removed toll-gates and that he was to do so at once and also get rid of all the mercenaries that garrisoned his castles. Weeping in frustrated rage, Raymond returned to Toulouse and did nothing.[2]

At the beginning of 1211 while the prelates plotted and schemed at the count's downfall Pedro II, the Catholic King of Aragon, tried to act as an intermediary and peacemaker. Finally accepting the homage of Simon de Montfort as the Viscount of Carcassonne he followed medieval tradition and strengthened the alliance by pledging the marriage of his four-year old son to Amicié, de Montfort's daughter. The king's sister, Sancha, was betrothed to Raymond, son of the Count of Toulouse, who was already married to Pedro's other sister, Eleanor. By these marital bonds Aragon, Toulouse and Carcassonne became nuptially interlinked.

To Arnaud Amaury it was without significance. Raymond VI was summoned to yet another meeting, this time at Montpellier in February and while Pedro, Raymond and their men were left outside the hall in the cold, 'exposed to a high wind', the clerical assembly inside formulated a collection of demands that were certain to be refused.

A secretary read them out to the Count. In his domains all mercenaries were to be expelled within twenty-four hours, an impossibility; there were to be no usurers, the Catholic clergy were to be paid, Jews were to be persecuted, heretics were to be banished 'within a year', there were to be no illegal tolls, crusaders would be fed and sheltered, and Raymond's lords must demolish their own castles.

None of this was feasible but what followed was calculated to demean. The count and his nobles were to have no meat for five days a week and then only two dishes on the remaining days, they were to wear coarse, plain-brown robes, knights in the towns and cities were to be exiled to the countryside and live like peasants.

Raymond himself was to enrol either with the Order of the Templars or the Hospitallers and go to the Holy Land and stay there until recalled by the legates.[3]

He turned his back on the gathering and left next morning with no farewell. To him the flight of a buzzard flying from right to left was a bad omen. At town, village and hamlet, all the way from Montpellier to Toulouse, he had the document read aloud 'that it might be clearly understood of all knights, burghers and Mass-chanting priests'.

It was a declaration of war. 'When the vassals of the fief, the knights and citizens heard this read to them, they said they would all rather be dead or imprisoned than endure those conditions or do what was required, that it would reduce them all to the status of serfs, villeins and rustics'. The people of Moissac and Agen said they would rather sail to Bordeaux, a terrestrial impossibility, than have a Frenchman lording it over them. On 6 February the Count of Toulouse was excommunicated at the Council of Montpellier. On 17 April the decree was confirmed by the pope.[4]

Simon de Montfort was active in other matters. On 10 March Cabaret and its two neighbouring castles on the heights of Lastours had surrendered to the crusaders following the agreed release of Bouchard de Marly. Peter-Roger, the murderous opponent of the crusaders, was given a fief near Béziers.

The previous year, when grapes were ripe for gathering, all the vineyards near Lastours had been uprooted on the Count's orders and there had been a miracle. 'One of our adversaries shot at one of our men with a cross-bow, and hit him in the chest, just where the sign of the cross was fixed. Everyone thought he must be dead, since he wore no armour; but he was found to be quite unhurt – the bolt had failed even to penetrate his clothing, but had rebounded as if it had hit the hardest stone. Such is the wonderful power of God, his immense strength'.[5]

Towards the middle of March Simon de Montfort with a small army came to Lavaur, a Trencavel town of no strategic importance but known as 'La Citadelle de Satan', a place, according to Guillaume de Puylaurens, who was no more than eleven years old at the time, 'in which through the heretics the Devil has prepared a synagogue for himself'. It was almost the capital of Catharism, an asylum and a stronghold for believers. The name of Lavaur, 'the washing of gold', is reminiscent of the Roman place-names for the mines in the vicinity of Rennes-le-Château.[6]

Lavaur stands above the River Agout on the watershed between a plain to its west and a countryside green with hills and strewn with Cathar villages to the east. Lacking men to surround the town the crusaders set up their tents on one side by the Naridelle stream outside the Tour des Rondes. They prepared for a long siege. The defences would not be broken quickly. It had been besieged before in 1181 by Henri de Marsac, Bishop of Clairvaux, but with little success. Only two believers had recanted. Simon de Montfort was to be more resolute and ruthless.

Lavaur is a pleasant small town today, typically Occitan, a huddle of old streets and orange-red brick houses inside vanished ramparts that had stood in a long horseshoe setting, a neater spread of modern roads outside them. In medieval times it was protected by steep cliffs above the river to the west, and dismayingly heavy walls and towers to north, east and west. No 'man had ever seen in flat country, higher ramparts or deeper ditches'.[7]

The battlements formed an enormous U-shape whose open mouth ended at the cliffs above the river. Dismantled in 1229 by the Treaty of Meaux-Paris they had been impressively thick and high, so broad that armoured defenders rode their horses along the ramparts taunting the pygmies camped on the ground below 'to show their contempt for our side and demonstrate that the walls were substantial and well fortified. What arrogance!'[8]

Today the outline of these defences is preserved in the long curve of the allées Jean Jaurès overshadowed by plane trees on either side of the street. At the south-eastern terminus of this formidable barrier was the castle of the Plô, 'the plateau', high above the river. Unlike Minerve the town had several wells inside the walls and was plentifully supplied with provisions.

'Tents were pitched all round the castle, trebuchets and mangonels built. But nothing they did could harm the defenders . . . It was a place no one could ever take or storm. The gate was shut'. Lavaur seemed secure.[9] The substantial garrison had been strengthened by the arrival of many *faidits*, those knights made landless by the crusade. There were now several hundred trained, well-equipped fighting men inside the town. There were also refugees.

For generations the seigneurs of the town had protected Good Men, one of whom, Guilhabert de Castres, was in charge of an entire community there. It was predictable that Lavaur would refuse to hand over its Cathar inhabitants and those others who had fled to its sanctuary from Villemur and elsewhere on the news of the approaching army.

One of them was the eleven-year-old Arnauda of Lamothe, already a Good Woman, who stayed at Lavaur with another, Alzalais, but got away to Rabastens as the crusaders approached. Hers is a pathetic but remarkably well-documented life. Thirty-three years later in August, 1244, she was questioned by the Inquisition and in terror chose to save her own life by denouncing those '*amis, des fidèles, ces croyants*', the very friends, faithful companions and believers who had protected, fed, and loved her. Jacques d'Odors, the Ribière brothers, others, they all died. Already in 1213, with her older sister, Peironne, she had publicly renounced her vows in Montauban.[10]

She was just one of many guarded by the commander of Lavaur, Aimery, once a great land owner but now deposed, of Laurac, of Montréal, and the services of more than two hundred knights. His bitterness guaranteed a prolonged resistance with no thought of surrender.

With him was his sister, Guirauda, 'Na Geralda' in Occitan, whose husband, William Bernard, had been killed only the year before in one of the petty local skirmishes that were the social weakness of the Languedoc. His widow, the chatelaine of Lavaur, was the epitome of *paratge*, a word meaning not merely courtesy but the virtues of tolerance, hospitality, charity and justice. Guirauda was the daughter of Blanche of Laurac who had presided over a convent for Cathar women with her other daughter, Mabilia. Blanche's three sons were Good Men. To the Catholics such associations made Guirauda 'a heretic of the worst sort'.[11]

While the siege-engines, the catapults, the towers and battering-rams, the cats, were being prepared there were religious and military disagreements miles away in Toulouse between Raymond VI and the bishop, Foulques of Marseilles. While an excommunicant like the count remained in the city no Catholic services could be held. Foulques proposed that Raymond should briefly go outside the walls to allow his subjects to worship. The distrustful count refused. Indignant and resentful, Foulques quitted the city and did not return for almost four years.

He had already arranged for a considerable battalion, five thousand of his well-armed White Brotherhood, to join the crusaders at Lavaur. Raymond VI forbade them to leave. They ignored him but could not take any supplies with them.[12]

Duplicitous as always, the count sent provisions to Lavaur for the crusaders and ordered his seneschal, the steward of his palace, and some knights to assist the defenders there. Weeks later they were captured and held chained in prison for years.

At Lavaur a desultory bombardment of the north walls began. Until more men came it was almost symbolic, causing damage inside the walls but hardly affecting the walls themselves. Then, a survivor brought de Montfort news of a disaster.

Fourteen miles away hundreds of crusaders and pilgrims had been massacred. An untidy straggle of German horsemen, foot-soldiers and followers had left Carcassonne to join the siege. Casually passing through the long, low hills they were ambushed at a small wood near Montgey by Raymond-Roger, Count of Foix, his son, Roger-Bernard, and that violent enemy of the Crusade, Gerald of Pépieux.

There was a fierce and murderous fight in which nearly all the crusaders were killed. Those that fell, wounded and helpless, were abandoned to the sticks and clubs of peasants who beat them to death and rifled their clothing. A dying crusader who was also a priest staggered and crawled to a nearby church but was followed by Roger-Bernard and killed. To permit villeins and serfs to harm knights was an outrage against the code of chivalry and might explain the savagery that followed at Lavaur. Leaving the villagers to their profitable butchery, the Count of Foix and his companions raced to Montgiscard with their loot, weapons, supplies, clothing, money, enough 'for weeks, for months, for a year'.

Outside the church wall in the nearby hamlet of Auvezines there is a standing stone with a plaque of dubious statistics in remembrance of the slaughter. *'Ici ou environs réposent 6000 Croisés surpris et embuscade fin d'Avril 1211'* ('Here or nearby, lie 6,000 crusaders ambushed at the end of April 1211') ten times the probable number. But, as O'Shea drily remarked, the memorial 'must be unique in France for deploring the demise of an invading German army'.

Four years later at a Lateran Council the Count of Foix was defiant about Montgey. 'Those robbers, those traitors, those oath-breakers adorned with the cross who have destroyed me, neither I nor mine have laid hands on one of them who has not lost his eyes, his feet, his fingers and his hands. And I rejoice to think of those I have killed and regret the escape of those that got away'.[13]

At Lavaur, meanwhile, the reinforcements arrived. A wooden bridge was constructed across the river. The town was surrounded. Siege-towers were winched closer to the walls. One with a cross standing on it had its arm broken by a mangonel to the derision of the garrison. But the towers came closer and, underneath their protective 'cats', sappers began filling the ditch with earth and brushwood to make a firm platform on which scaling-ladders could be set up.

Warfare in the Middle Ages was not always brutal carnage. There was ingenuity. From inside the town men dug a tunnel beneath the wall, reached the ditch, dragged the brushwood away and set fire to the 'cat'. It was extinguished. More brushwood was pushed into the ditch. It was removed. There was more ingenuity. Instead of dry branches the attackers pressed green wood into the tunnel, ignited it. The thick smoke swirled chokingly into the subterranean passage making it impassable.

Unimpeded, the miners probed and levered at the wall's foundations. A section collapsed. Crusaders rushed into the breach. It was Tuesday 3 May, the Day of the Holy Cross, over six weeks since the siege began.

Street by street the defenders were driven back, killed. 'They fell so thick and fast that till the end of time men will tremble to think of it'. For those that lived there was no mercy. Too many crusaders were dead. That does not excuse the excesses that followed but it does explain them. Aimery, still in the weight of his armour, was hanged on an improvised gallows. It toppled. Impatiently, de Montfort ordered that the lord and eighty or more of his surviving knights should have their throats cut.

It was not the end of horror. Guirauda was discovered in the castle. She was a cultivated and refined woman who enjoyed the learned company of mathematicians, Arab astrologers, Jewish doctors. She had protected Cathars, welcomed Good Men from the Lauragais. On 3 May 1211, she was treated like an animal. *'Elle fut livrée à la soldates qui la dénudé, en abusa, avant de la jeter dans un puits aussitôt comblé de pierres'*. Screaming, she 'was offered for the amusement of the soldiery, stripped, abused and finally thrown down a well and buried under an avalanche of stones'.

It was, perhaps, the most disgraceful event in a series of shameful episodes as the 'crusade' steadily mouldered into a vicious, cut-throat war of reprisals. Guillaume de Tudela regretted the woman's death. It was 'a shame and a sorrow, for no one in this world, you may take my word for it, ever left her presence without having eaten'. The shame is shown in the reticence. Even Vaux-de-Cernay said only that she was 'thrown into a pit and stones heaped on her'. So did Guillaume de Puylaurens.[14]

After the mayhem the bishops and the priests entered Lavaur along today's cul-de-sac of the rue de la Brèche singing *Veni Creator Spiritus*. The road is probably misnamed. To the south of the town the course of the Naridelle river made that approach difficult. More probably the walls had been broken across the level ground at the north where the cathedral of St.-Alain now rises in triumph. The old Romanesque church there was so badly damaged that it had to be rebuilt.[15]

There is also uncertainty about the whereabouts of the well which may have been in the courtyard of the castle where Guirauda had been found. On the shutters of another well on the rue Père Colin near the Plô is a painting of her escorted by two armoured soldiers. Her martyrdom is commemorated annually on the third Sunday in May.

On the rather neglected Plô a stele was erected in 1995. The shape of a dove is carved through the slab as a memorial to her and to the many others who died on that day. Paradoxically and ironically the greatest memorial, literally the greatest, is the monstrous and gloomy church of St.-Alain with its almost windowless walls of red brick and its huge hexagonal tower. Erected in 1254 it is a statement of Catholic victory. Around it are English-style gardens with a menagerie of topiarism: a donkey, cockerel, snail, swan, a horticultural prettiness incongruously close to the atrocity of eight centuries ago. But the towering mass of the church is itself an unintended reminder of its beginnings.

Simon de Montfort, warrior and Catholic crusader, had not forgotten his mission. The Cathars of Lavaur were gathered up in their hundreds: Guillaume de Puylaurens said three hundred; Guillaume de Tudela said four; Pierre des Vaux-de-Cernay, 'innumerable'. Outside the town in a meadow a vast fenced pyre of stakes and a forest of bundled matchwood had been prepared for the largest conflagration of the entire crusade. It was a voluntary auto-da-fé. No one was snatched from the flames. No one abjured. All of them, men and women, went willingly to their appalling deaths 'and there we burnt them with joy in our hearts'.[16]

There were riches in Lavaur, bay and sorrel horses, armour, corn and wine, cloth, rich clothing but none of it went to the crusaders. Everything was given to Raimon de Salvagnac, usurer of Cahors, who had subsidised de Montfort's expenses and who also collected the hearth-tax imposed by the pope, handing it to the Knights Templars of Paris to pass on to Rome.

Cahors was notorious for its money-lenders, to Christians those despicable Shylocks whom Dante condemned to the fearsome seventh circle of the *Inferno*:

> So the third ring sets its seal on the double shame
> Of Sodom and of Cahors . . .

There, the usurers were doomed to endless pain, imprisoned and writhing on the scorching agonies of an expanse of burning sands:

About the neck of each a great purse hung
Whereon their eyes seemed still to fix and feed.[17]

After the siege was over Simon de Montfort left his wife, Alice, in the safety of Lavaur and returned to the war. In May the crusaders entered the nearby castle of Puilaurens whose commander, Sicard, and his men deserted on hearing news of Lavaur, close by. The fort was given to Gui de Lucy. It was a modest place, often known as Lapradelle-Puilaurens to distinguish it from the imposing bastion of Puylaurens high on the jagged chain of the Arquières near Quillan sixty miles to the south. Nothing remains of it today.

Beyond Puilaurens they came to Montgey. In retribution for its peasants' bloodthirsty despatch of the dying German knights and the theft of their belongings the village was burnt down and every one of its briefly-enriched inhabitants killed.

Late in May, near Castelnaudary in the deep heartland of heresy the army captured Les Cassès, 'the fortress of Lauragais', little more than a small walled town but whose heretics hiding in the tower were burnt, '*bien soixante, avec un joie immense*' although instead of sixty victims Guillaume de Tudela thought ninety-four.[18] Among them was Alazaïs, a Good Woman and mother of the town's lord . The deaths did not eradicate heresy. Thirty years later there were three Good Women living in the neighbouring woods, spinning wool for their upkeep. In the town hall there is a rough stone statuette. It is not, as often claimed, of the crucified Christ but of the living Jesus holding out his arms in prayer. It may be a very rare example of Cathar art.

Towards the end of May on the old Roman road between Toulouse and Carcassonne the crusaders laid siege to the run-down castle of Montferrand. It was defended by Baudouin, the younger brother of Raymond VI but no close friend of his. Baudouin was the son of Constance, sister of Louis VII. She had married Raymond V in 1154 but left him and his truculent ways in 1165 and returned to the royal court of Paris. Baudouin was born there that year. He went to Toulouse in 1194 only after the death of his father but was coldly suspected of being an impostor by his brother and had to return to

Paris for documents that proved his legitimacy. Even then, despite distinguishing himself in conflict on Raymond's behalf, he received no honours but was fobbed off with meagre gifts and disregard.

Despite seventeen years of fraternal indifference he resisted the crusaders gallantly at Montferrand and on his surrender he and his garrison were chivalrously rewarded by being permitted to retain their weapons. Baudoin then distinguished himself by restoring their stolen money to some pilgrims.

Montferrand became yet another possession of Simon de Montfort.[19] It was a double-edged acquisition. Men had to garrison it. Being in charge of a crusade continuously added to by forty-day levies wanting the papal benefits and hoping to gain plunder, continually depleted when they left, was like being the guard of a local cross-country train stopping everywhere, passengers boarding, others alighting, never knowing what change the next station might bring. Simon de Montfort never had the comforting stability of a standing army.

He was undeterred. With the excommunication of Raymond VI, the Count of Toulouse was no longer a crusader and his city could be legitimately attacked. But not instantly. After Lavaur many of his forces had gone home and until more came there was no possibility of overpowering a citadel whose walls alone extended over three miles.

Instead, de Montfort went sixty devastated miles northwards from Montferrand, crossed the Tarn and pressed into the eastern Albigeois taking towns: Montégut; Gaillac; St.-Marcel, Languépie. St.-Antonin, now St.-Antonin-Noble-Val, surrendered to him. He was indefatigable. Raymond VI, less resolute, was in the castle of Bruniquel only a few miles to the south.

There were spies everywhere, a bush telegraph that warned of the army's movements but also, without prejudice informed the army of its opponents' whereabouts. At this point in the story of the Crusade, three men briefly intermingle: Raymond VI; his brother Baudouin; and the chronicler-to-be, Guillaume de Tudela.

Baudouin had learned where his brother was and went to Bruniquel entreating the count to rejoin the crusaders and have his excommunication annulled. Raymond refused and prepared to set fire to the castle before leaving for the safe walls of Toulouse. Baudouin objected. Rather than destroying Bruniquel, let him become commander there. A bush telegraph can be defective. Raymond VI was unaware that his brother had become a vassal of Simon de Montfort but did know that Baudouin was an excellent and doughty warrior and believed that he could be trusted. He handed over the keys and departed.[20]

Guillaume de Tudela was a Catholic monk of Montauban, a pleasant, pink-bricked bastide half a day's ride from Bruniquel. Rather like that genius of siege-machinery, the archdeacon of Paris, Guillaume appears somewhat unfocussed as a cleric, being more interested in warfare than worship. Believing that the persistence of heresy in the Languedoc would inevitably ruin the entire countryside he took a chance, left Montauban at the first opportunity, 'and went to join Count Baldwin . . . at Bruniquel where the count was delighted to welcome him'.[21]

On 17 June, reinforced by some half-hearted and lacklustre German troops, de Montfort ambitiously committed himself to a siege of Toulouse. It was a powerful city occupied by three important but quite different men: its indecisive Count Raymond, the hot-headed Count of Foix who rode out to attack the crusaders, and Foulques, the Bishop of Toulouse, who urged his Catholics to give help to de Montfort.

Foulkes was another unusual priest. He had been a rich merchant of Marseilles and a famous troubadour who had abdicated fortune, family and fame to join the church. So deep was the spiritual change that when, in Paris, he heard a minstrel singing one of his love-songs, he was so shamed that he committed himself to a harsh penance.

Of his sincere piety there was no question. But with it went a single-minded righteousness and this led one of the finest of troubadours, Peire Cardenal from the volcanic town of Puy-de-Velay, to condemn him and all Catholic clergy for their hypocrisy. They gorged. They enriched themselves. Preaching chastity, they raped:

Monge solon estar dins los mostiers serratz,	Once monks in monasteries were shut
On azoravan Dieu denan las magestatz;	To worship God, saints, martyrs, but
E can son en las vilas on an lurs pöestastz,	Now into towns they come to rut.
Si avetz bela femna o es homs molheratz,	They'll grab some lovely wife, no slut,
El seran cobertor, si.eus peza o si.eus platz.	Force her down astride their gut.
E can el son desus e.l cons es sagelatz	The cunt-cursed cock thrust jut, jut, jut,
Ab las bolas redondas que pendon al matratz,	Bollocks bouncing on her butt.
Con la letras son clausas e lo traucs es serratz,	Out spat the spunk in spurts, a glut
D'aqui eyson l'iretge e li essabatatz.	To generate more godless smut.

It was bitter and justified. Nor did the Catholic clergy confine their carnality to the Languedoc. Two hundred years later in Paris the poet, François Villon, complained about the Carmelite friars:

Carmes, chevauchent noz voisines	Carmelites straddle our neighbours' wives.
Mais cela ce n'est que du mains.	Wring hands in disgust? It's just 'holy' lives.[22]

Like the lecherous Pierre Clergue of Montaillou a century later, hundreds of clerical kneecaps were calloused more by copulation than by prayer.

The vitriolic Raymond-Roger, Count of Foix, was even less polite about the bishop. At a Lateran Council in 1215 he denounced Foulques as 'the bishop who is so violent that in all that he does he is a traitor to God and to ourselves, has gained by means of lying songs and beguiling phrases which kill the very soul of any who sing them . . . this bishop has gained such power, such riches, that no one dares breathe a word to challenge his lies . . . and once he was elected Bishop of Toulouse, a fire has raged throughout the land that no water anywhere can quench, for he has destroyed the souls and bodies of more than five hundred people, great and small . . . he is more like Antichrist than a messenger from Rome'.[23]

Despite the presence inside Toulouse of the bishop with his belligerent White Brotherhood, de Montfort's siege became almost a farce, no more than a metaphorical shake of the fist. The walls were too long. Supplies from outside could not be stopped. Toulouse, 'the flower of cities', third in Europe after Rome and Venice, a city of life, laughter and solemnity whose wondrous cathedral of St.-Sernin is the largest surviving Romanesque church in the world, with its conspicuous octagonal belfry tower. Such a great city could not be overrun by de Montfort's meagre and unenthusiastic force. After a frustrating fortnight the crusaders went away.

Psychologically, the affair had been worse than a fiasco. When the news broke that a siege was threatened, many of the Catholic citizens entreated Foulques to intercede so that Toulouse could be spared. They had supported the Crusade, they had sent troops to Lavaur, they had given hostages to prove their loyalty to the cause. The over-confident Foulques and his priests spurned them. 'Expel the count and his henchmen from the city', the suppliants were told, 'renounce your allegiance to him, and accept instead whatever lord the church may appoint in his place. Otherwise we shall crush you and you shall suffer the fate of heretics and their protectors'.

To the churchmen diplomacy was unnecessary. De Montfort would attack and conquer as he always did. They were wrong. The siege failed and they had alienated their own supporters. When the burghers indignantly rejected the terms the stiff-necked Foulques ordered the provost of the cathedral and all his priests to leave the city. Deprived of their church services, insulted by the peremptory demands, the citizens suffered further hardship. They watched the besieging army despoil the unprotected suburban gardens of food and fruit, rip up the growing vines and kill men working in the fields.

'Some thirty-three villeins of the district died at the edge of a meadow', wrote Guillaume de Tudela. In retaliation a crusader, Sir Eustace of Cayeux, was trapped and slain by a blow from an 'ash-shafted lance decorated with blue and white shield-shaped trimmings, a blow so heavy he could not get up again'. After more savage and unsuccessful fighting de Montfort, already weakened by some of his 'forty-day' crusaders returning to Germany, gave up on 29 June. By that time the Catholic inhabitants of Toulouse were wholehearted supporters of Raymond VI, their count.[24]

Disheartened and enfeebled by desertions the crusaders left Toulouse in the hope of taking the lesser citadel of Foix, five weary days away. They overran the countryside, damaged crops, endured the sweating days of summer but never threatened Foix. It was too strong.

Tucked at the juncture where the River Arget flowed into the heavier Ariège, the city stood at the mouth of a jaggedly peaked glacial valley with the snows of the Pyrenees rising a few miles to the south. The place was unassailable on its 60m high crag, 'a huge rock which seems to have fallen from the sky into the heart of the old town' like an upturned knee of solid gneiss.[25] On it were the ramparts. Inside those curtain walls was the castle with prisoners' graffiti in its dungeons. Today, rising above everything like a fairy tale fortress, are three tall and slender towers, two rectangular, one round and 34m high, a fifteenth century addition. In it is a museum with a stone from the wall of the old graveyard at Ussat. The outline of a fish is engraved on it. 'It is a truly authentic piece of Cathar work' like the doves from Montségur and from the grotto at Ussat, 'a rare piece of Cathar artistic symbolism'.[26]

The Count of Foix was the implacably fierce Raymond-Roger, supporter of Good Men and Women and merciless persecutor of Catholics. His faith was almost a family tradition. His son, Roger-Bernard III married a Cathar, Ermessende of Castelbon. In 1269 her heretical corpse was exhumed from a Catholic cemetery and burned by the Inquisitor of Aragon. Roger-Bernard's own death was a contradiction. Dying in March, 1302 he was consoled by the Good Man, Peter Autier, in the hall of Tarascon castle. Days later his funeral was conducted by the Catholic Bishop of Carcassonne in the presence of several abbots.[27]

Raymond-Roger himself had attended the ordination of his sister, Esclarmonde and four other noblewomen at Fanjeaux in 1204. His wife, Philippa, was also a Good Woman and the count provided her with a house in Pamiers despite the angry but futile opposition of the canons of St.-Antonin's cathedral in the town.

In his lifetime monkish scribes reacted differently to his deeds – or misdeeds. To Guillaume de Tudela, equivocal monk but enthusiastic military historian, Foix was a fine speaker, a valiant warrior and deservedly famous. Pierre des Vaux-de-Cernay condemned the traitor unambiguously as a monstrous persecutor of the church and a cruel dog whose 'wickedness exceeded all bounds . . . and never lost his thirst for blood'.[28]

Yet, in the autumn of 1209, after the massacre at Béziers and the capture of Carcassonne, Raymond-Roger with many nobles had thought it politic to swear allegiance to Simon de Montfort. As the crusading army dwindled, however, defections began: knights like Gerald of Pépieux; towns such as Castres.

Foix himself may have turned against de Montfort because of the death of Raymond-Roger Trencavel in the November of 1209. History suggests that he had personal reasons for his apostasy, suspecting that the young viscount had been murdered.

Born in 1185 the boy had endured a harsh tutelage as a page under Bertrand, Lord of Saissac, until reaching his majority at the age of 14 in 1199. Two years earlier it had been the same Bertrand who had religious objections to the choice of the new Catholic Abbot of Alet-les-Bains, five miles north of Rennes-le-Château. He acted on them. Forcing his way into the abbey, happening to kill some monks on the way, he imprisoned the unacceptable appointee, dug up the corpse of his predecessor, Pons Amiel, placed the dead body on the throne and in its macabre presence elected Boson, a man favourable to the Cathars. Boson remained abbot until 1222.[29]

In 1199 the young Trencavel became a squire to the Count of Foix and under his tutelage the lad acquired the military skills demanded of a knight, mounted on his destrier tilting with a lance at the quintain whose heavy sandbag could swing round and unhorse him if he were clumsy. He learned to carry his small shield on his left arm, learned to wear the heavy helmet with its ventilated holes and its eye-level slit so narrow that he could only see straight ahead. Days, weeks, months passed of practice with sword, mace, ball-and-chain, battle-axe, dagger, riding straight-legged in his high-backed saddle, controlling his ever-more spirited horse until, late in 1201, he spent a night-long vigil on his knees before the altar on which the pieces of his armour were placed. Next morning, he made his confession to a bishop who blessed his sword and touched the viscount on the shoulder with it. The Count of Foix shod him with the golden spurs and presented him with the banner of a knight.[30] He was the protégé of Raymond-Roger and news of his death in a dungeon of Carcassonne's Tour Pinte may have embittered his patron. Stories had spread that he had been killed.

Que pensez-vous qu'il arriva?	What do you think happened to him?
Simplement qu'on l'empoisonna.	Simply that someone poisoned him.

A woman may have been involved, 'Louve' of Pennautier, the beautiful woman that some fifteen years earlier had been adored by the troubadour, Peire Vidal. Still married she had disgraced herself by becoming the mistress of the Count of Foix. At the age of 47 it was murmured that she had tried to seduce the 16-year old Raymond in the castle of Foix and been refused.

There were rumours, unsubstantiated, that for revenge she became part of a trap to lure the unsuspecting viscount into the crusaders' camp at Carcassonne in 1209 where he was falsely arrested and imprisoned in the cell where he died.[31] Gossip, imaginary, even false, that Trencavel had been done to death may have caused Raymond-Roger's defection. If so, the crusaders were to regret it. Hot-tempered, rashly impulsive, ruthless, the count exacted vengeance on Catholic pilgrim and monk alike and in that inevitably catastrophic collision between spiritual certainty and physical violence it was the count's brutality that dominated.

Pilgrims were imprisoned and tortured in his castle. Travelling on the Via Tolosana from Arles to St.-Gilles on their way to Compostella, the plan of whose church was a copy of St.-Sernin in Toulouse, some of them visited the shrine of St.-Volusien in Foix, a fifth century Bishop of Tours who had been martyred at Varilhes just north of Foix by Visigoths going to Carcassonne and Rennes-le-Château.

The pilgrims sensibly used the helpful twelfth century *Pilgrims' Guide* by the monk, Aimery Picaud. With its recommendations of churches to see and comfortable places to stay at it read like a medieval *Michelin*: Tiermes, with its royal baths in which the water was always hot; Estella, with good bread and excellent wine; Sahagun, overflowing with all delights. Perhaps it was not coincidental that these were all Cluniac establishments, an order to which Picaud may have belonged.[32]

Going to Foix could be disastrous. Sadism was obligatory in the castle whose garrison 'made a frequent practice of suspending priests and other servants of the Lord's ministry, and on occasion, most dreadful to relate, tied cords to their genitals, and pulled them violently. What cruel barbarity, what unheard-of madness!'

Priests were persecuted in their own churches. Two knights had brought their mother, a Good Woman, to the seeming safety of Pamiers only to learn that the abbot had contemptuously driven her out of the town. In retaliation, one of the sons murdered a priest at mass in a nearby village church, and the 'altar is still red with the blood of the slaughtered priest'. The same man mutilated a monk in St.-Antonin's monastery by gouging out his eyes.

Even that was not sufficient for the men of Foix. Their count went to the monastery, demanding the keys which the abbot attempted to conceal in the tomb of St.-Antonin the Martyr. Raymond-Roger snatched them and locked abbot, monks, priests and laymen inside the church for three entire days without food, water, with no means of relieving themselves 'for so long that they were driven by thirst to drink their own urine'. The count ransacked the library, the treasury, anywhere there were valuables, roistered bawdily with harlots in the desecrated library before driving his prisoners into the open air almost naked. He then dismantled part of the church for material to strengthen his castle in Pamiers.

Marching on the monastery of Ste.-Marie he removed all the furniture and sacred vessels, smashed the bells. With only the walls standing he demanded, and received, 50,000 sous as ransom for the ruin. In an astonishing blasphemy one of his knights jested, 'We have destroyed St.-Antonin and Ste.-Marie; it only remains for us to destroy God!'

Everywhere around Foix Catholic property was attacked, images of the crucified Christ were damaged, legs and arms broken, hands broken off. Any priests, any crusaders that were captured were chained and their tormentors 'applied themselves diligently to thinking up new and original tortures'.[33]

In all this Simon de Montfort with his depleted army was helpless and eventually abandoned all thought of Foix, departing for Cahors a dragging hundred miles to the north where he bartered with money lenders for further advances before moving on devoutly to the miraculous village of Rocamadour in the Dordogne.

A constant drain of his 'forty-day crusaders' from Germany, dissatisfied unpaid mercenaries vanishing, his force dwindled to little more than a band of loyal knights with their soldiers. When Raymond VI, vacillating Count of Toulouse, learned how tiny a group of his enemies remained, 'he summoned his host from every corner of the fief and sent to tell all his servants to prepare at once'. It was to be the first full-scale opposition that de Montfort was to encounter.[34] It proved yet again how formidable an opponent he was.

According to Guillaume de Tudela, the southern army was enormous. 'More than two hundred thousand they are, as they stand arrayed in the field. Villeins urge on the beasts pulling carts laden with bread and wine and other supplies; buffaloes and heavy oxen haul the catapults'.[35] By the end of July the stupendous army was moving from Toulouse towards Carcassonne. Simon de Montfort abandoned Montferrand. Encouraged by the approach of the southerners the villagers at Puilaurens ejected the few crusaders of the garrison.

It was a desperate time. De Montfort's wife, Alice, was cut off in Lavaur. Amaury, his son, was ill in Fanjeaux. His infant daughter, Petronilla, was with her nurses at Montréal. They were all miles apart and he was helpless to save them.

A second-rate general would have shut himself in a stronghold like Carcassonne, defying capture, but a long siege would gain de Montfort nothing and would probably hearten more enemies to join the Count of Toulouse. Instead, he took the advice of an English crusader, Hugh de Lacy. 'Go to the weakest castle you possess, wait for the enemy to come up and then, once you have reinforcements, attack, and I am sure you will defeat them'.

It was sensible. The crusaders' experienced heavy cavalry, even though out-numbered, was likely to be more effective than the untried horsemen that would oppose them. De Montfort left Carcassonne and went to the shattered walls and water-shortage of Castelnaudary. With him were no more than five hundred men, some of them undependable.

By early September, with de Montfort inside the feebleness of Castelnaudary, Raymond VI camped on the nearby hill of La Pech, not threateningly, but digging deep trenches and raising sturdy palisades so that his army seemed more besieged than besieging. He had a trebuchet but no good stone. It broke harmlessly on impact and the bombardment was useless. The count's jester mocked him, 'Why are you expending so much effort on this machine? Why are you trying to break down the walls of this place? Do you not see that every day the enemy are coming right up to your tents, yet you dare not go out to meet them?'[36] The frightened people of Castelnaudary abandoned their homes. The Count of Foix and his son attacked the town but were driven off. In return, de Montfort made reckless personal assaults on the outworks of Raymond VI, endangering his own life, achieving nothing.

But reinforcements were arriving. With the Bishop of Cahors came the mercenary, Martin Algai, with twenty men from Saissac, and Bouchard de Marly with a further hundred from Castres. Circuitously avoiding ambushes, they brought supplies. The sight of a white falcon seemed auspicious. But near Castelnaudary their entry was blocked by the troops of the Count of Foix .

Next morning after the crusaders had celebrated mass the two armies met at St Martin-Lalande, a hamlet a few miles east of Castelnaudary alongside the little Lésquel river. The previous night de Montfort had sent forty more knights to Bouchard, who had a strength of perhaps four hundred men. It was insufficient. 'Foix and his allies numbered a good two thousand and had fast horses, hauberks, [quilted jackets] strong shining helmets or good iron headpieces, sharp spears, strong ashen shafts and crushing maces'. It was to be the first set battle of the crusade. It proved what was already suspected, that the Count of Toulouse was a coward and it was an occasion when the impulsive fieriness of the Count of Foix failed against the military ability of Simon de Montfort.[37]

Foix arranged his battle-lines in a traditional, rather outdated, formation, armoured cavalry in the centre, dismounted light horse on one wing, foot-soldiers with lances on the other. De Marly, seeing that the defences were at the sides, audaciously attacked the centre.

But there were too many against him and slowly, bloodily, his men were driven back. The fighting was merciless. That bitter enemy of the crusaders, Gerald of Pépieux, charged, encountered a Breton in a wood, and 'Through shield, through arm-guard and hauberk and deep into the rear saddlebow he struck, and his pennon was red with blood. That one fell dead unshriven'.[38]

Outnumbered, Marly began to withdraw in order to regroup. But the mercenary, Algai, panicked. 'We are all dead', he shouted, and fled. The Bishop of Cahors who had reproved him also decided that discretion was preferable to death and left the field.

Characteristically, Raymond VI, Count of Toulouse, dithered and did nothing. Just as characteristically, Simon de Montfort did. Leaving a mere five knights in Castelnaudary, he took fifty with him to meet Marly who, surprisingly, had not been pursued. The southern mercenaries were pillaging the crusaders' baggage-train.

The crusaders returned to the battle and attacked, de Montfort on one flank, de Marly on the other, slashing, hacking and thrusting into the sides of the enemy. The struggle was fierce. Some thirty crusaders were killed but the southerners were massacred. 'Only the Count of Foix fought back, and his shield was split and his sword notched from all the blows he had struck'. With his son and some knights they dealt out 'mortal blows. If the others had done as much, the battle would not have been so quickly lost nor Foix and his men defeated'.[39]

The pusillanimous Raymond VI, safely protected, was told of the defeat and quitted the camp. Behind him he left his trebuchet. 'I don't think they would have brought it away with them for a hundred thousand marks of silver'. De Montfort went to Castelnaudary 'and went straight to the church with feet unshod to give thanks to the Almighty for the favours he had received. In the church our soldiers sang *Te Deum Laudamus* with great devotion and joy'.[40]

The battle of St Martin-Lalande was the event that changed the Crusade. It provoked the resistance of desperation. The invaded southerners, especially those with Cathar leanings, had been reluctant to fight against fellow Christians until the Crusade had deteriorated into a war of conquest. Southerners resented the northern invasion and the loss of their lands.[41] The Albigeois rose in rebellion so successfully that, despite his craven behaviour, Raymond VI recovered his fiefs.

The Count of Foix, cunning as well as courageous, broadcast rumours that the crusaders had been defeated and Simon de Montfort hanged.[42] There were uprisings, at first local, becoming widespread. A carpenter at Lagrave, a village just east of Gaillac, invited the commander of the garrison, Pons de Beaumont, to inspect some new water casks, and as the man leaned over, killed him with an axe. A few days later the brother of Raymond VI, the southern renegade, Baudouin, came to Lagrave. Deceived by his golden cross of Toulouse, the citizens welcomed him. Every one of them, fifty or more, man, woman, child, was slain, 'almost in a single day'.[43]

Despite the horror, defiance persisted in the Languedoc. Castles and towns returned to their Occitanian allegiances. Men who had sworn fealty to the Crusade reneged. William Cat, a southerner, deserted. Such changes of allegiance multiplied. Gerald of Pépieux had done so. So had Bernard IV, Count of Comminges. Pierre des Vaux-de-Cernay cursed him as one of 'that villainous and damned trio, the Counts of Foix and Comminges and Gaston de Béarn'. Worst of all was that 'son of the Devil, servant of the Antichrist, Savary de Mauléon, more evil than any heretic, worse than any infidel, assailant of the church, the enemy of Christ. O most corrupt of mortals – or should I say himself a mortal infection? . . . himself the devil incarnate'.[44]

De Mauléon was the seneschal of Poitou for King John of England. With his Poitevin mercenaries and crossbowmen he joined Raymond VI, fought bravely at St Martin-Lalande but later kidnapped Raymond's son because the Count of Toulouse owed him ten thousand golden *livres*. Fidelity and steadfastness were fragile qualities during the Albigensian Crusade.

Among the many defections was the castle of Coustaussa. Just west of Rennes-le-Château it is one of the neglected forts of the Languedoc. Few visit it. It was never a massive fortification like

Peyrepertuse or elegant like the goldenness of Arques; nor was it the scene of a dramatic siege and bloodshed like Montségur. It was just one of a hundred similar castles in Occitania.

Built in 1157, its garrison had fled in 1210 when they learned of the surrender of Termes even though that stronghold was fifteen mountainous miles to the east through the gorges of the Orbieu. After the propaganda of Castelnaudary, the inhabitants pledged fidelity to Toulouse – but they quickly abandoned it after a brief siege by de Montfort. To prevent further treachery, he had the walls dismantled.[45]

The castle, never big, was rebuilt as a cramped rectangle and was occupied on and off in a slovenly manner until the early nineteenth century when its chambers and roofs were allowed to decay. Today, with a weed-thick wandering path below shabby walls it seems of no importance. Yet the village had a singular history.

Good Men still lived there in the early fourteenth century as they did in nearby Arques. 'While I was at Arques my mother told me Peter Autier, the heretic, was with Gilles Bothold', William Arzelier informed the Inquisitor. From the hamlet of Coustaussa the woman, Cassagnas, had gone to Ax-les-Thermes and the house of Sibylla d'En Baille for her twelve torturing weeks of *endura*. Many centuries later the Abbé Saunière's friend, Abbé Antoine Gélis was buried in the village's hillside cemetery. He was savagely murdered in his presbytery in 1897, killed, it is claimed, by someone searching for the explanation of Saunière's sudden wealth.

Coustaussa is a quiet place now, a tortuous meander uphill from the main road. It was not always peaceful. Napoléon Peyrat encouraged its unquiet by the publication of his *Histoire des Albigeois*. In its pages, having already over-estimated a million deaths during the fifteen years of the Crusade, he transformed the Good Woman, Esclarmonde, into an unlikely female, as lovely as Helen of Troy, as valiant as Joan of Arc and as saintly as Mother Theresa. He also transformed the Cathar 'treasure' smuggled out of Montségur in 1244. Over the years it romantically mutated from material wealth into a priceless archive of ancient wisdom and finally, as ideas merged into imagination, into the Holy Grail itself, the chalice from which Jesus and his disciples drank at the Last Supper and in which Joseph of Arimathea caught Christ's blood at the Crucifixion.

Enthusiastic followers of Peyrat were convinced that Mary Magdalene had brought it to the Languedoc where, over the unrecorded centuries, it eventually became the hallowed property of the Cathars. For that reason the church at Rennes-le-Château was dedicated to her.

Predictably, from the late nineteenth century onwards Coustaussa suffered as one of the places ravaged by credulous treasure-seekers, optimistic mystics, even of Heinrich Himmler's SS in search of evidence for Christ's Aryan ancestry. There is no record of any worthwhile discovery. Abandonment, weather, digging made the place so dangerous from falling stones that by 2001 entrance was forbidden. '*Accés au Château Interdit. Chutes de Pierres!*'

At the end of 1211 de Montfort was struggling for control. His ally, Baudouin, returned to Bruniquel, recaptured some castles. But the Crusade was failing. Virtually all that had been won was lost. Only Lavaur remained. Even the arrival of Robert Mauvoisin with a hundred knights and several thousand foot-soldiers was small consolation. Desertions continued throughout the Languedoc.

FIVE

1212–1213. Miravel, Moissac and Muret

The beginning of 1212 was less than two and a half years after the massacre at Béziers yet those brief months had transformed the Languedoc into a war-zone. Walled towns had been devastated, castles demolished, villages burned, crops and vines uprooted, nobleman, troubadour and serf alike left homeless.

In a time when an army could move only at the pace of its infantry and its wagon-train de Montfort travelled hundreds of determined, almost fanatical miles; ninety from Béziers in the east to Toulouse, from Foix in the south into the hills of the Lauragais and northwards to Cahors at the edge of the Dordogne, a further hundred miles. He twisted and turned for uncounted miles through valleys, over uplands, across rivers, seeking out opponents. He was tireless. Yet, often un-remarked, the mission to rid Occitania of its Cathars steadily became secondary to a war whose aim was the establishing of a minor kingdom for the military leader of the Crusade. Only his Catholic clergymen looked on the capture of a town less as a territorial gain than as a means of discovering and punishing of heretics. From 1212 to 1213 their zeal was not matched by their influence.

Before 1212 some six hundred Cathars had gone willingly to their deaths, a few at Tonneins, one at Castres, about one hundred and forty at Minerve, perhaps four hundred at Lavaur, sixty or more at Les Cassès. In empty contrast, from 1212 to 1213 there is not one record of an execution. Not one. Even that enthusiastic monk, Pierre des Vaux-de-Cernay, was silent.

111

It was not because de Montfort had become half-hearted. To the contrary, reinforced by Robert Mauvoisin and his knights and with the welcome addition of his brother, Guy, returning from the Holy Land at Christmas, 1211, in the twenty months from January, 1212 to August, 1213 he campaigned in the far north beyond Albi.[1] He took possession of more than fifty towns and castles: La Pomarède whose inhabitants fled, Albedun, Les Touelles where there was a mass slaughter, Cahuzac after a hard siege, Montégut, Rabastens, St.-Marcel unsuccessfully besieged, Hautpoul and a troubadour's castle, then Cuq, Montmaur, St.-Félix, Les Cassès retaken, Montferrand, Avignonet, St.-Michel, totally destroyed 'and many others'.

Puilaurens fell, St.-Martin Laguepié burnt down, St.-Antonin taken without the need of swords, Montcuq, Caylus, Penne d'Agenais on its pinnacle, Agen, Penne d'Albigeois, Marmande, Biron where a traitor was hanged, Moissac where de Montfort was wounded in the foot, Montauban, Castelsarrasin, Saverdun, Muret abandoned by its townsfolk, the peaceful surrender of St.-Gaudens, seventeen more castles and a siege of Puycelsi that could not be sustained, Pujol captured and handed to three knights who had volunteered to harry the country around Toulouse, and finally Roquefort late in 1213 when, after all his exertions, de Montfort was once again 'virtually alone and deserted'. In all this subjugation and terror not one Cathar had been persecuted.[2]

The Languedoc remained rebellious. 'The whole of the Albigensian area was in a confused and unstable state. The enemies of the faith and the King of Aragon's knights . . . were visiting our fortresses and inviting the inhabitants to desert and surrender'.[3] The year 1212 started in crisis. 1213 ended in one.

The first months were a strange period. Raymond VI, Count of Toulouse, had a vast army in the field, lumbering uneasily after de Montfort, killing stragglers, half-hearted siege following irresolute siege, a powerful force whose leader never dared to attack the many fewer crusaders, a timid enemy who existed powerfully in the neighbourhood, never a danger, always an irritant.

Northern Languedoc was almost unknown territory for de Montfort, far from Carcassonne in the unexplored, rustic, sometimes spectacular wave of hills in the Vère and Cérou valleys south of the River Aveyron. In this *terra incognita* he achieved little at first. By 12 March when Arnaud Amaury, that haughty cleric, became Archbishop of Narbonne the crusaders had captured just two castles and were optimistically laying siege to the sturdy walls of St.-Marcel, a stronghold commanded by Gerald of Pépieux twelve miles beyond Albi. Even though de Montfort had sent for Baudouin to join him his men were still too few to blockade more than one side of the stronghold.

Some impotent days later Raymond VI, Count of Toulouse, arrived with the Counts of Comminges and Foix and an immense body of soldiers. Yet although he outnumbered the crusader knights by at least five and arguably ten to one and the foot-soldiers by a hundredfold, instead of attacking, Raymond set up a watchful camp on the far side of St.-Marcel.

Nothing happened. De Montfort did nothing. So did the Count of Toulouse. Guillaume de Tudela was scornful of the crusaders' tactics. 'They laid siege to St.-Marcel and acted very stupidly, not achieving anything there worth a rotten apple, nothing but expense, may God bless me!' He added that Toulouse was as culpable because the count 'could easily have destroyed them but he and his men were so much afraid . . . that they made no attempt at an attack'.

His comments were not completely fair. Predictably, the Count of Foix did try to destroy the crusaders' catapults but was driven off. Then, short of provisions, with no bread for days, de Montfort raised the siege on 24 March and retreated to Albi, where they were met by the Abbot of Vaux-de-Cernay and the other chronicler of the crusade, his monk, Pierre.[4] There was an interesting aftermath to the St.-Marcel impasse. Returning to its walls in May de Montfort found them undefended and despite the begging of its citizens he levelled the defences and burnt everything down. St.-Marcel-Campes never recovered.

Ten years later in November, 1222, Raymond VII, a more resolute commander than his father, founded the double-walled town of Cordes-le-Ciel on an imposing, cloud-touching hill a few miles away.

Named after Cordoba because, like it, Cordes had leather and textile workers, the new town was privileged to pay neither tax nor toll. It flourished as a centre of Catharism with a workshop of 1224 for weavers and their apprentices. It provided a perfect disguise for Good Men such as Sicard de Figueras who could combine preaching with weaving.

By that time there had been a change in the attitude of some believers. When two Inquisitors interrogated an old woman of Cordes, condemned her as a heretic and had her burnt alive the enraged population lynched them, dragged them scraping along the mud-encrusted streets and, perhaps mindful of the disgraceful death of another woman, Guirauda in Lavaur many years earlier, with poetic revenge, hurled them down a well.[5]

Wrecked by Huguenots in the sixteenth century, medieval Cordes has been charmingly restored and, despite the steep, cobbled walk up to it, the old town, with its almost intact walls, barricaded gates and narrow streets is an attractive place to visit. So is the countryside with its wooded hills sloping into the vineyards of Gaillac.

Numerous reinforcements had been arriving for de Montfort, some of them forty-day noblemen, knights and soldiers, the Count of Berg from Germany, Leopold IV from Austria, French knights from the Auvergne, Normans, all of them gathered at Carcassonne where they received instructions but no maps. Some losing their way in the unfamiliar wildernesses were hacked to pieces by the remorseless Count of Foix.

Other reinforcements were not so welcome, untrained, often unarmed volunteers anxious to take part in a holy war. Despite their limitations, de Montfort accepted them. They had younger contemporaries.

A time of religious hysteria in Europe, 1212 was the year of the pathetic Childrens' Crusade, some of its participants almost infants, no older than six. Led by a French peasant boy, Stephen of Cloyes, and a German, Nicholas of Cologne, tens of thousands from France and Germany hoped to reach Jerusalem. Few did. Many died of starvation or disease. They may have been fortunate. Others reached

Marseilles where unscrupulous sea-captains took them to North Africa and sold them as slaves. The tragic episode may have inspired the thirteenth century legend of the Pied Piper of Hamelin.[6]

Simon de Montfort, Viscount of Carcassonne, had always possessed ability and courage. Now he had power. With so many men at his command he decided to split the ample forces and take the war into the lands of his most persistent opponent, the Count of Foix. Placing his brother Guy at their head he sent the French contingent southwards.

Some miles north of the hamlet of Montaillou, where Béatrice of Planisolles would live, the crusaders met their first resistance at the fortified town of Lavelanet. One of its several lords was Raymond of Péreille, the man whom Cathars had asked to restore the mountaintop castle of Montségur. For all its walls, Lavelanet was not as challenging as that sky-touching refuge. It fell. No quarter was given to a garrison that did not surrender. The people of Lavelanet were slaughtered.

News of the massacre spread. There was panic. Castles were set on fire by their occupants. Townsfolk and villagers fled to Toulouse. Everywhere, the crusaders came to abandoned settlements and everywhere, in a war of terror, they ravished the countryside, uprooting, burning, killing livestock, finding crops, leaving a wasteland. In his castle even the Count of Foix was helpless against such an army. The smoke of a scorched landscape clouded the skies.

In the north de Montfort rode out of Carcassonne and into the Lauragais. There, on 8 April, in the steep hills and low mountains near Mazamet, he arrived at the castle of Hautpoul that had once submitted to him, only to defect.

Built by the Visigoths and systematically strengthened over the centuries, it seemed to the awed Pierre des Vaux-de-Cernay utterly unapproachable, it was so high on such a huge crag. 'Even if the gates were opened', he gasped, 'and no resistance offered from inside, it would be impossible without the greatest difficulty to walk through the castrum and climb up the keep'.

During the siege catapults were used but to little effect. When some crusaders scrambled through a breach they were bombarded with heavy stones and had to fight their way back to safety through the flames of a spreading fire that the defenders had ignited behind them.

Yet, maybe dismayed by the sight of the gigantic host below them, after sunset on the fourth day when a thick mist made them invisible some of the garrison sidled out and disappeared. Hearing noises de Montfort's men scrabbled their way up to the walls, made prisoners of those that remained, came upon others trying to get away in the darkness, and slew every one. Next day the keep was demolished and the houses of the crowded settlement burnt down. Today all that survives are some roofless walls and gaping, round-arched windows. What did persist in the rebuilt village was Catharism. There were workplaces for Cathar weavers in the nearby woods. And, around 1240, Hautpoul became the bishopric of the Good Man, Jean de Collet.[7]

Like the holocaust at Lavelanet, news of the disaster at Hautpoul rippled frighteningly outwards into the hills and the halls whose defences were swiftly abandoned. At the unimpressive minor castle and village of Miravel-Cabardès some miles south of Hautpoul, Raymond, one of its three fraternal lords, left with his wife and his retinue of forty men. They had no choice. The crusaders would have killed them without compunction both for being Cathars and for having given aid to an enemy. The nearby house of Good Men had sheltered a southern knight who was dying of his wounds. There was even a house of Good Women, including Blanche of Miravel, inside the walled settlement itself.

Raymond of Miravel became a *faidit*, a knight deprived of his lands. He was also an accomplished and well-mannered troubadour, one-time admirer of 'Louve' of Pennautier. He had known the court and the Count of Toulouse for twenty years. The Monk of Montaudon, another troubadour, mocked him for his airs.

> And the third is from the Carcassés –
> Miravel – whose pretensions have no peer –
> Always giving men his castle, but he's
> Never there more than once a year
> And never for the Feast Day. So
> Why should he care if he lets it go?

A year after Hautpoul that exiled poet and his poetess wife, Gaudairenca, were at Toulouse. So was Pedro II, the King of Aragon. Raymond praised him. 'The king has promised me that in a short time I shall have Miravel again and my Audiart shall recover his Beaucaire, the ladies and their lovers shall regain their lost delights'. It was the optimism of a romantic. History proved it unrealistic.[8]

There were other desertions. Raymond VI, lurking in the dubious safety of Puilaurens castle, fled to the guaranteed protection of Toulouse. De Montfort gave it to Guy de Pucy and continued with his victories, helped by an unlikely conquest by his scruffy hangers-on.

During May at St.-Antonin the Bishop of Albi had entreated the defenders to surrender. Its viscount jeered at him. 'Let the Count of Montfort know that a crowd of stick-carriers will never take my castrum', referring disparagingly to the staves that the crusading knights carried. His were mistakenly prophetic words. The knights needed neither staves nor swords, not even armour. Camped on level ground by a stream, they were pestered by long-range arrowshots throughout the day and then at night, retired into their tents, the enemy bowmen came closer and the irritated knights found arrows piercing the flimsy walls of their shelters.

But before they had time to gird themselves, it was the unarmed riff-raff that attacked the garrison, howling and shouting, rushing at the walls, pelting the surprised defenders with stones 'and in the space of one hour captured three strong barbicans', three of the four great gateways into the town. 'A fight without swords', marvelled Vaux-de-Cernay, 'a glorious victory'. It was reminiscent of the affray at Béziers. 'You would hardly have had time to cook an egg before they took the place that night', marvelled Tudela.

After argumentative negotiations the ordinary inhabitants of St.-Antonin were spared. Some of the garrison had already died, drowned in the river as they ran away, or cut down. The commander and his remaining knights were imprisoned in Carcassonne. St.-Antonin was given to Baudouin, who made Guillaume de Tudela a canon there. 'And then Guillaume composed and wrote this book. Once he began it, he thought of nothing else till it was done and indeed scarcely gave himself time for sleep'.[9] He must have died in the following year for, from the middle of 1213 onwards, the *Chanson de la Croisade Albigeoise*, his *Song of the Albigensian Crusade*, was continued by a very different chronicler, unnamed and unknown, presumably a southerner, less sympathetic to the Catholic cause. A poet.[10]

The campaign had been easy and in June there were more easy acquisitions as other towns in the lower Quercy region, like Montcuq, submitted. Confidently, de Montfort advanced westwards into the lovely Agenais countryside of the Tarn and Lot rivers with its meadows, woodlands and vineyards. It was lovely but by the time he reached Penne d'Agenais the crusader was isolated, over a hundred miles from Carcassonne, with his brother's army the same distance to the south near Foix. The Count of Toulouse was nowhere near him but neither were reinforcements. With only a few mounted knights, just battalions of armed men on foot, he laid siege to Penne d'Agenais not far from Agen where had already been well received.

Penne was different. It is a vertiginous ruin today but on 3 June 1212 it was forbidding. So was its garrison. On the long, contested frontier between France and its English possessions from Poitiers down to Agen, a frontier of strong castles, Penne was one of the strongest, modified and improved in the 1180s by that master of military architecture, Richard Coeur de Lion. It lacked nothing. It had thick, high walls, a heavy keep rising above them, it had a new well, and within the ponderous outworks there were two forges, a bakery, even a windmill.

On its sharp-sided natural crag it was commanded by a seneschal of Raymond VI, a Navarrese mercenary from Aragon, Hugues d'Alfaro, who had married a bastard daughter of the Count of Toulouse, Guillemette. With him were four hundred Spanish mercenaries.

Like most castles, Penne had a civilian settlement for its servants, serfs and farmers who lived in the cottages and makeshift shelters on the long slope at the top of the rock. D'Alfaro levelled everything and sent the occupants away. With no concealment any attackers, once they struggled to the crest, were completely unprotected across the wide exposed approach. It was a killing ground for defenders armed with heavy, long-range crossbows. D'Alfaro's confident, well-provisioned garrison retired into the castle and keep.

As with many well-paid Spanish mercenaries, Penne's garrison was equipped not with the ordinary crossbow whose string was wound tight by hand but by a much more powerful winched weapon with a foot-stirrup to be pressed down. With a range of some 400m, almost a quarter of a mile, with metal bolts feathered for increased accuracy, the bolt or so-called quarrel, from the French *carré*, 'square', the four-sided projectile was sometimes barbed to cause even crueller injury. Even if the pyramid-shaped head did not always pierce armour the slamming impact of the bolt could shatter bones, hurl riders from their mounts, kill the almost defenceless horses.[11] D'Alfaro was confident.

There were attacks and counter-attacks, there were rains of bolts and arrows, bombardments with mangonels, a German catapult managed to open part of a wall but the assault that followed was hurled back by a barrage of stones from the defenders' own catapults. Guillaume, archdeacon of Paris and enthusiastic inventor of lethal machines, devised the largest trebuchet yet seen. While carpenters and smiths laboured at its construction de Montfort sent for his brother Guy.

It was midsummer and very hot. Some crusaders complained of illness and planned their departure. The Archbishop of Rouen and the Bishop-Elect of Laon wished to go. There were few arrivals. The gigantic trebuchet dented the keep's square corners but the damage was superficial. Inside the castle d'Alfaro decided to send out the women and children to preserve his supplies. Simon de Montfort sent them back. Vaux-de-Cernay thought this admirable. 'What noble and princely conduct! He did not deign to kill those he had not captured, and believed he would win no glory from the death of those whose capture would not help him to victory'.

It was stalemate but psychologically, though slowly, the besiegers were winning. Guy arrived with his large French army. It was a dispiriting sight. 'When they saw Count Guy arrive, together with Sir Foucaud de Berzy riding a dappled grey and his brother Sir John clad in ermine and miniver . . . and many more barons than I can tell you . . .' the defenders lost heart.

Aware that failure to withstand even one attack would end in the deaths of them all, d'Alfaro offered to surrender in return for a promise of safe conduct for him and all his men. De Montfort accepted and after a valiant defence of eight long weeks the mercenaries walked out of Penne d'Agenais.[12] It became one of de Montfort's finest strongholds. He had the walls repaired with mortar and lime and turned inexorably to his next objective, Biron, a few miles north in the Dordogne.

At a cliff's edge, it was the castle of Martin Algai, the mercenary captain who had fled from the battle of St.-Martin-Lalande. He was almost legendary, a Navarrese of low birth, superstitious, who had fought for Richard I in Aquitaine and had been a seneschal of King John's in Gascony and Perigord. John had a high estimation of him. 'No misfortune has happened which we have taken more to heart', he wrote to Algai's mercenaries, 'than what has befallen our beloved and faithful Martin Algais [sic], for, as God is our witness, we are greatly irritated and incensed thereat'. Others had a different opinion. Courageous as Algai was he was also brutal and impious, half-celebrated, half-condemned in troubadour poems. De Montfort wanted him.

The crusaders stormed the walls and attacked the tower, whose frightened garrison quickly offered to betray their commander in return for their lives. Algai was allowed his prayers and then, dressed in black, was set in a pillory to be mocked by the expectant soldiery. He was deprived of his knightly rank, tied to the tail of a fresh warhorse that dragged him bloodily and humiliatingly between the ranked files of contemptuous crusaders, out and around the walls before his remains were displayed on a gibbet in the meadows 'in the sight of all', recorded Guillaume de Tudela. 'Ravens and vultures ate what was left of him'.[13] De Montfort began the long, slow return to Carcassonne.

Reinforcements had already reached him. Pierre des Vaux-de-Cernay described how he had accompanied Alice, wife of the viscount, and the Bishop of Carcassonne. The cloudless days were blazing. The journey was hard and exhausting, seemingly endless, parching in the open, sweltering in the forests. Many men, almost fainting, could hardly continue. Something remarkable for the Middle Ages occurred. 'The Bishop and the Countess took pity on their condition and allowed them to ride behind them on their own horses all day; indeed from time to time they each allowed two crusaders to ride on their horses and themselves proceeded on foot. What pious compassion on the part of the Bishop, what noble humility shown by the countess'.[14]

They had joined de Montfort at Penne d'Agenais, went with him to Biron and then on to the defiant walls of Moissac. They arrived there at nine o'clock on the morning of Thursday, 14 August, camping on the banks of the Tarn outside the 'settlement by the water'. Unknown to the crusaders a large body of mercenaries had reached the town the previous evening, sent by Raymond VI.

Moissac was rich, levying taxes on the many villages that its Cluniac abbey of St.-Pierre had established in the neighbourhood. It was also divided, its ownership and government claimed both by the abbot and by the Count of Toulouse, who had briefly imprisoned the abbot some years before. Today, it is a place of caramel-coloured brick and large grey shutters, quiet, but in the thirteenth century it was an important stage on the pilgrims' road from Le Puy to Spain. The exquisitely carved tympanum of the church's belfry porch and the early eleventh century cloisters are masterpieces of Romanesque art, perhaps the finest in the whole of France in a countryside abundant with ecclesiastical sculptures of genius.

Moissac had none of the natural defences that had protected Minerve and Termes but its walls were ponderous and tall and its ditch was wide and deep. The town was too large to be surrounded by de Montfort and its mercenaries were able to leave freely and make sallies from a nearby hill, firing irreligious crossbows at the crusaders while the Bishop of Carcassonne was addressing his congregation. In turn, the besiegers assailed the walls, only for de Montfort to be wounded in the foot and his horse killed, leaving him surrounded and saved only by the desperate courage of Guillaume de Conques.

Pierre des Vaux-de-Cernay was lucky too. A bolt penetrated his saddle and 'pierced my robe, missed my flesh by a finger's width or less', proving that Divine intervention had prevented 'the enemies of religion' from injuring a monk. Others were less fortunate. A gentlewoman was killed. The nephew of the Bishop of Rheims was captured, dragged inside the town and systematically hacked to bits. Pieces of his dismembered body were gruesomely mangonelled out of the town.

Catapults bombarded all day long. The ingenious archdeacon of Paris designed 'cats', those protective sheds covered with fresh cow-hides to prevent fire that sappers could wheel up to the ditch. Defenders splashed oil and fat on to the shelters, flung straw and dry wood, fired burning arrows. The flames were extinguished. The assaults continued.

The siege ended in an almost comical anti-climax because the vineyards were reaching fruition and the townsfolk did not wish to lose a vintage year. They offered to surrender. Knowing that there would be many more casualties before Moissac could be taken by force, de Montfort accepted on the condition that the mercenaries were given to him. It was agreed and on 8 September after almost four weeks of resistance the crusaders entered the town. Carnage followed. Some three hundred mercenaries were slaughtered 'with great enthusiasm' because they had been sent by the Count of Toulouse.

For their gift of a hundred gold marks the citizens were promised that there would be no pillaging in the town. More loyal to Raymond VI than to the abbot, the inhabitants excluded the abbey from their petition, and it was so thoroughly ransacked that the abbot complained to King Philippe-Auguste that the church was completely wrecked and he was impoverished.[15]

The damage is still apparent. Most of the church, no longer an abbey, is fifteenth-century red-brick Gothic. Only the realistically carved tympanum of the porch with its glorious Vision of St John in which the lifelike Elders of the Apocalypse, all different, gaze in amazement at the majesty of Christ the Apocalypse, and the arcades of the cloisters, with their delicately slender marble pillars, escaped destruction. They endured during the Hundred Years' War and the wars of religion. In the Revolution they were sold, soldiers decapitated saints, hooves of their horses damaged the glazed brickwork, but the cloisters remained almost intact.

Peace proved more perilous than war. After all the mayhem and bloodshed commercialism became the threat. In the mid-nineteenth century latter-day Philistines recommended that the cloisters be demolished to make way for the Bordeaux-Sète railway line. There was a compromise. The proposed line was diverted, but by an arms-length. The cloisters with their elegant pillars and charming capitals are a delight to visit except when a train passes, rumbling by and almost brushing the north-west corner of the north gallery.[16]

After the fall of Moissac, de Montfort placed towns under the command of trusted deputies. Baudouin was given Montech, Guillaume de Conques received Castelsarrasin. Pierre de Cissey obtained Verdun-sur-Garonne where, in 1250, five hundred Jews were butchered by a gang of Christian thugs known as *Pastoureaux*, 'Shepherd Boys'.

In September, Marmande capitulated. Only Montauban held out. Elsewhere, everywhere, the crusaders were successful. In the south-west of the Languedoc the town of Muret, strategically placed between Toulouse and the Pyrenees, was taken. To its west in Gascony the lands of the Count of Comminges and of Gaston de Béarn, vassals of the King of Aragon, were conquered. It was rashly provocative. To risk the anger of a powerful monarch such as Pedro II was dangerous.

In the winter of 1212–13, their forty days completed and their pardons gained, many crusaders went home. It was of small significance. De Montfort was in control of almost the entire region. Only Toulouse remained to be captured.

It was time for the south to become a province of the north. 'Now that the heretical filth which had corrupted all those territories had been driven out, [it was necessary] to ensure the establishment of a sound set of customs'.[17]

In November Simon de Montfort, Viscount of Béziers and Carcassonne, summoned a 'parliament' at Pamiers, a town provocatively close to Foix, to codify new laws for the south, laws in reality introducing northern customs and disrupting the southern ways of life. They would also confirm de Montfort's standing as the lord of Languedoc.

A tribunal of clerics, knights and southerners was appointed. Superficially democratic, the selection of its members was anything but impartial. Every man was a Catholic and a supporter of the viscount. The four clerics were the Bishop of Toulouse, Foulques, and of Cousterans, Navarre, and a knight each from the Orders Hospitaller and Templar. The four lay knights were all from northern France. The four southerners were two knights who had sworn allegiance to de Montfort and two burghers sympathetic to his cause.

Their recommendations were comprehensive. The Catholic Church would retain its guaranteed immunities and privileges. The Crusade would pursue Cathars and hand them to the Church for examination. Southerners, especially lords and their ladies, would attend Mass on Sundays and Feast Days on penalty of heavy fines. Serfs could free themselves by living in towns. Justice for all would be free. New toll-gates would be abolished. Taxes would be reduced.

The changes were hard but just acceptable. What followed was not. There were to be no more mercenaries. The vassals of de Montfort would attend him on demand with a specified number of knights, all of whom, for the next twenty years, were to be northeners. Instead of estates being split between families on the death of a lord the northern practice of primogeniture would be enforced whereby only the first-born son could inherit. Should a widow be the heiress then for the following six years she could marry only a northener.

It was, wrote Vaux-de-Cernay, 'the best possible code to ensure the safety and protect the interests of the Church and indeed the whole body politic'. De Montfort and his knights swore on the Four Gospels to uphold the laws.

Inevitably there was opposition and not all from the south. The convocation that endorsed the Statute of Pamiers on 1 December 1212, consisted almost entirely of bishops. Few legates were present.

Prelates such as Arnaud Amaury would have reminded de Montfort that he was at Pamiers as an avowed crusader whose commitment it was to eliminate heresy, not to aggrandise himself. Ironically Amaury, Archbishop of Narbonne, had just ennobled himself in exactly the same self-important manner by becoming Duke of Narbonne and accepting homage from the city's viscount, Aimery, thereby making himself a secular rival to de Montfort.

There was another powerful man to whom the outcome of Pamiers was unacceptable. Pedro II, King of Aragon, had many vassals in the Languedoc, one being de Montfort himself. A medieval vassal more powerful than his lord was a constant danger to kings, princes and noblemen alike. The 'lord of the Languedoc' had passed laws convenient to himself and confirmed his own status but in doing so had simultaneously created new and more insidious dangers for himself. The King of Aragon was already indignant over the demeaning of vassals such as Comminges and Béarn and the loss of towns like St.-Gaudens. Towards the end of 1212 he appealed to Pope Innocent III.[18]

At that time Pedro was highly esteemed by the papacy. Only six months earlier there had been a much more serious threat to Christendom than the Cathars. A horde of heathen Moors of the emir of Morocco had invaded Castile and had blocked all the passes through the Sierra Morena mountains. Since the eighth century Moors had occupied the greater part of Spain. There had been sporadic Christian victories by leaders such as El Cid and in 1085 the King of Castile, 'the land of castles', recaptured Toledo. It did not bring peace. In 1195 an army of fanatical Berbers defeated Alphonso VII at the battle of Alarcos.

In 1211, having gradually regained power, the King of Castile and father of the future queen Blanche of France, asked for the Pope's support and Innocent III 'appealed to the faithful to unite against the Moors'. In 1212 he proclaimed a crusade. An enormous, cosmopolitan army came together, a combined force of French crusaders under Arnaud Amaury, Catalans, Navarrese, Aragonese and Spaniards. According to Guillaume de Puylaurens no fewer than five kings, including Alphonso, Pedro and Sancho VII of Navarre, joined the 'Spanish Crusade'. The host was led through a little-known valley by a shepherd boy and the battle that followed on 16 July 1212 at Las Navas de Tolosa was decisive. Hundreds of thousands of infidels were killed and it had been the onslaught of Pedro II, King of Aragon, in command of the left flank of the Christians, that was chiefly responsible for the victory.[19]

Fervent Catholic, dutiful servant of the Church, he convinced Innocent III that the Count of Toulouse had been unfairly treated and his own vassals illegally forced to yield the king's property to their northern victors. Now, he told the Pope, he was prepared to act as guarantor that any heretics remaining in the Languedoc would be captured and that he himself, King of Aragon, would take responsibility for this.

The Pope was persuaded by that champion of Christendom. On 15 January 1213 a letter was sent to Arnaud Amaury informing him that Catharism was extinct and that the crusade should end. 'Foxes', he stated, '*were* destroying the vineyard in Provence; they *have been captured*'. Innocent III was as plain-spoken to Simon de Montfort.

The King of Aragon had told him that 'not content with taking up arms against the heretics, you have also fought, under the banner of the Crusade, against Catholic people; that you have spilt innocent blood, and have invaded, to their detriment, the domains of the Count of Foix, and those of the Count of Comminges and of Gaston de Béarn, his vassals, though the population of these said domains was in no way suspect of heresy. . . . We order you to restore to him [Pedro] and his vassals all those seigneuries which you have appropriated by force'.[20]

The King of Aragon and his people in Occitania were jubilant. There was a grim reaction from Arnaud Amaury and his colleagues. Calling a Council at Lavaur they refused to allow Pedro to speak on behalf of the Languedocians, and insisted that his arguments be submitted in writing for them to consider, vowing to excommunicate him if he continue to protest the innocence of those evildoers.

Having silenced him, the Council then sent a delegation to Rome and wrote letter after letter from bishop after bishop to the pope, emphasising the equivocations of Raymond VI, the brutality and

Pope Innocent III (1160–1216) (*The Bridgeman Art Library*).

The Tour Magdala, Rennes-le-Château.

The reconstructed ramparts and towers of Carcassonne.

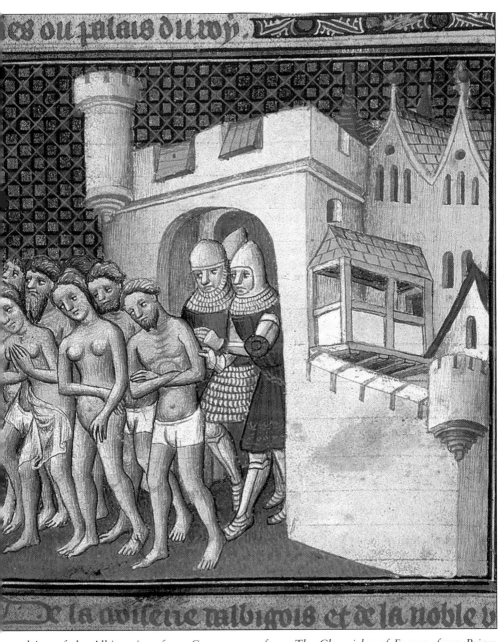

The expulsion of the Albigensians from Carcassonne, from *The Chronicles of France, from Priam of Troy until the Crowning of Charles VI*, by the Boucicaut Master and Workshop (*Cott Nero bt2 f.20v The British Library/The Bridgeman Art Library*).

The elegant west front of the abbey church of St.-Gilles, all that remains of the twelfth-century church.

The vault of St.-Gilles. The tomb of Pierre de Castelnau was in the recess on the left. On the right are the stairs by which Raymond VI left the church.

Two of the four castles at Lastours. The round tower is the Tour Régine. Beyond it is the keep of Cabaret.

The castles of Lastours across the river-valley of Grésillon. From left to right they are Cabaret; then the Tour Régine, the latest; then the ruinous Surdespine and finally Quertinheux.

Toulouse. The cathedral of St.-Sernin with its octagonal bell tower.

The splendid tympanum above the west door of St.-Sernin cathedral, Toulouse. It shows the Ascension of Christ. His apostles stand beneath him.

The cathedral of St.-Alain, Lavaur, in its ornamental gardens.

Moissac. The Romanesque cloisters, the finest in France. They were to be destroyed in the nineteenth century to make room for the railway line which now passes just beyond the far wall.

Carving of a minstrel in the Musicians' Room, Puivert castle. He is playing a cornemuse, a medieval bagpipe.

Statue of a crusader at the gateway of Avignonet, scene of a massacre of monks in 1242.

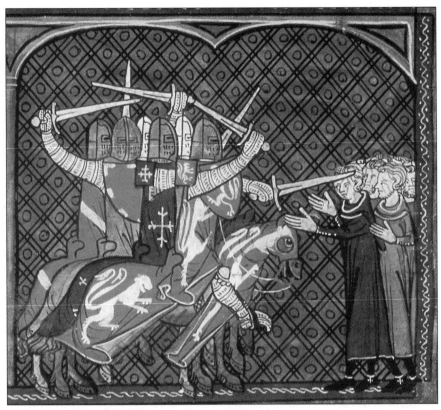

Soldiers on horseback wielding swords attack a group of Albigensians. From *Chroniques de France ou de Saint Denis (Roy 16 G VI.f.374v The British Library)*.

Moissac. The early twelfth-century masterpiece of the tympanum showing Christ surrounded by angels. Below them the Elders of the Apocalypse gaze upwards in wonderment.

The ravaged fortlet of Penne d'Agenais.

The castle of Peyrepertuse. The later fortification to the west (right) 'has never been accessible to horses or even mules'.

Peyrepertuse. To the east, the oldest remains of the castle.

The grandiose cathedral of Ste.-Cécile in Albi.

The pope excommunicating the Albigensians. From *Chroniques de France ou de Saint Denis (Roy 16 G VI.f.374v The British Library)*.

The 'unreachable' castle of Montségur on its steep-sided mountain.

Montaillou. The ruined castle. Nothing remains of the village and its houses.

The fine castle of Villerouge-Termenès.

The castle of Arques. A small-scale replica of a mangonel stands near the gateway.

The church of Ste.-Marie-Madeleine, Rennes-le-Château.

viciousness of the Count of Foix and the wrongdoings of Comminges and Béarn. Almost certainly overstated, these were not direct lies and, after some vacillation, the Pope wrote to the King of Aragon on 21 May retracting his promises.

'We are amazed and disturbed that, by using your envoys to suppress the truth and give a false account of matters, you have extorted from us a papal letter ordering the restitution of their territories to the Counts of Foix and Comminges and Gaston de Béarn, bearing in mind that – to pass over their many other monstrous misdeeds – they have been bound with the chains of excommunication for their support of the heretics, whom they openly defend'. His letters of remission were withdrawn.[21]

The results were disastrous. After his peremptory dismissal at Lavaur, Pedro II had gone to Toulouse and formally placed the city under his protection. Leaving a small band of his knights behind he returned to Aragon to raise an army, instructing his vassals to summon all their men. He also sent word to Simon de Montfort that the viscount's homage was renounced and he was no longer the king's man. War had been declared.

De Montfort himself had lost most of his crusaders. With the papal uncertainty being widely known there were few newcomers to Carcassonne. At the same time his enemy, the Count of Toulouse, was encouraging his former castles and towns to reassert their loyalty to him. Some did.

On 24 June at Castelnaudary de Montfort's son, Amaury, was formally knighted in an occasion of pomp, the Bishops of Orléans and Auxerre conspicuously present in a gathering of bright pavilions and shining raiment. The gorgeous ceremony was intended to be the foundation of a dynasty for the de Montfort family, the hopeful beginnings of a lineage that would rule in the Languedoc for many generations.[22]

Next month came the confusing affair of Pujol. Today, it is no more than the scattered hamlet of Pujolet, but, eight hundred years ago, it was a nondescript castle eleven miles east of Toulouse. As an episode in the Albigensian crusade it merits no more than a phrase in a footnote. As a revelation of how accounts could be distorted by the prejudices of their reporters it deserves several paragraphs. For the first time there is a remarkable difference between the accounts of Pierre des Vaux-de-Cernay, Catholic monk and northener, and the nameless chronicler of the *Song of the Cathar Wars*. That man stressed the valour of the soldiers of the Languedoc. The monk railed against the treachery of the people of Toulouse.

A problem in any reconstruction of episodes in the distant past is the reliability of the evidence. Archaeologically, the remains of castles, towns and battle-grounds offer fragmentary but unbiased elements of the past that with care can be assessed. Quite differently, historical chronicles are suspect. They are not dispassionate and objective accounts of what happened. Their writers were not impartial. They were partisans whose descriptions are better accepted as propaganda than as trustworthy records. This is as true of the nameless man who followed Guillaume de Tudela as it is of Guillaume or of Vaux-de-Cernay.

Who he was is unknown. He says nothing about himself, his name, his life, his occupation. He could write but does not seem to have been a monk. He may have been one of the many troubadours in Occitania for he was far more of a poet than his predecessor. Perhaps when Guillaume died or was unable or unwilling to continue his work his inheritor was given or took the manuscripts from St.-Antonin and deserted the protection of Baudouin in favour of the court of Toulouse.

Full of admiration for Raymond VI, he wrote that, in July 1213, the count was aware that the Catholic garrison at Pujol intended to ravage the harvests around Lanta two or three miles to the south. To prevent it, Raymond assembled a fearsome army. With him was the Count of Foix and his son, the Count of Comminges, a regiment of Catalans from Aragon and a well-armed crowd of militant civilians. For the attack they had catapults, siege-machines, battering-rams, crossbows with feathered quarrels, 'cats' to reach the ditch, fill it and storm the defences because 'inside the castle are the flower of all the crusaders'.

Once the ditch could be crossed by the participants, knight, foot-soldier and townsman alike, miners sapped the walls 'with massive picks'. The defenders fought back savagely with 'blazing fire and a torrent of rocks and dressed stones and after that boiling water'.

In vain. The archers of Toulouse shot so many arrows so quickly, and so accurately that no crusader dared show himself above the parapet for fear of being hit in the jaw or tooth. The ramparts were dripping with blood and littered with the dead. The castle was stormed and every Frenchman, noble or commoner, was put to the sword or hanged. Sixty knights were slain before the victorious army returned to Toulouse. Guy, brother of de Montfort, arrived too late to save the garrison and 'he could not hold back his tears'. It had been an epic battle against stalwart defences and redoubtable opponents, almost as great a triumph as Joan of Arc at Orléans two hundred years later. But not according to Pierre des Vaux-de-Cernay.

The castle, he knew, was 'weak and poorly fortified', manned only by the three knights who had offered to maraud in the lands around Toulouse. Their men were insufficient to withstand a gigantic army and after a few days they offered to surrender on an assurance of liberty. It was promised and dishonoured. Taken to Toulouse the three were degradingly dragged through the streets behind horses and hanged outside the city walls.

Writing thirty years later, Guillaume de Puylaurens provided a gloss. It had been a civilian militia that had besieged Pujol. The three knights had taken refuge in a tower but gave themselves up under a *'garanti des conditions de sauvegarde'*. They were spared but imprisoned in Toulouse only for a mob to break into their dungeon. It was undisciplined townspeople who mutilated the knights, tied them to horses and hauled the maimed carcases out of the gates, where they dangled mockingly on the gallows. Clearly, the 'truth' of what happened at Pujol depended on the selected choices of the writer.[23]

What happened at Muret on 12 September is less equivocal. It was the first battle of the crusade between two Catholic sides and it was decisive. Innocent III had instructed the King of Aragon not to interfere in the religious struggle of the Languedoc. Pedro II ignored him. With a vast army of vassals, their knights and foot-soldiers and with great numbers of mercenaries he crossed the Pyrenees early in

September, was greeted with joy everywhere, and was joined by the Counts of Foix and Comminges with their followers. From Toulouse six heavy siege-machines were taken by barges down the Garonne to Muret ten miles down river. It was a massive concourse, over-estimated by Vaux-de-Cernay to contain a hundred thousand armed men but still awesome, that assembled outside Muret's ramparts, men, horses, foot-soldiers, well-armed, even with the deadly curl-shaped and exceptionally powerful Turkish bow with its long killing range. Troubadours sang of filling 'the fields with helmets and hauberks, lances and fluttering banners'.[24]

Against that army there were just thirty French knights inside Muret. Pedro II had eight hundred cavalry. Two hundred more were expected. The Counts of Toulouse, Foix and Comminges may have had another six hundred between them. That alone was twice as many as Simon de Montfort had forty miles to the east at Fanjeaux. Aware of the dangers but undaunted, he prepared to leave. His wife, Alice, had a nightmare in which blood poured from her arms as if in warning. Simon reassured her. He was not a superstitious Spaniard. Even if he knew he would be killed he would still go to Muret just to prove that he had no trust in 'dreams and auguries'. He was different from the emotional Raymond VI, who 'put great faith in the flight and song of birds and other auguries'.[25] De Montfort asked Alice to go to Carcassonne and send any men there to his assistance.

He doubted the resolve and commitment of his enemies. According to Guillaume de Puylaurens, the count had intercepted a letter from Pedro to a married noblewoman of Toulouse telling her that it was for love of her that he had come to the Languedoc to drive out the French. De Montfort was contemptuous. '*Je ne crains pas un roi . . . pour une courtisane*'. He had no fear of a king who was infatuated with a whore, unlike the crusader who was fighting in the cause of God.[26]

Of his Christian sincerity there is no question. On his way to Muret he stopped at the church in Boulbonne. He put his sword on the altar. 'Loving Lord, Bountiful Jesus! You have chosen me, unworthy as I am, to fight your battles. Today I take my arms from your altar, so that as I prepare to fight your battles, I receive from you the instruments of battle'. At Saverdun, ever a realist, he made his will.[27] The Catholic bishops with him, openly apprehensive of the outcome of the battle asked Pedro for a safe-conduct so that they might negotiate peaceful terms. The king answered that no man of God would be injured by him.

Early on the morning of 11 September Raymond VI's trumpets blew, Muret was bombarded and soldiers swarmed into the lower town driving the defenders into the bourg and the citadel. While the captives were being put to death, de Montfort was seen across the Garonne. There was panic. The triumphant attackers did not even attempt to defend or destroy the wooden bridge across the river. They ran. De Montfort entered the town unopposed. Apologists for Pedro claimed that it had been intentional so that the crusader would be trapped inside the walls. Lack of nerve is more likely.[28]

Muret could not be defended. There was food for no more than a day. The defences were inadequate. The ever more fearful bishops pleaded with the King of Aragon, Foulques, Bishop of Toulouse, argued with the Count of Toulouse. They had no success but, during the talks, Muret was assailed for a second time, more resolutely, and 'both sides made blood spurt so freely that you would have seen the whole gate dyed scarlet'.[29]

Reinforcements arrived from Carcassonne and de Montfort made his battle plans. Nothing could show more clearly his military intelligence and the thoughtless incompetence of the opposition. He divided his cavalry into three squadrons, the first commanded by Guillaume de Contres and the second by Bouchard de Marly. As was the sensible custom to safeguard a leader, de Montfort headed the reserve. The horsemen were to advance directly on the enemy. The instructions were brief.

Against him, a mile away across a flat and open plain was the army of Aragon and Toulouse. Unlike the unquestioned orders that the crusaders had received, there had been disagreement and anger amongst his enemy. Raymond VI proposed that they should fence their camp with a palisade and starve de Montfort out. He was derided by the Aragonese, especially by Michael of Luesia, who sneered that his king would never do anything so dishonourable. 'And it is a great pity that you who have lands to live on should have been such cowards as to lose them'. Raymond retired to his pavilion in a sulk.[30]

The situation deteriorated further. It was rumoured that Pedro had spent the entire night with a woman and by the morning was so exhausted that he was unable stand during the reading of the Gospel.[31] Nor could he think clearly. Not waiting for more men to arrive, uncaring that none of the Toulousian knights was present, he placed his army at the head of a slight rise, his right flank protected by a stream, his left by marshy ground.

The position was good, the disposition of his force was not. Each of his knights picked his place indifferent to any thought of strategy. Dressed in ordinary armour, Pedro II chose to be in the second confusion of horsemen rather than in the reserve. Lacking instructions, having no clearcut leader at their head, the mass of soldiery converted itself into a self-constructed disaster. Years later Pedro's son, Jaime, explained what happened. 'Those on the king's side did not know how to draw up the battle lines and go forward closely together, and each nobleman acted independently and against the nature of arms'.[32]

To avoid harm to his horses from the enemy infantry outside Muret, de Montfort led his knights through the enclosed Sales gate at the south, hidden by it, turned out onto the narrow path behind the walls of Muret alongside the Garonne, always out of sight, and across the St.-Sernin bridge at the north-east.[33]

He led his reserve towards the right of the enemy. At a steady canter the two other bodies of the crusaders charged directly at them bellowing 'Montfort', 'Auxerre', 'St Denis'. The armies clashed. Safe in the distant camp Raymond's young son heard the impact like 'a whole forest going down under the axe'. It was annihilation. Pedro's disorganised horsemen scattered blindly into each other, were felled, trampled down. Puylaurens celebrated the defeat 'as the wind sweeps dust along the ground'.[34]

Unnoticed in the melee de Montfort's cavalry came to the marsh, noticed a faint path along a 'ditch', perhaps the inconspicuous River

Pesquiés, and smashed into the side of the battle. Unrecognised in his plain armour the King of Aragon was unhorsed and killed by the crusader Alain de Roucy. De Leusia, who had jeered at the Count of Toulouse, also died. Few survived. Many of those who managed to get away were drowned as they plunged frantically into the streaming Garonne.

Two-and-a-half centuries later, in 1461, the battle of Towton in England was 'the longest, biggest and bloodiest battle ever fought on British soil'. Some twenty thousand men were killed in ten vicious hours of carnage. Perhaps half that number perished at Muret. But that conflict had lasted just twenty minutes.[35]

Quite indifferent to the calamity crusader foot-soldiers roamed the field, finishing off the wounded with their daggers, stripping the dead of anything valuable. When de Montfort learned of the death of the king he demanded that the corpse be found. By the time it was discovered, like all the others Pedro's body lay robbed and naked. He was buried by the Knights Hospitaller. Seven hundred years later a stone obelisk was erected to commemorate the place where he fell. It was moved, then moved again when a four-lane highway was constructed past Muret. The place where the king died now lies under the concrete of the N117.[36] The Count of Foix survived. Raymond VI and his son fled to the safety of the walls of Toulouse. De Montfort did not pursue them.

Instead he walked barefoot to the church in Muret 'to render thanks to Almighty God for the victory He had granted'. He gave his horse and his armour as alms for the poor. It had been, exulted Pierre des Vaux-de-Cernay, 'a marvellous battle and a glorious victory'. The unknown chronicler demurred. 'It dishonoured the whole of Christendom, it dishonoured all humanity' for it destroyed *paratge*.[37]

It was also the beginning of the end for troubadours in Occitania. Once there had been happy nights in the great halls, people in the dark around a bright fire, playing chess, in conversation, a minstrel singing and playing 'and each person, after listening to one with pleasure, returned to his earlier occupation'. At one time there had been so many patrons around Béziers and Carcassonne, recited

Raymond of Miravel, that it would have taken forty verses to name them all. It was ending. Now there was to be a 'decline into decadence that began with Muret'.

The benefactors had disappeared. 'Most of their patrons were struggling for their existence . . . when the invaders succeeded in establishing themselves, they had no desire for court poetry. The troubadours' occupation was gone, and those who wished for an audience were obliged to seek beyond the borders of France'. 'After the Battle of Muret in 1213, however, the whole world of patronage began to fall apart. The noblemen were now fighting for their very lives and were no longer concerned with enhancing the splendour of their courts. And of the great poets who had made up the golden age, some were now dead, others had entered monasteries, and yet others fled abroad'.[38]

Simon de Montfort, some fifty years of age, holy Crusader, escheated Earl of Leicester in England, titular Viscount of Béziers and Carcassonne in France, was effectively master of the Languedoc.

SIX

1214–1218: Toulouse

De facto lord of the Languedoc de Montfort may have been, the great nobles of Occitania dead or in hiding, castles occupied by crusaders, towns terrorised; but his titles had not been confirmed by Philippe-Auguste, and there remained three severe threats to his status: the Pope, the King of France and the dispossessed *faidits*.

Innocent III had begun to mistrust his Legates who were over-compliant to the wishes of a soldier. 'Two things are above all, dear to me', he said, 'the liberation of the Holy Land, and the reform of the Universal Church' and he was determined that the reasons for his crusade should be honoured. It had been corrupted by militarism. Heresy had been forgotten. He appointed yet another Legate, his sixth, Pietro di Benevento, who was to absolve the southern nobles but was forbidden to agree to any permanent arrangement in the Languedoc without the Pope's direct consent. Most importantly, he was 'on no account to be molested by Simon de Montfort'.[1]

These were religious considerations. There were also political ones. Philippe-Auguste, King of France, permanently engaged on the fringe of war with England, steadily but very slowly regaining lands in Normandy and Aquitaine, had reluctantly accepted that his realm was being eroded by the expanding territories conquered by de Montfort. Unable to retaliate, he longed for a chance of fate. 'My Lords' he sighed, 'I still have *hope* that, before it prove too late, this Count de Montfort and his brother, Count Guy, may die in harness'.[2]

135

The Pope, the king, both too powerful to ignore, were many miles and therefore weeks, even months, away from interference. The *faidits* were not. They had nothing, nor had their supporters and families, and it would remain so unless they fought in battle, in ambush, in treachery. 'A thousand noblemen were condemned to wander penniless across a land where they had once ruled', lamented a troubadour.[3] In October and November of 1213 there were outbreaks in Provence. Narbonne, Montpellier, Nîmes refused to open their gates to crusaders. The citizens of Moissac rebelled. Worse still, Raymond VI had gone to the court of King John in England, his brother-in-law through Raymond's fourth wife, Joan, daughter of Henry II and sister of John and Richard I. The count pleaded with the king to help him regain his dominions.

Tempted by the prospect of repossessing parts of Normandy John, aptly nicknamed 'Lackland', agreed. An invasion was planned. On 15 February 1214, an English army landed at La Rochelle. In April it advanced to La Réole near de Montfort's castle at Marmande only a few miles from his successes in the Agenais. Almost immediately the unreliable castle seceded and became an English garrison.[4]

A joint campaign was planned. The English army was to wait for the troops of the Holy Roman emperor, Otto IV, to invade from the north of France and the combined forces would then overcome Philippe-Auguste. It came to nothing. De Montfort was too decisive. In June the crusaders laid siege to Marmande, whose men retreated a few miles to La Réole – and then many more to the port of La Rochelle, constantly harried by Prince Louis, the twenty-seven year old son of the French king.

On 27 July Philippe-Auguste brilliantly out-thought and out-fought Otto at the battle of Bouvines near Lille. The feeble alliance collapsed.

The king took advantage of the situation. His son, genuinely pious and morally decent, had vowed to join the Crusade in the Languedoc. His presence there, Philippe realised, would emphasise to Pope, Legates and de Montfort that Toulouse was a fief of the French crown and not to be commandeered by the crusaders even though de Montfort himself was a northern Frenchman.[5] By 19

April 1215, Louis was at Lyon and a month later he joined de Montfort at Toulouse. Long before that time there had been devastation.

There were disaffection and disloyalty everywhere. Just as defeat at St. Martin-Lalande had led to resistance, so the disaster at Muret provoked uprisings as lords and commoners realised how close their way of life was to extinction. Especially in the north on the fringes of de Montfort's conquests there was rebellion.

Trust was a traitor to those naive enough to believe in it. Months before the English quitted France in the middle of 1214, long before the victory at Bouvines in that year, Baudouin, brother of the Count of Toulouse, was betrayed on 17 February by traitors among his men. Having little regard for their commander, a renegade crusader whose northern accent contrasted sharply with the broader speech of Occitania, one night they unbarred the door of his castle at Lolmie near Montcuq.

Two southern knights in the neighbourhood, Ratier de Castelnau and Bertrand de Mondénard, both of whom would suffer for their treason, broke into Baudouin's bedchamber where he was sleeping 'quite naked'. They took him to Montcuq, imprisoning him there without food. Then, chained, he was removed to Montauban to wait for his brother's arrival. Raymond VI came with the Count of Foix and his inseparable son. Baudouin was condemned to death, forbidden prayers or confession and hanged on a walnut tree by the city walls. His executioner was assisted by an Aragonese knight, Bernard de Portella, who had not forgiven the death of Pedro II. That king had been buried by the Knights Hospitaller. It was Knights Templar, more sympathetic to the crusade, who took down Baudouin's body and interred it by the cloisters in their cemetery at La Villedieu.[6]

In the following months there was an astonishing expedition. In part to avenge Baudouin, more to suppress the growing dissatisfaction, mainly to prevent revolt spreading into previously unvisited northern borders of his acquisitions, Simon de Montfort and his brother Guy started upon an arduous campaign. In the absence of the Legate, Benevento, the two crusaders persuaded a more amenable Legate, Robert de Courçon, to grant them freedom to recapture lands in Quercy and the Agenais and, illegally, to suppress resistance in 'other territories yet to be conquered'.[7]

From May to November they rode nearly a thousand miles, sometimes dividing their forces, Guy searching for the murderers of Baudouin, rejoining his brother, the two armies criss-crossing, merging in a bewilderment of journeys like a scrawl of lines scratched by a vandal on a stained-glass window.

In those unpaved days the distances were exhausting, over a hundred anti-clockwise miles of tracks from Carcassonne to Sévérac-le-Château at the north-east, another hundred to Beynac at the north, a hundred and fifty more to Marmande at the south-west. It was never so symmetrical. It was forwards, sideways, returning over old ground, ceaseless but never aimless. The campaign was unrelenting. The policy was not scorched earth. Suppressing an outburst of discontent here, another there, across the Languedoc would have been as vain as pricking bubbles of simmering fat. Terror was demanded and physical destruction. Enemies were slain. Fortifications were methodically demolished. Even today there are only shattered walls and broken towers at castles like Sévérac-le-Château.

History can be selective. Of those implacably destructive eight months in 1214 neither the anonymous chronicler nor Guillaume de Puylaurens mentions anything. In contrast, Pierre des Vaux-de-Cernay could hardly stop, writing fourteen detailed pages of death and demolition in the Agenais, then in Quercy north of Cahors and finally across the driftingly lovely Dordogne into the Perigord.[8]

First to be attacked from 13 to 16 April was Le Mas d'Agenais near Marmande; but without siege-machines, the town could not be taken, and, after three days, the crusaders went away.

They were receiving numerous volunteers. Guy, Bishop of Carcassonne, had been preaching all over France, exhorting men to join the crusade. The response was startling. 'There were about a hundred thousand of us, taking mounted men and foot-soldiers together', bragged Vaux-de-Cernay, who was accompanying de Montfort.[9]

In early summer the host came to the strong defences of Morlhon-le-Haut a hundred and fifty miles east of Marmande. Resistance, mocking for a few days, faltered, probably dismayed at the growing galaxy of pavilions and tents below it. 'Our men completely destroyed the place'. It was the forerunner of many other places to be wasted.

A religious bonus for the Legate, Robert de Courçon, who like Vaux-de-Cernay was with the Crusade, was the discovery of seven 'heretical' Waldenses. They were followers of Peter Valdes of Lyon 'who emphatically did not wish to part from the official hierarchy'. Known as 'clog-wearers' from their avowed extreme poverty they preached in the vernacular but accepted the authority of the Catholic church. This equivocal attitude confused many clergymen but led Innocent III to regard them as 'Poor Catholics . . . imitating the poverty of Christ'. His Christian understanding did not save the seven at Morlhon. 'The crusaders seized them and burnt them with great rejoicing'.[10]

Then came the turn of Castelnau-Montratier, home of the treacherous Ratier of Castelnau who had arrested Baudouin at Lolmie a few miles to the west. It was destroyed. De Montfort then 'razed to the ground numerous strong castles in the area' including the abandoned Cazes-Mondénard five miles south of Lolmie, whose owner, Bertrand, had accompanied Ratier.

By this time many of the 'forty-day' crusaders were returning home, their sins forgiven, their purses filled. Reduced in numbers but assured of God the de Montforts headed for the recently strengthened defences of Montpézat. It was empty. It was destroyed. The nearby castle and town of Marmande occupied by the troops of King John was besieged. It surrendered.

Only Casseneuil to the east fought back and for over seven weeks from 28 June to 18 August it defied its attackers. 'Most of its inhabitants were heretics, thieves and perjurers, full of iniquity and sins'. Catapults battered the almost impervious walls. Relief by the English was promised but never came. Weeks passed. Despite the bombardment the walls stood almost unharmed and de Montfort decided there should be a direct assault.

The moat, however, was deep and wide. The only bridge had been demolished by the defenders. Ingenious engineers devised a pontoon whose linked sections were to float on large casks. The contraption was dragged to the moat down whose steep, high bank it was lowered. It instantly sank under its own weight. A smaller one was constructed. To the derisive jeers of the garrison it was too short.

There was more military invention. Carpenters assembled a flat-roofed house protected by a gated outer palisade. On top of the roof they built a five-storeyed tower from which crossbowmen could fire straight into Casseneuil. The improvised machine was pushed to the moat. Sappers poured earth and lumber into the water until men could cross the improvised ramp. A night attack on the walls failed because there were no ladders.

Carpenters built some. When they were climbed the crusaders found a deserted town whose mercenaries had fled in the night. Casseneuil was set on fire and its 'walls razed to the ground'. De Montfort donated all the revenues to Dominic who had moved from Fanjeaux to Toulouse.[11]

Late in the summer the crusaders crossed the Dordogne. It was the first time that the army had entered the Perigord although de Montfort himself had much earlier been to Rocamadour. In 1214 it was not piety but suppression that took him there. Any incipient opposition was to be quelled.

Of de Montfort's unquestioning faith in the Catholic church there is no uncertainty. Years after 1214 when Philippe-Auguste and his son Louis VIII were dead, in the mid-thirteenth century Jean, Sire de Joinville, had gone on the Seventh Crusade to Egypt with Louis IX, who remembered what his father had told him about the viscount:

The sainted king told me that several people among the Albigenses came to the Count of Montfort, who was then guarding the land of the Albigenses for the king, and asked him to come and look at the body of our Lord, which had become flesh and blood in the hands of the priest. And the Count of Montfort said, 'Go and look at it yourselves, you who do not believe it. As for me, I believe it firmly, holding as Holy Church teaches of the sacrament of the altar. And do you know what I shall gain', asked the count, 'in that during this mortal life I have believed as holy Church teaches? I shall have a crown in the heavens, above the angels, for the angels cannot but believe, inasmuch as they see God face to face'.[12]

It is an anecdote that Prince Louis, later Louis VIII, may have heard when in the Languedoc in 1215.

It was de Montfort, devout Catholic and ruthless warrior, who led his men into the Perigord. Four vital castles were taken: Domme whose tall and attractive keep was 'undermined and pulled down'. One gateway of the walls on the cliff remains; then the fortress of Montfort whose 'cement as hard as stone' caused 'men . . . to spend several days on the task', from early morning to evening before it was demolished; then Castelnaud, and lastly Beynac, whose 'lord was an evil man, a cruel robber and a violent oppressor of churches'. Gaillac was offered the choice of returning the stolen goods or witness the destruction of his castle. He refused. The walls were levelled. 'For a hundred years or more Satan's seat had been in these four places, from them iniquity had gone forth on the face of the earth . . .'. De Montfort returned to the Agenais. 'Now that the opportunity had arisen he arranged for the demolition of all the fortified places in the diocese of Agen'.[13]

The capture and destruction of Montfort brought retribution. It had been the property of Bernard of Cazenac whose wife, Hélis, was 'far more beastly and cruel than Jezebel, more evil than any woman ever!' The horrified Vaux-de-Cernay reported that the pair had desecrated churches, persecuted widows and, when Catholics came to the Benedictine monastery of Sarlat monastery, they found the remains of men and women mutilated, with hands or feet lopped off, blinded, women's thumbs severed leaving them incapable of work, nipples tortured.

Whether the barbarity was exaggerated is unknown. The anonymous chronicler described Bernard of Cazenac as 'a more active knight, as fair-minded as he is powerful', with 'wisdom, generosity and a fine troop of men'.[14]

From the Perigord the crusaders went south-east to the Agenais, to Figeac, and in October to Capdenac, 'a nest and a refuge for mercenaries'. It was a region of long-established heresy where the final objective was the subjugation of Sévérac-le-Château, another 'haunt of mercenaries'. Standing on a rocky outcrop on the outskirts of the wild and mountainous Causse de Sauveterre it was a bleak place made worse by the withering chill of the winter. Under the excuse that it was infested with outlaws de Montfort decided to add it to his possessions.

Guy stormed the town, whose defenders retreated uphill to the boasted impregnability of the castle. Their abandoned houses provided an abundance of shelter for the crusaders. Taken by surprise by the unexpected attack and having made no preparations against it, short of food and water, without fuel, clad in inadequately thin clothing, the besieged men were forced to surrender on 30 November. De Montfort gave the town and castle to the Bishop of Rodez just as he had given other places to churchmen, gaining their support.[15]

Having returned from Aragon, Pietro di Benevento summoned a Council of Montpellier to convene early in 1215 and on 8 January the Council recommended that de Montfort be made the lord of the county of Toulouse. The Legate demurred. Innocent III had insisted that such resolutions should be referred to him and despite the objections of the assembled bishops and priests an embassy was sent to Rome asking for the Pope's decision.[16]

Everything was changing. Already in April 1214 at Narbonne there had been contrition. The Counts of Comminges and Foix, Raymond VI, Count of Toulouse all expressed their shame and asked for the forgiveness and absolution of the Church. Foix and Comminges each surrendered a castle as evidence of their good faith. Raymond VI conceded the Château Narbonnais and volunteered to go into exile while the Church decided his future.[17]

In the count's absence, on 4 February Foulques, Bishop of Toulouse, returned to his city after an absence of almost four years. He was rigorous in his religious convictions, openly critical of corruption. The poet Dante in his *Paradise* praised him for rebuking popes and cardinals alike for their worldly greed and neglect of pure Christianity. The Vatican would 'soon be freed from these adulteries'. He saw Foulques as

> . . . one
> Illustrious, [who] now flashed forth in brilliance clad
> Like a fine ruby smitten by the sun . . .
> Foulques' men called me . . .
>
> Canto IX, 47–142.[18]

In April, Prince Louis, later Louis VIII 'the Lion', fulfilled his pledge to be part of the crusade – although now that the fighting was over his was more a pilgrimage than a military intervention. On his fine Arab courser, with a gorgeous retinue of nobles and bannered knights, with an immense army, his royal presence was an earthly godsend to de Montfort.

In front of the prince he asked Benevento to grant him the cities of Narbonne and Toulouse. The request embarrassed the Legate. Toulouse was under the protection of the Pope. Narbonne was the dukedom of Arnaud Amaury. But a prince and an army were considerable barriers to refusal.

The mere size of the royal army persuaded the citizens of Narbonne that it would be folly to encourage a siege. At the request of Louis they agreed to break wide gaps in the city walls and accept de Montfort as their lord. The futile protests of Arnaud Amaury were ignored – although not by the angry Innocent III in Rome, who asserted that de Montfort had usurped the rights of the Archbishop.

In May the history of Toulouse was similar. Its consuls yielded, walls were breached, moats filled, chains for barricading streets removed, fortified houses and towers pulled down. Ramparts connected to the Château Narbonnais were removed and the castle stood detached from the defences, palisaded and a gateway added to allow access to the open countryside.

Satisfied with the effect his influence had achieved, by 8 June the prince was back in Paris with a holy relic, the jawbone of St Vincent, fourth century martyr of Saragossa, tortured and scorched to death during the reign of Diocletian.

It was a busy time. On the same day the Council of Montpellier received Philippe-Auguste's permission for the city to be placed under the protection of Jaime, the young King of Aragon. On 2 July the still furious Pope insisted that Arnaud Amaury was the rightful Duke of Narbonne. And in Toulouse a rich Catholic, Pierre Seilan, gave Dominic several houses. They were to become part of the headquarters of the Inquisition.

During the summer and autumn Simon de Montfort was in Toulouse supervising the dismantling of the defences and in November, still occupied, he sent his brother, Guy, to Rome to attend the Fourth Lateran Council, the meeting that would confirm the annexation of the Languedoc.

On 30 November it was an enormous concourse that crowded into a cramped space. Almost three thousand people pressed into the ancient basilica, clergy and laity, the Pope, two patriarchs from Constantinople and Jerusalem, scores of archbishops, four hundred bishops, eight hundred abbots, counts, nobles, *faidits*, a representative of King John, all gathered to debate the outcome of the Albigensian Crusade. Everywhere was packed, suffocating. It was noisy and unruly.[19]

Innocent III, stern but a peacemaker, proposed that, now that heresy had been eliminated, Simon de Montfort should retain the Trencavel lands. Everything else should be returned to their original owners. There followed uproarious dissent. Accusation and denial followed.

The Count of Foix was outspoken in his protestations of his innocence. 'I can honestly swear that I have never loved heretics; that I shun their company; and that in no respect are my feelings in agreement with theirs . . . Holy Church has in me an obedient son'. Foulques sardonically reminded the audience of the man's cruelty, of 'those pilgrims whom the Count slaughtered and cut to pieces, so many of them indeed that the field of Montgey is still covered with their remains'. He was also a liar, a protector of heretics. 'His whole county is crammed and seething with heresy, that the peak of

Montségur was deliberately fortified so that he could protect them, and he has made them welcome there. And his sister [Esclarmonde] became a heretic when her husband died and she then lived more than three years at Pamiers where she converted many to her evil doctrine'. Foix damned Foulques, shouting that he had 'no responsibility for a heretical sister'.[20]

It went on for hours. Finally Innocent III retired to his garden to contemplate a solution to the ecclesiastical/territorial impasse. He was allowed no peace. The Catholic bishops of Occitania followed him. Raymond VI was guilty, Foix was guilty, Comminges was guilty. Considerations of the young son of the Count of Toulouse were irrelevant to the punishments that those who had resisted the crusade merited. Foulques stressed the efforts de Montfort had made, the peace that he had brought to a region of unbelievers. Innocent III replied that the man was not a saint. 'He destroys Catholics just as much as heretics. Serious complaints and bitter accusations reach me every month. God is being brought low and evil exalted'.[21]

It was useless. The pope, whatever his charity, was a realist. Condemnation, anathema, excommunication were words. Soldiers and weapons were physical

On 14 December it was agreed that Raymond VI, Count of Toulouse, had refused to control his subjects in spite of repeated orders to do so and he was therefore exiled 'beyond his frontiers', where he was to do fitting penance and to be stripped of his lands and titles which were given to Simon de Montfort. He was to be allowed his wife's dowry and a pitiful 400 marks yearly for subsistence. For his son, Raymond, there was a small reward. On the death of his father he would be allowed the Count's possessions in Provence.

Two commissioners were appointed to investigate the activities of the Count of Foix and to report to the Pope within three months. If their recommendations were favourable the count would regain his castle at Foix.[22]

In January, 1216, the resentful Arnaud Amaury, Archbishop of Narbonne, excommunicated de Montfort for his appropriation of

145

the title of Duke of Narbonne against the specific orders of Innocent III. De Montfort, fervent Catholic, was unperturbed. He was God's soldier.[23]

In April, having quelled some unrest in Toulouse he rode to Paris to pay homage to Philippe-Auguste. They met at the Pont de l'Arche and rather unexpectedly the crusader was well received by the king who made him Duke of Narbonne and Carcassonne and Count of Toulouse. He was acclaimed everywhere in the surrounding towns and on a magnificent progress crowds applauded him, supplicants touched his robes. Those whom the gods intend to destroy they first make mad. At the summit of his glory, with the entire Languedoc at his command, he could only descend. And the decline had already begun.[24]

While he was there, enjoying the acclamations, in the same month, Raymond VI and his nineteen year old son left Rome, sailed from Genoa and landed at Marseilles. Their return was as celebrated as de Montfort's ride of triumph through the north of France. From Marseilles they went to Avignon, the land of wine, honey, limes and olives. They entered the city to thankful cheers, then were given 'a rich banquet where every variety of fish was served flowing with delicate sauces and washed down with red, and rosé wine, scented with cloves, while jugglers and musicians, singers and dancers performed for their delight'.[25]

Knights and *faidits* at Orange and elsewhere told the pair how they longed for the return of *paratge* and urged their count to recapture his lands. Towns and cities rejected their French garrisons and were reoccupied by their former owners. Provence was in rebellion. Raymond VI departed for Aragon to recruit troops to recapture Toulouse. His son went to Beaucaire on the Rhône, a city critically placed to control the river-traffic. Even today the castle's ramparts are a pleasure to walk. In late April Raymond besieged it. His mother, Joan of England, had given birth to him there.

With him was a swelling Provençal host of disaffected soldiers, an army daily increased by volunteers from all over the province. Raymond was a very different person from his father. He was decisive, resolute, and brave but not as unthinkingly impulsive as the

Count of Foix. Despite his youth his men followed him willingly and with trust.

On his arrival the citizens of Beaucaire instantly opened the gates of the town and the Provençals rushed in to attack the French garrison commanded by Lambert de Croissy, lord of Limoux. 'Toulouse!' was the war-cry. 'Darts, lances they flung, bolts, arrows, axes hatchets, they fought with spears, with swords, with clubs and staves . . . But the French fought back like heroes'. For all their courage they were forced back to the castle. Just beyond it, to the north, was a redoubt, an outlying triangular tower. It was set on fire and its defenders surrendered the same evening.

The siege continued through four months of constant, unyielding combat. Guy and Amaury, his nephew, came to help. On the hill he found a well-entrenched enemy that had already built a temporary wall extending from the town to the burnt-out tower, a barrier that prevented access to the castle. It had been erected by a workforce of 'distinguished stonemasons'. Knights and their ladies had carried sacks of mortar and cement, girls and youths shouldered timbers and dressed stones.[26] It was a very different response from the negative immobility of Raymond VI.

Learning of the uprising de Montfort left Paris. On 5 June he reached Beaucaire with a hasty collection of troops from his scattered garrisons, some mercenaries and a motley band of foreign knights. He had no siege-machines. He camped below the hill, besieging the besiegers.

He attacked ferociously. He was beaten back savagely and bloodily. 'Many were the horses you would have seen running loose, iron-clad, riderless, their masters fallen and killed. Sir Guy of Cavaillon, riding an Arab mount, struck down Guillaume de Berlit that day, and they hanged him there and then from a flowering olive tree'.[27]

For de Montfort and for the trapped garrison it was a desperate time. A massive trebuchet was methodically smashing down the keep. An enormous iron-shod battering-ram was thumping against the quaking walls. The Provençal army had plentiful supplies, the defenders no bread, wine or corn. The Rhône was blocked both to the trapped garrison and to the crusaders futilely barricaded from the castle.

De Montfort did have a siege-tower and a 'cat' but the newly built wall blocked his way to the castle and the machines were 'just an enchanter's dream, they are a spider's web and a sheer waste of material'.[28] Reinforcements for Raymond were continually arriving on their thousand-shilling horses, bringing hordes of men with them.

In spite of the garrison's valiant resistance there was pessimism. De Montfort could not reach them and they could not reach him. They were prisoners in their own keep. 'Not of us can get out without turning into a sparrowhawk'.

They could see vineyards with bodies of captured knights hanging from the trees. Every Frenchman taken was maltreated, whether priest or soldier. One knight was caught, injured, hanged, his hands and feet were cut off, and the feet were mangoneled over the ramparts of the despairing castle. Lambert de Croissy raised a pessimistic black flag. A day or two later empty napkins and an empty bottle were waved from the starving keep.

De Montfort's men were as hungry. They had eaten their mules. One crusader suggested cannibalism, and 'the one who fights worst and gives way to fear, it makes sense to eat him first'. His distasteful comrades were against the idea.

On 15 August the crusaders advanced again, charging on Raymond's camp. Again they were repulsed, leaving a field of dying horses and wounded men. 'The battle ended, the remains left lying there made a feast for dogs and birds'.[29]

Eventually one defender did get through the enemy lines and found de Montfort. The situation was hopeless. The keep would have to surrender. On 24 August terms were agreed. The heroic garrison was allowed out with full honours but they kept no equipment. For de Montfort it was a psychological disaster. It was his first considerable defeat. For the people of Provençal and the Languedoc it was their first real success, a brightening sky of hope.[30]

During the prolonged siege on 16 July Innocent III had died of fever in Perugia. His body was shamefully neglected. In the church next day the corpse was found stripped of its rich vestments, naked and decaying in the summer heat. His cardinals were far more concerned with the election of his successor, the much milder Honorius III.[31]

On 29 August a furious and frustrated de Montfort galloped the two hundred miles to Toulouse for retribution, an angry, horse-killing ride of five days accomplished in three. Raging at his defeat he was convinced that the city of Raymond VI had betrayed him.

To the welcoming delegation of burghers he brusquely informed them that they were turncoats and traitors. He put them in the cells of the Château Narbonnais. All the inhabitants of the city were told to assemble outside the south gate. De Montfort planned to have their empty houses looted.

The pillagers were detected by laggards late for the meeting and news of the robbery caused a riot. In the narrow streets where swords were difficult to wield hundreds of townsmen with clubs and axes and daggers overwhelmed the few crusaders. Some had fled to the sanctuary of the bishop's palace. Others hid in the house of the Count of Comminges or took shelter in a bell-tower. Less successful ones were lynched, battered and stabbed to death in a carnage of madness.

Outside the walls de Montfort organised parties to break down the damaged east and south gates but his enemies were too many. The attacks were beaten off. Late in the night the crusaders withdrew from the walls, spitefully setting fire to wooden houses during their retreat. Livid at so many setbacks de Montfort went to his captives in the Château Narbonnais. He threatened vengeance. 'You cannot escape, and by the most holy cross on which God hung, no riches in the world can stop me cutting your heads off and throwing you from the battlements'.[32]

He meant it but first the city had to be entered and subdued, almost an impossibility because its dense population could block what was now obvious, that the destruction by Prince Louis in 1215 had been inadequate. The breaches were too few and too narrow. Nor was a siege practical. By the time Toulouse surrendered all the crusaders taking refuge in it would have been killed.

Since the Holy Crusade's beginning in 1209 there had been uncountable disgraces: deceit, treason, ambush, broken promises of release, mutilation and murder. Now the Catholic Church itself lied. De Montfort pacifically offered the city's leading citizens safe-conduct if they would meet him in the Villeneuve 'new town' suburb outside the Bourg to discuss solutions to the conflict. Any suspicions the men had were allayed by the assurances of their bishop, Foulques.

'My lords, listen to this', he said to them, 'holy Church has promised you safety, and the count is neither so stupid nor so arrogant as to do anything to you from which he could be blamed. And if he did injure you, the Church would shout so loud that Rome and all Christendom would hear it. Don't be afraid of the next step, honour the count'.[33]

A hundred or more of them went to the suburb. The refugees were released from their hiding-places and escorted to safety. With no delay or explanation the guileless burghers were taken prisoners and sent to the cells of a scatter of castles across the Languedoc. Knights and ladies, men of substance, rank or worth were all expelled into the homeless countryside. Still unsatisfied, demanding retribution for the city's imagined disloyalty, needing money for his mercenaries and his own expenses, de Montfort imposed an enormous tax of 30,000 silver marks to be extorted from the households of Toulouse. The door of any building failing to pay was marked with a cross and destroyed.

'He ordered his officers to send men with picks all over the town to break it down so flat that a man could run straight into it without a pause. Then you would have seen solars and towers knocked down, ramparts, halls and tall crenels overthrown. Workmen demolished roofs and workshops, passages and fine painted chambers, doorways, vaults and lofty pillars. Such was the noise, the dust and damage, the confusion and heat in every quarter of the town, such the mingling of sun, air, haze and fog, it was felt like an earthquake, like thunder or the beat of drums'. Vaux-de-Cernay wrote one short, uninformative paragraph about the despicable episode. He did not mention the lies of Foulques.[34]

Increasingly blatantly behaving as he had always been, a foreigner in a strange land, de Montfort decided to annex the profitable fief of Bigorre in Spain, despite it being the property of the King of Aragon, and married his younger son, Guy, fifteen, to the Countess of Bigorre, Petronilla of Comminges, thirty-three. Unconcerned that she was already the wife of the cousin of the King of Aragon he had the contract annulled by the complacent Archbishop of Auch.

Power corrupts. So does vengeance. So do unexpected defeats. Like a megalomaniac, de Montfort ravaged the lands of the Count of Foix, who had assiduously remained at peace since the edicts of the Lateran Council. For his inactivity he was rewarded. In November, 1216, the pope's commissioners exonerated him of all guilt and restored his castle. Ignoring this de Montfort seized it the following May.[35]

He had already besieged and captured the count's newly-built castle of Montgailhard, today Montgrenier, insolently disobeying the pope's orders. Then, leaving Alice in the secure gloom of the Château Narbonnais, he marched into Provence where the young Raymond and his allies had been taking control of towns and cities. Rapidly de Montfort recaptured fortresses around Nîmes and Vauvert: La Bastide, Monteil, Pierrepertuse. But while he occupied himself in those relatively military trivialities, a hundred and fifty miles away, Toulouse was in revolt.[36]

The untroubled garrison had been taken by surprise. With a small body of men Raymond VI left Aragon and taking advantage of a fog he entered his city through the Bazacle gate on 13 September. His welcome was almost hysterical, his people cramming the streets, cheering and shouting, mixing their near-manic noisy celebrations with their equally noisy, enthusiastic murder of any crusader caught in the open.

The French inside the Château Narbonnais heard the yelling and screams and Alice asked the reason. When she was told of Raymond's reception she grieved. 'I can see that my happiness is over and my sorrows must increase. I am afraid for myself and my children'.[37] Vaux-de-Cernay cursed the city for its duplicity, punning its name of Tolosa with Dolosa, 'Toulouse, city of ruse', and was dismayed to see how quickly the defences ruined by de Montfort were being repaired, churches converted into forts, the vulnerable south-east walls rebuilt.

In the Château Narbonnais, a thousand year old Roman fortress, dark, chilly and overcrowded, the occupants were cut off. Guy came from Carcassonne but could not free them.

As the year ended more and more recruits from the Périgord and Quercy, nobles, knights, *faidits*, reached Raymond. Inside the city every person, rich or poor, man or woman, laboured at the defences. 'Those that were not fighting at the walls were directed to watch-duty or trench-digging. Rich merchants and civic dignitaries hauled rubble through the streets. Women worked the siege engines'. Faint-hearts sneaked away.[38]

Simon de Montfort arrived from Provence and on 8 October a ten-month long siege commenced. Its outcome was to be catastrophic. Characteristically he attacked but this time the crusaders encountered defenders as resolute as themselves. No one was spared. The Count of Comminges aimed his crossbow at Guy, younger son of de Montfort. 'So hard did the bolt strike the damascened mail that it drove in through silken surcoat and ribs and out the other side. Down fell Sir Guy and they carried him away'. Others were hacked down, the fortunate ones killed, the injured abandoned in their agony to be tortured, maimed and brutally despatched. The crusaders were driven back. 'Such wounds, such injuries they suffered, that they strewed the battlefield with white and red'.[39]

In December, accepting that he had insufficient men to break into the city, de Montfort sent his wife and Foulques to Paris, Alice to ask for the king's help, the bishop to travel from town to town urging men to join the 'Crusade'. He was successful. From January to May hundreds of 'forty-day' volunteers reached Toulouse. On 30 May after a torrential downpour the Garonne flooded, bridges were swept away by the swirling waters, sludge and pebbles surged into the river partly blocking it and crusaders were able to cross up to the walls of Toulouse.

There were assaults and counter-attacks. On 6 June Bernard of Cazenac came from the Dordogne with five hundred men. A few days later, Raymond VI's son came from Beaucaire. They saw mounted men and foot-soldiers picking their way between sharpened stakes and deep ditches to smash at the gates under a cascade of stones, boiling oil, missiles of every kind. 'Wherever they could find each other, there they fought . . . Swords and halberds, quarrels and firebrands, lances, maces, stones and setts, javelins and axes, pikes and clubs, broad arrows and slender children's bolts came at the French from all sides, from front and back. None could remain unafraid, not the fiercest man among them'.[40]

There were no prisoners. The Count of Foix hurtled out of the gates and forced the attackers back towards the river. De Montfort calmly retreated, steadily nearing the waiting boats but some in front of him panicked, began rushing and de Montfort slipped and fell into the Garonne. A man close by saved him but 'his horse, wearing armour, was drowned'.

At last, after months of indecisive battle with little success, de Montfort believed that he could safely approach the Montoulieu gate at the south of the city and scale the walls. For weeks his carpenters had been preparing 'cats', one of them gigantic, as large as a mansion with a tower for archers to fire at anyone exposing himself on the battlements.

On 24 June the shelter was pushed forward, only for a great boulder from a trebuchet to crash onto it, smashing its axle and killing several men. De Montfort ordered it to be repaired. The alarmed defenders knew that it had to be destroyed. 'Out they went down the ladders, deployed onto open ground and occupied the levels, shouting 'Toulouse! Now the fire's alight. Kill them, kill them' and charged at the French.

'The crusaders gave way and abandoned the shelters. Once they remounted their chargers, however, the bloodshed began again with such fury that feet, fists and arms flew off and the ground was red with blood and brains'. A squire rushed to de Montfort at Mass in the Château Narbonnais warning him of what could become disaster. De Montfort armed himself and led his men to the field.

'Now from the left-hand parapet an archer let fly and his bolt hit Count Guy's horse on the head and drove half its length into its head. As the horse turned, another crossbowman with a bow fully wound and ready shot at Sir Guy from the side and struck him in the left side of the groin, leaving the steel deep in his flesh; his side and breeches were red with blood'.

De Montfort dismounted, raced to his brother and as he was speaking to him, noblewomen, little girls and wives dragged a new mangonel, said to have been built in St.-Sernin cathedral, to the battlements. 'A stone arrived just when it was needed and struck Count Simon on his steel helmet, shattering his eyes, brains, back teeth, forehead and jaw. Bleeding and black, the count dropped dead on the ground'. The 'Lion of the Crusades', fifty-three years old, was no more. A commemorative tablet on the wall at the entrance to the Jardin des Plantes marks the place where he fell.[41]

The news and jubilation spread throughout the Languedoc. Women danced on the ramparts of Toulouse clattering tambourines. Grateful candles were lit on altars, bells rang from village to village, trumpets blared. Songs were written:

Montfort es mort, es mort, es mort	Montfort is dead!
Viva Tolosa	Long live Toulouse,
Ciotat gloriosa	city glorious,
es poderosa.	and mighty.
Tornan lo paratge et l'honor	Fortune and honour once more are hers
Montfort es mort, es mort, es mort.	Montfort is dead![42]

Simon de Montfort had been killed. His brother Guy was near to death, fearsomely wounded. In their absence Simon's young son, the callow Amaury, became the leader of a disheartened army. Fathers and sons can differ. The pusillanimous Raymond VI lacked the determination and bravery of the twenty-one year old Raymond. Amaury, only eighteen, was as courageous as his father but did not have his warlike intelligence. Nor did he have the personality of a natural leader.

There was one last attack on 1 July. Three weeks later the siege was abandoned and, wrapped in an ox-hide, the corpse of de Montfort was taken to Carcassonne. There, as was the custom, the body was boiled until the flesh dropped off, and the bones were buried in a chapel of St.-Nazaire cathedral. In 1845 a tombstone was discovered with the effigy of a thirteenth century knight having the armorial bearings of the Montfort lion and the cross of Toulouse. The burial had long been removed. In 1224 the count's remains were reburied in Rambouillet priory near Chevreuse southwest of Paris on de Montfort's original French estates.[43]

There is no surviving memorial. The unknown chronicler recorded that there had been an epitaph that the count had been a saint and a martyr to be seated in the kingdom of God. The anonymous writer was sarcastically unimpressed.

'If by killing men and shedding blood, by damning souls and causing deaths, by trusting evil counsels, by setting fires, destroying men, dishonouring paratge, seizing lands and encouraging pride, by kindling evil and quenching good, by killing women and slaughtering children, a man can in this world win Jesus Christ, certainly Count Simon wears a crown and shines in heaven above'.[44]

What had been a conquered land became a land of banditry. Lacking their respect Amaury had little discipline from his followers. One of them, Joris, had been given the lands of the Count of Comminges by de Montfort and was overpowering towns and slaying the inhabitants of any place that defied him. He was trapped and defeated at Meilhan by the Count himself.

Others created their own baronies, ruling as independent princes, flaunting concubines and confiscations in contempt of any attempt to restrain them. Two brothers, Jean and Foucaud de Berzy were little more than brigands terrorising the lands around Toulouse.[45] What had been a holy war in 1209 had become corruption by 1218. Over those years of devastation it has been calculated that over four hundred villages and towns disappeared. The Languedoc never recovered.

Late in December, 1218, the chronicler Pierre des Vaux-de-Cernay died.[46]

SEVEN

1219–1229: *Calm, Crusade, Collapse*

The twenty years that followed were decisive. At a time when the Mongol horsemen of Genghis Khan were overrunning China and Russia there were three quieter but equally disruptive phases in the Languedoc.

Fighting continued but now the aggressors were more usually the southerners. Interference from the Catholic church increased, culminating in the establishment of the Inquisition. More enduring in its outcome than either, the Languedoc became part of the kingdom of France.

Paradoxically, it had been three men, Pope Innocent III, Viscount Simon de Montfort, and the papal Legate, Arnaud Amaury, who had begun the process. But it was one woman, the daunting Blanche of Castile, Queen-Regent, the far-sighted person who, some believed, had removed the royal treasury to Rennes-le-Château, who completed the conquest. She permitted no resistance. Peyrat should have chosen her rather than Esclarmonde to be his heroine.

Apologist for the Cathars and the south as he was, he abominated her. 'Rome', he wrote, 'chose war, extermination. Rome was at the heart of the darkness, of bloody chaos, of clerical intrigue both feudal and royal when suddenly, like a flash of deadly lightning, appeared the foul and ferocious figure of Blanche. She dominated this history. She herself made it both great and tragic. . . . She possessed all the characteristics of her native Spain, she was fierce, proud, obstinate, unconquerable, always greedy, savage'.[1] She would, he added, do anything to achieve her ends. He chose not to mention that through her English mother, Joan, daughter of Henry II and the formidable Eleanor of Aquitaine, she had inherited the indomitable spirit of the Plantagenets.

Once Peyrat's prejudices are ignored the passage can be interpreted as Blanche doing what many mothers have attempted, to protect and improve the prospects of her child. She intended to make her young son, Louis, king of all France.

The downfall of Languedoc began when Prince Louis, later Louis VIII led a second crusade into the Languedoc. On 13 August 1218, Honorius III entreated Philippe-Auguste to allow his son to take up the Cross against the heretics. Eight months later on 16 May 1219, Louis left Paris, marching past Limoges to reach the market town of Marmande that Amaury de Montfort had been besieging for six months. It was to be a second Béziers.

Since Alice, the widowed Countess of Montfort, and Bouchard de Marly had brought more men after Christmas 1218, Amaury had been besieging the walled town but it was well-defended by its commander, Centule d'Astarac, and for months all attacks were beaten back. Amaury waited for the royal army.

A hundred miles to the south-east, on the far side of Toulouse, there was another conflict. The area and the Lauragais had become a rustler's heaven. Lawless bands took what they wanted. The two de Berzy brothers rounded up flocks of sheep. The Count of Foix, their enemy but always an opportunist, stole cattle and property from his base at Baziège. The young Raymond came to join him. Foucaud de Berzy came to fight.

Medieval standards of honour were strict. A southerner urged Raymond to take no part in the forthcoming battle. 'You would win no honour in this battle. Your rank is too great, you should not fight them unless they had Sir Amaury with them, or some other count or great noble'. Foucaud was brave but without wealth or power and his capture would be of no value to Raymond. Medieval standards of courage were just as inflexible. Raymond would fight.

The aftermath of any conflict was predetermined. Defeated knights who were not dead were held for ransom. Common soldiery were slaughtered without compunction. At Baziège Foucaud and his brother, Jean, were captured and taken to the cells of Toulouse.[2]

Miles away at Marmande, Prince Louis had an awesome army, twenty bishops, thirty-three counts, six hundred knights, ten thousand archers and foot-soldiers. The besieged garrison looked and sensibly surrendered. The bishops demanded that the commander, Centule, be burnt as a heretic or hanged as a traitor. To the Prince and his knights this would be a waste of a valuable asset. There was a compromise. Centule was imprisoned. The unarmed garrison was released. The civilians were to be massacred.

Men rushed into the defenceless town with sharp weapons. 'Lords, ladies and their little children, women and men stripped naked, all these men slashed and cut to pieces with keen-edged swords. . . . Not a man or a woman was left alive, neither young nor old, no living creature, unless any had managed to hide. Marmande was razed and set alight'. Another French chronicler, Guillaume le Breton, added, 'All the burghers, with their wives and children, young and old, every inhabitant, to the number of five thousand souls' were slaughtered.[3]

Pleased with his victorious atrocity the prince turned to Toulouse. 'So huge was this throng of murderers that the full host numbered thirteen hundred thousand. They brought carts, mules and pack-beasts, tents, pavilions, victuals and money, and travelled in stages to let those at the rear keep up'. Their intentions were genocidal. Bertrand, cardinal of Rome, was unambiguous. 'Death and slaughter must lead the way, that in and around Toulouse there will remain no living man, neither noble lady, girl nor pregnant woman, no created thing, no child at the breast, but all must die in fire and flames'.[4]

It was the city's fourth siege and it was as unsuccessful as the others. After forty-five days of failure, his 'forty-day' soldiers ready to leave, Louis had his siege-machines set on fire, left two hundred knights behind for Amaury and returned to Paris. He had already exchanged Centule d'Astarac for the de Berzy brothers, whom he liked. Amaury was left to do what he could with his weakened body of men.

Already Cathar Good Men were coming out of their refuges to resume preaching to their believers. Guilhabert of Castres who had debated with Dominic many years before left Montségur and travelled across the Languedoc to Fanjeaux, Laurac, Castelnaudary, Mirepoix and Toulouse teaching, administering the *consolamentum*, reviving the hopes and faith of a revived population.[5]

Years of attack and counter-attack followed. Irresolutely Amaury besieged Castelnaudary for eight months, achieving nothing. His younger brother, Guy, 'handsome, faithful and valiant in arms' was killed. His uncle, Guy, was recovering from his wounds at Lézignan. The crusade was at a standstill.

Quite differently, the south was active. Leaving his father in Toulouse Raymond and the Count of Foix campaigned to recover their lands. In the winter they came to the stronghold of Puilaurens between Toulouse and Castres. In it were the villainous de Berzy brothers. Since their liberation they had meandered from prosperous small town to small town amongst the hills of the Lauragais with their brigands, stealing cattle and sheep, maintaining a private harem.

Misnaming them Foulcaud and Jean Brigier, the censorious Sismondi wrote: 'In their seraglio were found married women taken from the most respectable persons in the province; they had fixed one hundred *sols d'or* for the ransom of their prisoners, and they suffered all those that could not pay this exorbitant sum to perish with hunger at the bottom of a tower'. They even compelled a man to hang his own son'.[6] Raymond caught them, had them decapitated and displayed their heads on spikes over the gates of Toulouse.

In the spring Servian was taken. Lavaur, scene of a massacre in 1211, was the scene of another in 1220 when the town was stormed and the garrison put to death. Some got away by swimming across the Agout. Others drowned. In February, 1221, Montréal surrendered after its commander, Alain de Roucy, was killed, struck on the head by a crossbow bolt. Fanjeaux and Limoux capitulated. Oliver and Bernard of Termes recovered the great castle of their fathers.

When it was captured in 1210 and its lord imprisoned in Carcassonne his wife had been released but his two young sons were held hostage in the custody of Simon de Montfort. In Carcassonne they met the even younger Jaime, son of Pedro II, who had been married in 1211 to Amicié, daughter of de Montfort for optimistic dynastic reasons. When Jaime was sent back to Aragon in 1214 it is likely that the Termes brothers went with him and were educated in that court where there was already another exile, Raymond-Roger Trencavel, son of the Viscount of Béziers.[7]

On 6 August 1221, Dominic died in Bologna. Thirteen years later he was canonised by Pope Gregory IX. His predecessor, Honorius III, appointed yet another legate, Conrad, warned Raymond in June that his actions could cost him the lands in Provence so bountifully allowed him by the Lateran Council. 'Do not congratulate yourself on the ephemeral victories that you have already won. Do not imagine that you can defeat God and defend your territories once we have deprived you of them'. Raymond ignored him. In October, 1221, the Church revoked his titles. At the end of the year Conrad persuaded Amaury to offer his Languedoc possessions to Philippe-Auguste.

In Spring 1222, the year he founded Cordes, unworried by the Pope's action Raymond took Millau and Moissac and moved through the Minervois and Narbonnais accepting the rather reluctant submission of towns unsure of how permanent his dominance would be.

Amid his triumphs there was a personal loss. The Languedoc had been a tragedy and, like a tragedy, death was claiming its leading actors. Within four years two de Montforts had been killed, two clergymen, Innocent III and Dominic had passed away. Two, perhaps three, chroniclers had gone, Guillaume de Tudela, Pierre des Vaux-de-Cernay, and probably their nameless associate. Now to that morbid list were added the names of three southern nobles. First came the death of Raymond VI, aged sixty-six, Count of Toulouse for twenty-eight years. Already ill, the August heat in Toulouse caused a stroke. He was carried to the shade of a fig-tree in a merchant's courtyard, where he died. Despite wearing Hospitaller robes he was denied the last rites by the Abbot of St.-Sernin because he had been excommunicated. No sacraments were administered. Nor could his body be buried in hallowed ground.

For centuries his wooden coffin lay outside the walls of the priory of the Hospitallers. By the fifteenth century rats had gnawed it to pieces 'and Raymond's bones had disappeared'. Nicolas Bertrand had seen a natural fleur-de-lys on one of them, the sign of royalty. The skull survived until the seventeenth century. It has gone.[8]

To many modern minds such treatment of the count's body is repellent but the excommunication is a matter of indifference. To the mind of a medieval Christian the opposite was true. Corruption of the flesh was a daily sight but to be deprived of the care and love of the Church was a catastrophe. 'We do cast you forth and reject you from the communion of the Church as an infected limb', her tribunal informed Joan of Arc. No prayers could be said for the living and death brought only everlasting purgatory for the soul, even descent into Hell. Fear of such a condemnation caused Raymond VII to plead for forgiveness when he himself was excommunicated in 1225.[9]

Then, early in 1223, after he had liberated Mirepoix, there was the death of the Count of Foix, Raymond-Roger. His son, Roger Bernard, succeeded him. Bernard, Count of Comminges, had died in February. All the major protagonists in the Albigensian Crusade were gone. Only Raymond VII, the new Count of Toulouse, and Amaury, son of Simon de Montfort, remained in contention.[10]

At that time Raymond was at Penne d'Agenais but the approach of Amaury with a powerful body of men caused him to retreat. It was a lone success for the crusaders. In May the legate Conrad sent a despairing letter to Philippe-Auguste, 'Here at Béziers we are surrounded by the might of the enemy and expecting to be killed at any time'. No help came from king or Pope.

In the summer a vague truce was agreed and Amaury and Raymond were seen joking together in Carcassonne. A conference to discuss possible peace terms was held in St Flour and when the disagreements remained strong another was arranged for Sens to be conducted in the presence of the king. But on 14 July Philippe-Auguste died in Nantes and his son, the husband of Blanche, became Louis VIII. Crowned in Reims, he was more concerned with maintaining the strength of his throne and resisting the constant threat from England and he ignored the Languedoc, merely sending Amaury ten thousand silver marks. War was resumed.

Weakened by desertions, with no likelihood of help arriving, besieged in Carcassonne by Raymond and the Count of Foix, Amaury capitulated. On 14 January 1214, he conceded Carcassonne, Minerve and Penne d'Agenais with a promise that in two months all other places would be abandoned. The following day he left the Languedoc, taking the bodies of his father, Simon, and brother, Guy, wrapped in ox-hides, to the priory of Hautes-Bruyères in the forest of Rambouillet near Paris. The sixteen-year-old Raymond-Roger Trencavel returned from exile and was given the titles of Viscount of Béziers and Carcassonne. He was in Carcassonne, the Count of Foix was in Pamiers. Raymond VII was in Toulouse. The Crusade was over.[11]

That Crusade was over but Amaury de Montfort was persuading the new king to undertake another. Even though he was occupied with recapturing land held by the English, Louis VIII appreciated the richness of the Languedoc and its proximity to the Mediterranean. With the gift of Amaury's former possessions there the south of France would be a valuable royal asset. With the expected support of Honorius III a second crusade could be proclaimed.

But not immediately. On 5 May Louis declared war on Henry III and French forces overran Poitou and most of Gascony north of the Garonne. Alarmed at the nearness of a royal army so close to Toulouse Raymond quickly asked for the pope's support. Beset by two opposing interests the ageing prelate dithered.

At a conference in Montpellier that August summoned by Arnaud Amaury, the apprehensive Count of Toulouse swore to obey the Church in all matters. He would restore church property, pay compensation for any damage, expel all mercenaries and would unremittingly hunt down any heretics in his realms. So did Roger-Bernard, Count of Foix, and Raymond-Roger Trencavel, Viscount of Carcassonne. The bishops were impressed.[12]

It was a time of plots and counter-plots, of treaties and treacheries. Busy as he was with his campaign against England, Louis VIII agreed to lead a crusade but only if Rome agreed to pay all of its expenses, allow the king to do as he wished and keep what cities and regions he wanted. The demands were harsh, perhaps deliberately so, and with the apparent submission of Raymond VII the Pope rejected them. He told the king that the invasion of the Languedoc would have to be postponed. Angrily Louis told Conrad, the uneasy bearer of the news, that the affair was no longer of any interest to him. Unknown either to king or Pope Raymond made a secret alliance with Henry III.

There was no stability. By the February of 1225, Honorius III had changed his mind. He appointed another legate, the imperious and high-born Romano Frangipani, Cardinal of St Angelo, who demanded the attendance of both Amaury de Montfort and Raymond, Count of Toulouse, at the Council of Bourges in November near the city's heavy cathedral, one of the darkest in France. Two months earlier, on 29 September, the elderly Arnaud Amaury, Archbishop of Narbonne, had died.

There was a huge assembly at Bourges, six archbishops, one hundred and thirteen bishops and abbots. Raymond repeated his solemn promises and again asked the Pope to grant him his inheritance. He was unsuccessful. Amaury reminded the congress of the conclusions of the Lateran Council ten years earlier and of the apostasy of Raymond's father. Partly suspecting that the son might prove as fickle, more concerned that a strong Count of Toulouse might retain those properties that the Church had acquired during the crusade, the Council voted against Raymond, stripping him of his possessions and excommunicating him for disobedience because he had 'failed to obey the orders of the church in the manner expected of him'. It was unfair but it was predictable. Amaury de Montfort claimed the county of Toulouse as a fief of Louis VIII.[13]

On 28 January the following year Romano repeated the excommunication in Paris. Rome declared that Raymond VII could not prove himself to be a true son of the Church and his lands were granted to the King of France. Two days later, at the urging of his wife, Blanche of Castile, and of Honorius III, Louis VIII took the Cross. The royal crusade was to assemble at Bourges after Easter on 17 May, 1216.[14]

In desperation Raymond begged support from Henry III, King of England, his cousin-german through the marriage of Raymond VI to Joan, daughter of Richard the Lion Heart, sister of King John and aunt of Henry. Raymond also enlisted Hugues de Lusignan, Count de La Marche, a bitter enemy of the French monarchy. The alliance was confirmed in the usual medieval manner by marrying the daughter of Hugues to Raymond's son.

It was a powerful coalition in theory but not in reality. Henry's English Council decided against any invasion, a conclusion based on a mixture of military realism and superstition. Their court astrologer said that Louis should be allowed to go on the crusade because he would die there. It was a prediction weirdly but quite independently repeated by the troubadour-turned-nun, Gormonda de Monpeslier.

Mas so que Merlis	But the thing that Merlin,
prophetizan dis	prophesying, said
de bon rey Loys	of good king Louis,
que morira en Pansa,	that he would die in Pansa, [Montpensier]
aras s'esclarzis.	Is now becoming clear.[15]

It was weird because both the astrologer and the mythical Merlin, unknown to each other, were excellent prophets. The king did die as they foretold.

The anti-Catholic troubadour, Guilhem de Figueira, blamed Honorius III for the mortality. 'Thou didst bring him to his death, for thy false preaching enticed him from his land'. Gormonda answered the condemnation rather feebly. 'In Rome all goodness is accomplished. He who disagrees lacks any sense'. Figueira's words of 1228 were so memorable, so popular, and so dangerous to know, that almost fifty years later in 1274 the Inquisition accused a man of having a manuscript of the troubadour's works.[16]

None of that was known in 1226 as the king's army travelled southwards along the Rhône reaching Lyon on 28 May, turning and twisting across the river at Vienne and Valence, reaching Avignon early in June. From there the river had to be crossed by the only bridge, St. Bénézet. Avignon was a powerful city, nominally a fief of the Count of Provence but in reality virtually an independent city-state with tall inner walls and three miles of outer ramparts and a confusion of tradesmen's streets: rue Banasterie for weavers; rue des Teinteriers, dyers' row; rue Fourbisseurs for sword-cutlers. In the fourteenth century Avignon was strong and attractive enough to to be chosen for the palace of seven anti-Lateran popes during the Great Schism of 1309–77.

The third was Benedict XII, 1334–42, formerly Jacques Fournier, Bishop of Pamiers, who, in July 1320, would question Béatrice of Planisolles about the years she had lived in the Cathar village of Montaillou.[17]

Avignon was also the home of the Italian poet, Petrarch, who met the chaste Laura there only to leave after her death, disgusted at the depravity of the Avignonese, 'an abode of sorrows, the shame of mankind, a sink of vice . . . a sewer where all the filth of the universe has gathered'.

That was in 1353. In 1226 Louis VIII was negotiating permission to cross the Rhône by the St Bénézet bridge. Today there are two good bridges to the south. In 1226 there was one, wooden, on Roman foundations, and it was narrow, used by pedestrians and horsemen but far too constricted for the legendary dancing. 'Sur le Pont d'Avignon on y danse . . .' should read,

'*Sous* le Pont d'Avignon
On y danse, tous en rond'

men and women revelling underneath it on the Ile de la Barthelasse halfway across the river, a popular pleasure-ground for dancing and drinking in the Middle Ages. Clement IV, one of the Avignon popes, replaced the bridge with a wider one of stone in the mid-fourteenth century but, repeatedly damaged by floods, it was finally broken in 1689 and only four of its twenty-two arches remain.

Louis VIII and Avignon came to an agreement. The citizens were willing for the king and a reasonably-sized retinue to enter the city and cross the bridge. The remainder of the army would have to use an improvised pontoon of linked rafts further upriver. It was inconvenient and would cause delay but it was accepted.

166

What went wrong has never been explained. One column of crusaders had got over the makeshift bridge. A second contingent was unexpectedly attacked. The assailants shut themselves inside the massive walls, where the city had been rich enough to pay for a large garrison of mercenaries. Assault being futile the king ordered a siege and, for three long, boring months of unseasonable tropical heat, the royal army watched, waited and writhed under a plague of black flies that spread disease. Three thousand crusaders, it was said, including Bouchard de Marly, died. Corpses began to fester in their open grave-pits and were thrown into the Rhône.

Neither side could win but on 9 September it was Avignon that asked for terms. They were settled. All the city's armoury and siege-machines were confiscated, a fine of three thousand silver marks was levelled and the walls were broken down. They and their thirty-nine towers were rebuilt, badly, in the following century and partly restored by Viollet-le-Doc in the nineteenth. The ramparts can still be walked.[18]

News of Avignon's surrender reached a war-weary Languedoc. After two years of near-peace the people had no enthusiasm for a return to fighting. From all over Occitania nobles came to yield to the king. 'We long to rest under your protective wing and live under your wise government' grovelled Bernard-Otho of Niort, whose grandmother, had been the Good Woman, Blanche of Laurac. She had persuaded her husband to shelter Cathars in his castles and later in life she took refuge in Montségur.

Sicard of Puylaurens was as sycophantic, and just as hypocritical, as Bernard-Otho. 'We bathe your feet with our tears, illustrious lord, and we crave the privilege of being received as slaves beneath your protective mantle'. Jordan of Cabaret was also on his way but Oliver and Bernard of Termes, brothers and landless *faidits*, kidnapped the traitor, who died two years later in the dungeons of Toulouse.[19]

Cities and castles opened their gates: Albi, Arles, Béziers, Castres, Narbonne, Nîmes, St.-Gilles; even Termes, where Oliver and Bernard submitted to the royal will. At Carcassonne the disheartened burghers expelled Raymond-Roger Trencavel and the Count of Foix.

It was a regal victory but with it came two problems. The season was late and many of the greater crusaders including the Counts of Brittany and Champagne wished to return home. After a meeting at Pamiers to appoint governors to control the newly-won lands, Guy de Montfort, brother of Simon, being given Castres, Louis deferred a march on Toulouse until next year. Overall military command was given to his cousin, the youthful but capable Humbert de Beaujeu with a company of fifty knights. Seventeen years later he was to besiege the last Cathar stronghold, the mystical and almost unreachable castle of Montségur.[20]

The king started for Paris but died less than halfway there, falling ill at Albi and dying at Montpensier on 8 November. Poison was suspected. Guillaume de Puylaurens piously attributed the royal demise to sexual starvation and excessive chastity, the ailing king having refused the solicitous, if not salacious attentions of a young virgin in his bed. Abstinence is unlikely. Fidelity may be the explanation. Since their wedding in 1200 Blanche and he had twelve children, four dying before Louis became king, three more before their eldest son, Louis, was of age. Rather than chastity death came more probably from dysentery contracted during the infected siege.[21]

The marriage between Louis and Blanche of Castile was happy yet it took place almost by a linguistic lottery. To choose a bride for Philippe-Auguste's son a royal delegation from France was led by the pro-French, ageing, but still strong-minded Eleanor of Aquitaine, widow of Henry II of England. Once the bride of Louis VII of France the union had been annulled because of consanguinity. The infidelities of her second husband, Henry, led her to encourage her sons, Richard and John, to rebel against their father.

Like so many wives of those centuries her life disproved the myth that they were no more than breeding machines and the acquiescent chattels of their husbands. Estranged wife of the adulterous monarch, malicious but improbable rumours muttered that she had arranged the murder of the king's lovely mistress, Rosamund Clifford, 'Fair Rosamund'. Known contradictorily as *Rosa-mundi*, rose of the world, and *Rosa-immundi*, rose of filth, she died in 1176 and was buried in Godstow nunnery near Oxford. The epitaph on her tomb was typical of the medieval fascination with the corruption of death.

Hic jacet in tumba Rosa mundi, non rosa munda;
Non redolat, sed olet, quae redolere solet.

'Here in this tomb lies the rose of the world, not a fine rose, its smell is not good. It stinks that once was sweet'. Yet the Tudor antiquarian, John Leland, recorded that when the tomb was opened 'a uery swete smell cam owt of it'.[22]

Rosamund would have been no more than a fragment of memory to Eleanor of Aquitaine when she was offered the choice between two attractive little girls, Blanche and her sister, Urraca, as the bride-to-be of Prince Louis. Urruca was rather more beautiful but her name with its double 'rr' and hard 'c' would have been 'harsh and alien' whereas 'Blanche' would be 'spoken easily' in the langue d'Oïl of the Ile de France.

Some women change history by chance. Helen of Troy's beauty launched a thousand ships from Greece. Jocasta did not recognise her own son, Oedipus. 'Had Cleopatra's nose had been shorter the face of the world would have changed', mused Pascal, the seventeenth-century French mathematician and man-of-letters, facetiously. If the lovely but unpronounceable Urraca had been called Isabella the destiny of the Languedoc might have been different.

Fate can amuse. Urraca was rejected. She became Queen of Portugal. The easily-spoken Blanche was chosen. Born in the mid-1180s, perhaps in the same year, 1187, as her future husband, she was in her early teens at her wedding yet their first child, Louis, was not born until 1215 when she was almost thirty.[23]

She was a devoted mother. A mid-thirteenth century 'Moralised Bible' shows her supervising her son's secular and religious education. Her psalter still exists. 'Dearest son', she wrote, 'I would rather you incur temporal death than by any mortal sin you should offend your Creator'. Louis, later St Louis, did not disappoint her.

In 1226 Blanche of Castile was resolute that neither anyone nor anything should interfere with his progress. A hurried coronation was held at Reims on 29 November, to prevent time for any rebellion. The French crown had enemies. It was significant that neither the Count of Brittany nor of La Marche, an implacable enemy of the French monarchy, attended the ceremony.

At the late king's last but clear-cut instructions Blanche acted as Queen-Regent during her son's minority. In effect she ruled the kingdom of France from 1226 until 1231 when Louis became sixteen. With unlimited authority she took control of everything, legislated, dealt with foreign powers, waged war, arranged marriages. She even had the power to fill ecclesiastical benefices. Constantly attended and advised by the attentive and attractive Cardinal Legate, Romano, 'in Paris tongues wagged about Romano and Blanche sharing more than just prayers'.[24]

True or not these were not comfortable years for Blanche. Three threats persisted until 1231: mutinous barons; England, which controlled half the lands of France; and the persistent attempts by southerners to overthrow their northern French invaders.

Of these challenges the nobles were the most troublesome. Led by magnates such as Pierre Mauclerc, Count of Brittany and Hugues de la Marche who was married to Isabel of Angoulême, widow of the English King John, they disobeyed commands, marauded across royal terrain, swore to depose the foreign woman who had usurped their throne. 'Queen Blanche ought not to govern so great a thing as the kingdom of France, and it did not pertain to a woman to do such a thing'. They were confident of help from England.[25]

In 1227 the two counts joined by those of Champagne and Boulogne assembled a host to challenge Blanche. She out-thought them. The Count of Boulogne defected when she gave him two castles and a thousand pounds. Then with a steadfast army she moved swiftly to Tours, to Chinon next day and confronted the rebels at Loudun. For four thousand pounds the Count of Champagne went home. Richard of Cornwall who was in Gascony during the turmoil simply accepted the reluctant truce and did nothing. Deprived of their own allies, abandoned by a dormant

England, the nobles retreated, sullen but defeated. There were sporadic mutinies until 1231. Blanche repressed them. Only the Languedoc continued with its two problems, a military one for Humbert de Beaujeu, a religious one for Honorius III.

A year before the death of Louis VIII, and for the first time in years, led by Guilhabert de Castres, almost a hundred Cathar bishops, deacons and Good Men assembled at Pieusse just north of Limoux near a Catholic abbey with its austerely attractive first-floor cloisters. After almost sixteen years of persecution the Council was still confident enough to create a fifth diocese in the Razès district of south-eastern Languedoc. Four already existed at Toulouse in the west, Carcassonne, east, Albi in the north and Agen at the north-west. The new bishop was Benôit of Termes and his region around the valley of the Aude from Quillan in the south to Limoux at the north was to become a major centre of heresy now that the Lauragais had been subdued. Despite the massacres at Minerve, Lavaur and elsewhere the Cathars had not been systematically persecuted. But they had learned. The mass burnings warned them not to gather in their misguided hundreds behind unreliable city walls. Now they would live as individuals and families in their own homes, almost undetectable unless betrayed.[26]

The Razès, so long a quiescent part of the crusade, only passed through by de Montfort on his way to military objectives, now developed into an area of warfare. In the winter of 1226/7 there was a surge of outrage. The Count of Foix and Raymond-Roger Trencavel, Viscount of Béziers, took possession of Limoux. Raymond VII defiantly captured Auterive near Toulouse, burnt by de Montfort in 1211, then swung thirty miles eastwards to Labécède in the Lauragais. In 1224 Oliver of Termes had offered his services to Raymond VII. As a reward the Count appointed him and Pons de Villeneuve joint commanders of the fortified town.

The actions were provocative and Humbert de Beaujeu did not ignore them. Louis VIII had entrusted him with the governance of the Languedoc and the king's trust was justified. With a secure base at Carcassonne the commander did not suffer from the perpetual weakness of Simon de Montfort who never knew when reinforcements would arrive. De Beaujeu was not fighting a crusade but a royal war. He had the assurance of continual replacements throughout the regency of Queen Blanche.

Until 1227 fighting had generally been to the north of the Garonne above a line from Toulouse to Carcassonne, mainly in the towns and villages of the heretical Lauragais. The south-east of the Languedoc had been quiet. With the exception of Termes there had been little opposition. Now along the valley of the Aude there were uprisings. It was a region with no great cities and very few towns: Limoux, Quillan, Lavelanet. But it was a land of immense castles: Peyrepertuse, Quéribus, Puylaurens and those strongholds were surrounded by many smaller fortifications: Aguilar, Arques, Coustaussa, Padern, Usson, and the formidable Cathar stronghold of Montségur on its unreachable mountaintop. It was a land that Humbert de Beaujeu would have to conquer.

In the spring of 1227 the French captain-general went on the offensive. On his way to Toulouse with the Archbishop of Narbonne and Foulques, Bishop of Toulouse, he diverted to Labécède and after a short siege recaptured it. Although some of the defenders, shamefully including the two commanders, slipped away during the night the reminder of the garrison were pitilessly slaughtered, 'some by the sword, some by the spear'.[27] It was a warning of what could be expected for those who opposed de Beaujeu.

During the siege some of the defenders had shouted down at Foulques, calling him the bishop with a congregation of devils. The former troubadour had a sardonic sense of humour. He agreed with the mockery but for a reason consistent with his Catholic faith. 'They are the devils', he pronounced, 'and I am their bishop'. As a good Christian he asked de Beaujeu to spare the women and little children in the town. There was no mercy for the heretics discovered inside Labécède. Gerald of Lamothe, some deacons and other believers were burnt.[28]

Then Toulouse was encircled. There was no attempt to storm the walls. There was no need for men to be lost. Nor, although Raymond VII and the Count of Foix were inside the city, was there any sally from the gates. For the citizens inside it was a summer of helpless despair. From their battlements they watched immature vines being uprooted for the fourth time in fifteen years. Orchards and olive groves were chopped down. Fields were scythed flat months before the harvest. Wells were poisoned. Cattle were driven off. It was pitiless and it could not be prevented.[29]

Leaving the mockery of a countryside behind him de Beaujeu forced his way into Limoux after heavy fighting, accepted surrender after surrender across a despondent Razès and installed garrisons in every town and many of the smaller castles. Not only the Razès was affected. Across Occitania it was accepted that there would be no peace unless it was a peace that Blanche and the kingdom of France allowed. There was little fighting anywhere but near Pamiers in January, 1228, Guy de Montfort, brother of Simon, was slain by an archer at the bastide of Varilhes, a town in which Béatrice of Planisolles was to live.

The story of the de Montforts was one of valiant futility. Simon had been killed at Toulouse in 1218, now his brother had perished. Simon's second son fell at Castelnaudary. Amaury survived the Languedoc only to go on a crusade where he was captured by Arabs and imprisoned for eighteen months. Released, he died at Otranto on his way home in 1241. Simon's third son, another Simon, became Earl of Leicester in England, defeated King Henry III at the battle of Lewes in 1264 but was slain at Evesham by Prince Edward the following year. It was a fifty-year family history of unsuccessful courage.

There was yet another notable death. Honorius III died and on 19 March 1227 he was succeeded by Gregory IX. Years earlier in 1216 Honorius had confirmed the Order of the Dominicans and by that had established the beginnings of the notorious Inquisition.

There were occasional setbacks for the crusaders. In the Spring of 1228 de Beaujeu was defeated at Castelsarrasin just south of Moissac and eight miles to the south-east at Montech a party of his men was ambushed, some killed in the fighting, others captured. Knights like Othon de Terrides were imprisoned in the dungeons of Castelsarrasin. Common soldiers were savaged. In retaliation for the bloodshed at Labécède their hands were cut off, their eyes were put out and they were abandoned to the blind wilderness of the forest.[30]

Humbert de Beaujeu was not deflected from his ruthless pacification. He besieged Cabaret and forced its garrison to surrender. At the end of November Oliver and Bernard accepted that any lasting success was impossible and presented their castle and lands to the Archbishop of Narbonne, the Bishop of Carcassonne and Guy de Lévis. Oliver asked to be returned to the Catholic church and was given some land in the forest of Crausse near St.-Hilaire.[31] The great castle of Puylaurens near Quillan became the property of the Count of Roussillon.

Late in that year of failure at the Treaty of Baziège through the services of Élie Guérin, Bishop of Grandselve, Raymond VII entreated Blanche, Queen-Regent of France, for a truce. It was a plea from a desperate man who could expect little compassion. Their second war had been costly for the French. It had seen the deaths of the King, Louis VIII, the Archbishop of Reims, the Counts of Namur and St Pol, Guy de Montfort, Bouchard de Marly and thousands of soldiers in 1226 alone. Any terms offered to Raymond II, recalcitrant Count of Toulouse, would be severe.

In November Grandselve went to Paris with Raymond's request for peace and in January, 1229, after three months of negotiations, a preliminary Treaty of Meaux in the county of Champagne laid down a set of demands to be met by the Count of Toulouse. They were to be ratified at Easter in Paris at a formal convocation organised by Cardinal-Legate Romanus of St Angelo, whom some suspected of being the discreet lover of Blanche.[32]

The terms had been modified since Meaux. The Archbishop of Narbonne demanded that Raymond, the Count of Foix and the 'so-called' Viscount of Bèziers – who had been disinherited – were to be deprived of their possessions 'for their refusal to discover and hand over heretics to the Church'. The mood was punitive.

There is no record of what the weather was like in Paris on Maundy Thursday, 12 April 1229, but there was no need of sunshine. The forecourt of the almost finished Notre-Dame was brilliant with colour. An excited child with a kaleidoscope could not have seen a greater jostle of reds, blues, greens, mauves than the scene of rich scarlets and yellows as gaily-apparelled courtiers and crimson-robed clerics mingled and moved from gorgeous group to group. It was spectacular. There were draped tapestries, lustrous canopies. There was the dazzle of great noblemen's rectangular banners, the long, narrow standards of lesser ranks, the slightest breeze shaking the red-dyed pointed pennons of mere knights and squires. By the cathedral's West Front stood the plumed Royal Guard with their glittering halberds and ceremonial scabbards. There were silks and furs, carpets for aristocratic shoes and sandals, richly cloaked cardinals and mitred archbishops, and at the heart of the gorgeous pageant were the high thrones of King Louis IX, just two weeks before his fourteenth birthday, and his mother, Blanche, the Queen-Regent.

Above them hung the flaming red silken oriflamme banner on its golden lance. Alongside them was the royal shield, its blue surface covered with gilded fleurs-de-lys, an innovation hardly fifty years old. To the right of the couple were the thrones of the prelates. To the left were the barons. Hollywood at its technicoloured best could not have outdone the scene.

In front of the king was a desk and on it was a Holy Bible. It was on that book in front of everyone that Raymond VII, Count of Toulouse, was to swear allegiance to Louis IX and obedience to the Catholic Church. Trumpets sounded. The King's Scrivener loudly, solemnly read out the decrees, one by demanding one. They were draconian.

Raymond swore fidelity to his king and to the Church until his death; he would unceasingly pursue, catch and deliver heretics to the Church; for that purpose he would pay for the church to examine all the accused; he would expel every mercenary from his lands; he agreed to restore lost properties to the Church and pay it 10,000 gold marks in compensation; he would give a further 4,100 gold marks to abbeys chosen by the Church; he would donate 4,000 gold marks annually to maintain the new Toulouse university and pay the salaries of four Masters of Theology, fifty marks yearly, two Decretalists in Canon Law, thirty marks, six Masters of the Liberal

Arts, twenty marks, and two Grammarians, ten. There was more. In two years' time he would go to the Holy Land for five years, although this condition was not enforced. Raymond promised to befriend all those who did wish to go on a Holy Crusade. The walls of Toulouse were to be dismantled in thirty places for a distance of five hundred *toises* of 1.94m, nearly two-thirds of a mile. The Château Narbonnais in Toulouse was to be held by the king for ten years assisted by a gift of 6,000 marks for its maintenance. Louis IX received all the intact castles in the Languedoc. Raymond accepted shamefully shrunken frontiers, in effect losing two-thirds of his territories including the cities of Avignon, Beaucaire, Carcassonne, Nîmes, St.-Gilles, virtually all his lands to the east of Toulouse.

The terms were brutal but there was worse. At the insistence of Blanche, always protective of her son and of the kingdom of France, Raymond's daughter, Jeanne, nine years old, was to be his sole heiress and betrothed to Alphonse de Poitiers, also nine, the brother of Louis IX. If the marriage were childless then on Jeanne's death the entire county of Toulouse was to go to the French crown. The betrothal was solemnised in June at Moret-sur-Loing.

Raymond had reluctantly agreed but hopefully asked Gregory IX to annul his marriage so that he could remarry and have a son. The pope refused. Some seven years later in 1236–7 when they were sixteen the youth and girl were married.

The humiliation of Raymond VII was still not complete. The following day on Good Friday, 13 April, inside a crowded Notre-Dame the excommunicated Count made a public repentance and in front of the assembly he was scourged at the altar by Romanus, the Cardinal-Legate, watched by Louis IX and Blanche.

Even Puylaurens thought the terms and the punishment over-harsh. '*C'était pitié . . . à l'autel*', 'It was great shame to see so noble a prince, who had long held his own against powers both mighty and many, thus hauled to the altar bare-footed, clad only in shirt and breeches'.

After the whipping, which had been far from token, he was held for six weeks in the Louvre prison while his daughter was escorted to the king's commissioners in Paris. Finally, on 3 June the excommunication lifted. Louis IX knighted him.[33]

Many troubadours disapproved. An anonymous woman wrote:

Vai, sirventesca, al bon rey d'Arago	Go, poem, to the good king of Aragon
e a la papa que.l sagramen perdo,	and to the Pope; let them undo the law.
car vilanesca an fag, si Dieus be.m do,	For it is villainous, God grant me grace,
e ribaudesca, nostre marit felo.	And shameful what our husbands allowed.

Another troubadour, Bernard Sicart de Marveljos, raged at the Treaty and the lands and cities that had been lost:

Ai! Tolosa et Provensa!	Ah, Toulouse and Provence!
E la terra d'Argensa!	And the land of the Agenais!
Bezers et Carcassey!	Béziers and Carcassonne!
Quo vos vi! quo vos vei!	How you go, how you all go![34]

Penne d'Albigeois castle and nine others had been promised to the king by the beginning of August, 1231. Once at liberty, Raymond imitated his father and did nothing. To him the Treaty of Meaux-Paris had been a 'forced treaty' and therefore only a provisional agreement that he proposed to ignore as far as he could. Others complained of the injustice. The author of the *Besant de Dieu* of about 1230, wrote:

Quant Franceis vont sor Tolosans	When Frenchmen attack Toulousains
Qu'il tienent a popelicans	whom they think are heretics
E la legacie romaine	And the Roman legate
Les i conduit et les i maine,	Leads them and incites them,
N'est mie bien, ceo m'est avis.	To me it is wrong because I know,
Bons e mals sont en toz pais.	There are good and bad in all places.[35]

In May Toulouse university was founded, its inaugural sermon given on the 24th of that month. Administration was entrusted to Dominican friars who were to be in charge of the persecution of heretics. Gregory IX knew that preaching and exhortation had failed repeatedly. Catharism could be successfully repressed only by a specially organised institution whose members ideally would be the preaching, theologically trained Dominican friars. Their attitude was defined during the summer when at a council, Foulques, Bishop of Toulouse, announced that every parish was to have a group set up to hunt down Cathars whose sin was so abominable to the Church that even if they had died their corpses were to be exhumed and burned. By ordinance all men aged over fourteen and girls of more than twelve were obliged by their faith to identify unbelievers, even their own families and friends.[36] In November the Papal Legate, Romano Frangipani, came to Toulouse to ensure that Raymond VII was keeping his promise to make 'diligent enquiries' into the whereabouts of heretics.

One war had ended. Another was beginning.

EIGHT

1230–1244: Inquisitors and Castles

One day in 1232 oxen pulled a cart out of Toulouse. There was no food from the countryside in it nor anything manufactured in the city. It was a cart of death. Surrounded by an escort of armed horsemen and preceded by the Bishop of Toulouse and his entourage it was carrying nineteen tightly-roped men and women, condemned as heretics, to their place of burning outside the walls. Thick posts, hung with chains and heaped round with dried wood, waited for them. So did an expectant crowd.

One of the prisoners was the aged Pagan, lord of Labécède, who had resisted valiantly against Humbert de Beaujeu during his castle's siege of 1227 but his loyalty then to the Count of Toulouse gave him no protection five years later. It was Raymond, his own Count, who had caught him and handed him to the judgement of the Bishop's tribunal. Pagan freely admitted that he was a Good Man, one of those Cathar preachers sarcastically termed *Parfaits* or Perfects by contemptuous Catholic clergy.

One night Raymond VII accompanied by Raimon de Fauga, the new Bishop of Toulouse after the death of Foulques in 1231, had led a search-party into the region of the Montagne Noire near Castelnaudary. Perhaps informed of a secret gathering of Cathars in the forest they surprised the nocturnal group and took the captives, including the old nobleman, to Toulouse. It was an act of betrayal by a feudal lord of one of his vassals. It may be that Raymond VII hoped that his treachery would prove his good faith, that he had

179

kept his promise at the Treaty of Meaux-Paris to persecute unbelievers and that he could then return to the ways of his father and live in religious inactivity. Whatever the count's motives, Pagan of Labécède and all his companions were executed.[1] Raymond gained nothing.

The five years from 1230 to 1234 were like the inevitable stages of a Greek tragedy for the Cathars. Once they had walked without concern around the Languedoc, respected, but now they fled the death-traps of towns with the danger of betrayal by terrified comrades. Now they skulked in temporary refuges or went to the walls of great castles. And, like hungry packs of hunting-dogs, Inquisitors searched for them with the prospect of pyres in their minds.

The first year, 1230, found Dominican friars obtaining houses in Toulouse for their tribunals. In 1231 the pope, Gregory IX, decreed that all heretics should be excommunicated. 1232 was the year when Pagan of Labécède was captured and killed. Raymond VII gained nothing for the disgrace for in the following year he was summoned to go to Melun and compelled to give his authority to twenty-nine detailed ordinances against heretics. It was the year when a General Inquisition, conducted by Dominicans, was established by the Pope. 1234 saw Raymond's 'Statutes Against Heretics' pronounced in Toulouse by order of the Count. That year powerful Inquisitors and their officials were installed in Toulouse, Albi, Cahors and Moissac.

An informative source for those five years and for many after was the Chronicle of Guillaume de Pélhisson, a Dominican of Toulouse, who himself had been an Inquisitor with Arnaud Catala at Albi. His journal began in the early 1230s. 'Just at the moment when the church thought to have peace in the land, heretics and their believers girded themselves more and more for numerous ventures and stratagems against her and against Catholics with the result that the heretics did more harm by far in Toulouse and the region than they ever had during the war'. His records of the depositions and the means by which they were obtained is a clear illustration of the tenacity and pitiless actions of the Inquisition.[2]

The friars had houses in Toulouse. One given to Dominic by Peter Seilan in 1215 is still there against a stretch of Gallo-Roman wall on the rue Fonderie near the former Château Narbonnais. In 1230, as it and the accommodation in the church of St.-Romain were too limited for their intended interrogations the Inquisitors acquired other properties and it was from those places that their questioning began.[3] In the beginning it was unsystematic, picking up lucky scraps; but it steadily developed into an organised and well-recorded set of written list of names that could be cross-checked, ensuring that what had been testified at one examination was in agreement with what was said at another. And informers such as William of Solier, a one-time Good Man who had recanted in dread of the agony of the stake, provided lists of the many believers that they had met. Having detailed information about the clandestine network that the Cathars had created he was able to betray the whereabouts of many preachers. It was with a mixture of relief and satisfaction that Guillaume de Puylaurens remarked, 'His witness should be efficacious against those about whom he knows the truth'. After the long years of frustration the Church might at last be able to destroy its enemies.[4]

Already, in 1227, under the guidance of the Papal legate, Romano Frangipani, Cardinal of St Angelo, adviser and friend of the Queen-Regent, a Council in Toulouse had codified the methods by which the persecution of Cathars by Inquisitors was to be conducted. The possession of the Old and New Testaments, psalters and breviaries was forbidden to anyone not in Holy Orders. To own them was to condemn oneself. The results were like a Gestapo of the Middle Ages, sleeping households awakened in the middle of the night by teams of two laymen and a priest, the home searched from cellar to outbuilding, books confiscated, people taken away for questioning. It was terror.[5]

A man in Toulouse, Jean Teisseire accused of heresy, denied it vigorously. 'Gentlemen, listen to me! I am not a heretic, for I have a wife and I sleep with her. I have sons, I eat meat, and I lie and swear, and I am a faithful Christian'. It was all irrelevant unless he were a Good Man. To the Cathars a credente or believer could do all those things without blame but many of his friends swore that what he had said was true and their evidence saved him from death. He was sent to the misery of the bishop's prison while further enquiries were made.

He doomed himself. Constantly in his cell asking for the blessing of Christ he was joined by a group of Cathars caught near Lavaur. Talking with them he admitted his true faith, withdrew his protestations and was received back into his religion by a Good Man. He went on trial with his fellows, refused to join the Catholic church and was burned with them.

There were consequences. 'All who had previously defended him were now covered with confusion, and they damned and cursed him' realising that they now would be subjected to fierce questioning about their false witness. Shortly afterwards his widow, Juliana, was sentenced to life imprisonment 'as an adherent of heretics and a perjurer'.[6]

It is occasionally written that in 1231 the Pope had announced a general inquisition in the south of France. The word is misleading. There would be no official body of the Inquisition until 1233, the year that Guillaume Arnaud began his years of an extensive Inquisitorial tour that included Laurac, inciting authorities to hunt heretics.

A better term for 'inquisition' would be 'investigation'. In 1231 friars were to explore the Languedoc for evidence of heresy. It could be perilous. In Italy that year Roland di Cremona, a Dominican preacher, was almost killed at Piacenza simply for preaching the Catholic faith. He was to be as fearlessly outrageous in Toulouse in 1234.[7]

Cathars took precautions. In the same year the death of Pagan of Labécède Guilhabert of Castres, the Cathar bishop of Toulouse, named the invincible castle of Montségur as the seat of the Languedocian church and convened a synod there. Yet all the time the menace became stronger.

On 20 April 1233, impatient with such little success in exterminating the irreligious sect, Gregory IX ordered a general inquisition throughout southern France. It was to be conducted by

Dominican preaching friars, an Order instituted by Dominic specifically to combat heresy. Trained in theology and law they were ideally educated to investigate, interrogate and detect inconsistencies in the answers scared men and women gave them. They were persistent and they were ruthless.

It was almost a hundred years since Bernard of Clairvaux had gone from town to town in the Languedoc futilely urging wrongdoers to repent of their sins and lessons had been learned. Since his failure in the mid-twelfth century and those of Arnaud Amaury and Dominic at the beginning of the next, the Dominicans realised that preaching by itself was feeble, achieving too little over too long a time. Nor had the military Crusade been more successful in the destruction of heresy, the sword striking at random, cutting down obvious targets but never reaching the roots. It was not a physical onslaught that was required. The sharpest weapon would be informers like William of Solier.

There was no equivocation about the orders issued to the Inquisitors. 'As to those you are to arrest no man can be exempted from imprisonment, on account of his wife, however young she may be; no woman, on account of her husband; nor both of them on account of their children, their relations, or those to whom they are most necessary. Let no one be exempted from prison, on account of weakness or age, or any similar cause. . . . If you have not succeeded in arresting them, hesitate not to proceed against the absent'.[8]

The methods of interrogation were superficially merciful but filled with traps. After preaching there was the promise of gentle penalties for those who confessed, a gift of alms, a short pilgrimage was all that was demanded. For the more obdurate there were stern punishments, the wearing of the shameful Yellow Crosses or, worse physically, imprisonment; at best demanding, at worst almost starved in filthy conditions, sometimes for life in cold, damp, darkness. These people were the *immurati*, 'the ones lost inside the walls'. Finally, for the truly impenitent and defiant, there was the stake.

It appeared straightforward but that was the trap. Seemingly a quick confession offered clemency but a confession made a person even more vulnerable to severe punishment. To admit having been a believer meant that they must have known others, friends, probably at least two Good Men and the names and whereabouts of the heretics were demanded. Refusal, even ignorance, placed the confessed Cathar into the second level of punishment. It was merciless and no defence was permitted.

The effective system developed into the official Inquisition. In April 1233, Gregory IX founded the Inquisition and appointed the legate, Jean de Bernin, Archbishop of Arles, to organise matters in the Languedoc. Tribunals were set up in Bordeaux, Bourges, Narbonne and Auch. After preaching that exhorted heretics to come forward a week of grace was allowed before the persecution began.[9]

Nothing was overlooked. The religious demanded action from the secular. In the autumn of that year Romano, dissatisfied with Raymond's inertia, 'lukewarm and negligent, and was seen to be lacking in enthusiasm in the pursuit of the Cause of Peace and the Faith',[10] took him to Melun a few miles south of Paris where, in the presence of Louis IX and Blanche, still the Queen-Regent until the young king's majority the following year, the Count accepted responsibility for enacting twenty-nine harsh conditions for the eradication of the Cathars. Among the ordinances he promised to execute anyone accused of killing an Inquisitor; to pay a silver mark to any informer; would pull down the houses of all condemned persons; would confiscate their goods; would destroy all cottages, refuges, anywhere that could become a retreat for heretics; would allow nothing to go to their children; and would deprive anyone helping the Cathars of all their possessions. Nowhere was the word 'death' mentioned, only the evasive but equally lethal phrase, 'delivering the criminal to the secular arm'.[11]

The Inquisitors brought widespread fright but they rapidly brought anger at their injustice and inflexibility. They also brought horror. It was not sufficient in their fanatical minds to hound the living. If they discovered that a non-believer had died they dug up the corpse and dragged its reeking, rotting remains from its grave to be burned. 'They seem to try to drive people into error rather than to lead them back to the truth: for they cause disturbance all over the land and by their excesses stir people up against convents and clerics', a perturbed Count of Toulouse wrote to the pope in 1234, knowing that it was only a year since the infuriated populace of Cordes had thrown two Dominicans down a well to put an end to their persistent and dangerous enquiries.[12]

Gregory wrote back in November but his commands to avoid excesses had little effect on the committed men that he had empowered. In January, 1234, the first Inquisitors had been installed: Pons of St.-Gilles for the church of St..-Sernin in Toulouse; Arnaud Catala and Guillaume de Pélhisson at Ste.-Cécile in Albi; Pierre Seila and Guillaume Arnaud for both St.-Étienne at Cahors, and St.-Pierre in Moissac.[13] In April Raymond VII ordered his resentful consuls to enforce the instructions of the Inquisitors. In turn, the apparently invulnerable inquisitors subjected their potential martyrs to a bombardment of tellingly constructed questions.

The accused shall be asked if he has anywhere seen or been acquainted with one or more heretics, knowing or believing them to be such by name or repute: where he has seen them, on how many occasions, with whom, and when . . . whether he has had any familiar intercourse with them, when and how, and by whom introduced . . . whether he has received in his own home one or more heretics; if so who and what they were; who brought them; how many times they stayed with the accused; what visitors they had; who escorted them thence; and where they went . . . whether he did adoration before them, or saw other persons adore them or do them reverence after the heretical manner . . . whether he greeted them, or saw any other person greet them, after the heretical fashion . . . whether he was present at the initiation of any amongst them; if so, what was the manner of the initiation; what was the name of the heretic or heretics; who was present at the ceremony, and where was the house in which the sick person lay . . . whether the person initiated made any bequest to the heretics, and if so what and how much, and who drew up the deed; whether adoration was done before the heretic who performed the initiation; whether the person succumbed to his illness, and if so where he was buried; who brought the heretic or heretics thither, and conducted them thence'.[14]

Scores, then hundreds of suspected Cathars were subjected to interrogations and scores, hundreds of names were collected. In their zest friars summoned not ten but fifty to a hundred suspects a day, witnesses against them testifying in secrecy with hoods over their heads, disguising their voices. There was instant cynicism and fear. 'At this rate every man who owes money, or whose wife is too pretty, or who has a bad reputation, will become a heretic', falsely accused of being a Cathar by enemies or perjurers hoping to gain some advantage from his death. The proclamation of the twenty-nine 'Statutes Against Heretics' by Raymond VII made lives feel even more insecure. It was that year, 1234, that brought the crisis.

Villagers and impoverished city dwellers at first passively accepted the persecution but even among them resistance developed against the cruelties. Aroused, the weaponless citizens who had fought de Montfort's soldiers in the streets of Toulouse could become brutal threats to two or three unprotected friars.

On 5 August 1234 Dominic was canonised. It was a great honour for the Dominicans of Toulouse. Already enriched by the munificence of Foulques and safeguarded by the protection of local Catholics, now with a patron saint, they could gladly claim that Toulouse was truly the 'home of their Order'.

But as they gained they also lost. Complacent in their righteousness, insensitive in their obsession to eradicate heresy, their blind bigotry against the living extended to the dead. To them even lifeless, decaying bodies had to be purged of their sin. The sight of rotting flesh and protruding bones was a despicable savagery too many.

The Inquisitor, Arnaud Catala and his colleague, the monkish chronicler, Guillaume de Pélhisson, had the burial of a heretical woman in Albi exhumed during the week of Whitsun. Knowing the mood of the citizens the civic officials refused to take part but recklessly Catala began the uncovering of Boysenne, wife of a

Cathar believer, Brostaion, by giving her grave symbolical blows with his mattock. Heavier blows followed. A violent opposition led by a knight, Pons Bernard, and a score or more of infuriated men beat the Inquisitor, hitting his face, drawing blood, tearing his clothes, kicking him, some trying to haul him into a shop to cut his throat, others dragging him by his hood towards the banks of the Tarn. The mob wanted to drown him and only cautionary words by some townsfolk allowed him, Pélhisson and a wounded priest, Isarn de Denart, to stagger to the shelter of the cathedral. From that sanctuary they could hear shouts. 'Why don't they cut off the traitor's head and stuff it into a sack and throw it into the Tarn?' It was the first of several revolts against the sickening exhumations.

In Cahors Pierre Seila and Guillaume Arnaud, had the body of Humbert de Castelnaud disinterred for burning but during the night his son secretly removed his father's remains from the cemetery.[15]

The mutilations at Bram were another atrocity. Desecration of the dead was despicable. More nauseating still was the sanctimonious deceit of the Bishop of Toulouse, Raimon de Fauga. In Toulouse on 4 August, by chance the first Feast Day of St Dominic, the bishop had celebrated Mass and just returned to the refectory where he was washing his hands when 'a person from the town' told him that an old, well-born woman was dying of a fever in the nearby street of l'Olmet Sec, today the rue Romiguières by the Capitole, a busy road dividing the original bourg from the later cité. She was a Cathar and had received the *consolamentum*.

With complacent hypocrisy, disguised, wearing no Catholic vestments, no cross, mitre, no rings, Fauga went to the house where the woman's alarmed son-in-law, Peitivin Borsier, a suspected believer, had time only to tell her that the bishop was coming. In her delirium she believed that it was a Cathar who approached her.

Apparently consolingly, in reality craftily, Raimon de Fauga sat by her bed encouraging her to speak of her 'contempt for the world and for earthly things', a conviction in Cathar dualism that material existence was sin and evil and only the Spirit was good. Like a hypnotic snake the bishop then urged her to be constant in her beliefs. Innocently she confessed her faith whereupon the double-tongued Man of God denounced her. Despite her sudden dread she refused to recant. Triumphantly Fauga summoned a magistrate, the representative of the 'secular arm', who condemned her, and she was carried in her bed to the Pré du Comte, the count's meadow, and burnt alive. The Christian bishop and his attendants returned to the refectory and 'giving thanks to God and the Blessed Dominic, ate with rejoicing what had been prepared for them'.

It seems an episode so disgraceful as to be unbelievable. But it was recorded by Guillaume de Pélhisson, the bishop's fellow-inquisitor, who could see only good in it. 'God performed these works . . . to the glory and praise of His name . . . to the exaltation of the faith and to the discomfiture of the heretics'.[16]

Without compunction the ferocious executions continued. Guillaume Arnaud and Pierre Seila condemned no fewer than two hundred and ten heretics at Moissac. Others were burnt at Cahors and Castelnaudary. In Toulouse a wine-seller, Arnold Dominic, hysterical with fear at the thought of the stake, offered to betray eleven Cathars that he knew at Les Cassès. Seven Good Men were apprehended there but three escaped. The wine-seller was released only to be murdered in his bed at Aigrefeuille near Toulouse.[17]

Encouraged by their achievements all the Inquisitors assembled in Toulouse on Good Friday to invite every sinner to confess and return to the true Church. So many men and women responded that the Dominicans had to ask clerics from other Orders to help them. Lines of people stood waiting to affirm their loyalty.[18] It was a victorious campaign but, as always, it was undone by unnecessary provocation. Instead of being content with their work the Inquisitors continued to exasperate and rouse the very city that they were endeavouring to convert.

In the middle of October Roland di Cremona led friars and monks to exhume a Cathar from its cemetery, then took a mob to a house where the corpse of a Waldensian heretic lay. The body was destroyed by fire. On Christmas Day, 1234 the same zealot discovered that a Catholic canon had been buried in the cloisters of St.-Sernin's cathedral. Learning that the man had been a covert Cathar he had the body dug from its grave and dragged to the town dump and the fire of extinction. Still unsatisfied he had the canon's house torn down and turned into a public urinal. The atmosphere in a city that should have been quelled instead became resentful, then antagonistic, finally violent. There had been too many similar incidents.[19]

From the pulpit of St.-Sernin in 1235 di Cremona preached that there were still too many heretics in Toulouse. Supporting him Guillaume Arnaud named twelve, all of them prominent citizens. The city consuls not only objected but demanded that the horrifying inquisitions cease. The Dominicans refused. On 5 November Guillaume Arnaud was forced out of the city, roughly handled as he went.

Learning nothing, the evicted Inquisitor wrote to Carcassonne asking the chief Inquisitor of Toulouse, Pons de St.-Gilles, for volunteers to return to the city, serve warrants and arrest the accused. With courage if not common sense four offered to go. They made their confessions, were given absolution for their sins by the Inquisitor and went on their mission.

'Diligently and fearlessly they executed it, so much so, indeed, that they were not content to seek out those persons in the streets and at their houses, but even sought them in their inner bedchambers. When they were in the house of Maraud the elder in search of them, his sons, Maraud and Raymond Maraud the One-eyed, came running and hustled the friars out of doors, heaping abusive words on them, dragging them by the hair and thrusting them out of the house, shouting as they struck them, and trying to slash them with knives'. Luckily more peaceable people intervened, one of them Peter of Coussa, a Catholic.[20]

It is an interesting question as to which religion such assailants belonged. Cathars were firm advocates of non-aggression. No Good Man would fight. It is possible that on those occasions of bruising frenzy it was Catholics, angry at the shameful interference with their ordinary lives, that struck out at their own clergymen. Certainly it was Raymond VII and his leading men, none known as a heretic, who debated whether to kill the meddlesome, murderous friars or expel them from the city.

During the protracted discussion the remaining Dominicans were locked in a church. Orders were given that no one was to assist them in any way, by money, food, drink, even sympathy. Their refuge was surrounded. They were cut off from their gardens and the river. Then on 9 November they were expelled, some forty of them, by the Count and his consuls. Next day Arnaud excommunicated Toulouse.[21] The curse was lifted next year when the friars were allowed to return to the city.

With promises of less rigorous procedures the Dominicans went back to Toulouse but their indoctrination had been too thorough. Very shortly Catala and Pélhisson were burning Arnold Giffre in Albi. In Toulouse itself Raymond Gros, a Good Man for some twenty-two years, volunteered scores of names both dead and living. Characteristically not one of his erstwhile fellow-preachers argued against him. 'Masters, you may know that it is all just as Master Raymond says it is'. The dead, important merchants, nobles, Good Women, were dug up and 'their bones and stinking bodies were dragged through the town', their names proclaimed by heralds who called, 'Who behaves thus shall perish thus'. Many of the living fled only to be discovered some years later in Montségur.[22]

It was a year of heavy rain in England. Anyone interested in the history of the thirteenth century in western Europe is fortunate to have the lively *English History* of Matthew Paris, a Benedictine monk at St Albans, who compiled a chatty diary of events, weather, anecdotes and gossip for the years from 1236 to 1259. He despised the avarice and weakness of his king, Henry III. He shared the anti-semitism of his times. Some Jews in Norwich were accused of circumcising a Christian boy, intending to crucify him. 'Four of the Jews, therefore, having been found guilty of the aforesaid crime, were first dragged at the tails of horses, and afterwards hung on a gibbet, where they breathed forth the wretched remains of life'.

He recorded storms, earthquakes, floods and plagues. He was an admirer of Blanche of Castile, 'a woman in sex, but a man in counsels, one worthy to be compared with Semiramis', a legendary empress of Assyria who conquered all the lands around her for the sake of her son and who made the city of Babylon the wonder of the world.[23]

The 1230s was a decade of religious unrest, people intimidated by the prying persistence of the friars, whose obstinacy occasionally made them reckless. Some, travelling alone, were trapped and killed. It was a political decade when the noblemen of the Languedoc attempted to recover possessions that had been confiscated, Raymond VII in Provence, Raymond-Roger Trencavel at Carcassonne. These were also the years of royal conflict when Henry III of England tried to regain lands that had been reconquered by the French. Such struggles were sporadic events. The Inquisitors were ceaseless.

As yet there was no official torture. That method of forcing the truth from unwilling lips would not be authorised by Pope Innocent IV until 1252 and even then it was permitted only under strict conditions. No clergyman was to be present. No life or limb was to be imperilled. No blood was to be drawn.

There was no rack, no thumbscrew, no bastinado but there were other exquisite methods of extracting information from reluctant witnesses. Francis of Assisi knew of a man who had been chained in an unlit, unwholesome cell for years, given only bread and water, never knowing when his next interrogation would be. Quite intentionally Inquisitors could take not days or months but years in between their examinations. Many prisoners confessed in desperation to end the dreadful uncertainty.

One suspect in Vienna was tied so tightly to a pillar that he shrieked, begging for mercy, offering to admit anything. Callously he was left in his agony for a further twenty-four hours. When he was cut free he retired, broken in spirit, mind and body, to a monastery.[24]

Frequently the most heartless of the Inquisitors were men who had recanted and proceeded to prosecute their former comrades with an enthusiasm that touched the extreme limits of what the Catholic church allowed.

Matthew Paris mentioned a notorious Cathar Good Man and recusant, Robert le Petit, who had joined the Dominicans. He was sometimes known as le Bougre, 'the bugger', perhaps because Cathar preachers were disgustedly suspected of sodomy. The man's nickname more probably was the 'Bulgar' because Catharism had developed from the heretical Bogomils of Bulgaria. Paris termed him the 'hammer of the heretics' and 'a lying imposter, false brother of the order of Preachers'. 'Within two or three months he caused about fifty people to be burnt or buried alive'.[25]

Reliable history rarely comes from rumour which exaggerates as it distorts from one mouth to the next. An example proves this. The Elizabethan poet and dramatist, Christopher Marlowe, was killed in 1593. Only four years later Thomas Beard wrote that the playwright had been slain in the streets, stabbed in the head with his own dagger. Next year Frances Meres said he was murdered by a bawdy serving-man, a rival for a woman. Quite shortly, the death left the open air and occurred in a tavern where Marlowe quarrelled with Francis Archer over payment for a meal. Even more improbably John Aubrey was told by Sir Edward Sherburne that the poet had been killed by Ben Jonson.[26]

The truth was completely different. Marlowe was neither killed in a street nor a tavern but in a respectable house in Deptford. There had been no argument over a bill. His killer had been Ingram Frizer, one of a trio involved in the political murder of Marlowe, not as a poet but as a troublesome secret agent. If such misrepresentation of the facts could develop within a brief seven years between 1593 and 1600 it is as plausible that Matthew Paris, in his 'buried alive' was simply reporting years-old, popular, but over-stated gossip on the grapevine about the fearsome Robert le Bougre.

In 1232 the interrogator had been given extensive powers in the north of France by Gregory IX, first in the Franche-Conté then La Charité-sur-Loire where his cruel methods led to his temporary suspension. Soon restored to his efficient and effective duties he reached the climax of his achievements by overseeing an *auto-da-fé* at Mont-Aimé near Chalons-sur-Marne. The day was described by Aubri, a monk of the nearby Cistercian monastery of Trois-Fontaines, who significantly called the captured heretics, 'Bougres'.

It was 13 May, the Friday before Pentecost. Mont Aimé or Montwimmer was the oldest centre of heresy in France and one of the traditional places from which Catharism had spread southwards into the Languedoc. Today there are only the ruins of a small castle.

The activities of Robert the Bulgar had brought almost two hundred unbelievers to punishment in the town. Their purging was an important occasion attended by the King of Navarre, the Count of Champagne, the Archbishop of Reims, fifteen bishops from Arras to Verdun and a huge crowd of onlookers, exaggerated by Aubri to an impossible seven hundred thousand spectators of both sexes and all ages.

Robert the Bulgar had granted an astonishing indulgence for thirty years to all who attended the burning of the one hundred and eighty-three Cathars, 'ces Bougres, pires des chiens', Cathars, worse than dogs'. Their 'archbishop' of Morains administered the *consolamentum* to all his followers. 'Only I am damned', he grieved, 'because I have no superior to save me'.[27] Robert le Petit's career lasted until 1241 when he was imprisoned and left history.

He had been one of the few Good Men who defected. There were others: Raymond Gros, Sicard of Lunels, Bernard Raimond, William of Solier, Rainier Sacconi, a Good Woman, Arnaude of Lamothe. There were deacons: Arnold Huc, Armand Pradier, Bernard Gaussbert and more but these were little more than a pathetic dribble when contrasted with the many hundreds, perhaps thousands at Lavaur and elsewhere who chose to die rather than renounce their beliefs.[28]

Not every Dominican was a tyrant. One of their friars, Theodoric de Lucca, son of a crusader, who taught in Bologna, pioneered the development of elementary anaesthetics to alleviate pain, sponges soaked in narcotics such as mandragora and opium being applied to the nose. He also recommended the use of mercury for skin complaints.[29]

Life in Languedoc was not as it had been ten years earlier. Now there was little fear of one's house being pulled down or a village set on fire, cattle driven off, crops and vines trampled. Now there were few armed soldiers. Instead there were many Inquisitors armed with fatal records of a person's complicity with heretics. The investigations were remorseless and never ceased. Inevitably there were betrayals, lapses of caution, callous perjurers lying a person's life away for profit.

In the 1230s it was fear of a family being destroyed, a father, mother, child taken away for the quiet question, the sly suggestion, the sudden revelation that the prisoner was known to be guilty, unnamed witnesses had sworn it. The Languedoc had become a land of triumphant Catholics and scared Cathars.

Yet in spite of the continual harassment there were still centres where Cathars felt safe. Cities and towns were death-traps. Heretics had to choose between the impregnable castle or a remote village for concealment, the cramped walls of Laurac being a typical example. Hiding-places existed in almost invisible retreats like that hamlet between Castlenaudary and Fanjeaux, near the horror that had been Bram. In Laurac Good Men camouflaged themselves as peasants working in the fields, as shepherds, carpenters, smiths. The disguises were successful because many of the men genuinely were peasants, shepherds, carpenters, smiths. They were secure in such a taciturn little community.

Having so many Cathars inside it, Laurac was almost a miniature equivalent of Mont Aimé four hundred miles to the north. Insignificant today, in no guidebook, it is a charming hamlet of old houses, a tiny ruined castle and a fortified church perched on almost a mountain and reached only by narrow zigzags of road. It was a good hideaway. Everywhere inside it were Cathars and there would be for years. The Good Woman, Arnaude Bénech, who was put to death as late as 1242, came from Laurac. In 1233 the Inquisitor Guillaume Arnaud had gone there on his arduous search of the Lauragais. When he left, having learned nothing, there were still heretics unharmed and unsuspected in the village. In 1245 the widow, Na Gauzio, testified that in the early thirteenth century Good Men had lived there openly. It was as much a stronghold of heresy as Les Cassès a few miles away. And as of past years noble families protected the Cathar preachers. Villages in the Lauragais were like an heretical hydra. When one head was decapitated, another took its place.[30]

A Cathar deacon Bernard Raymond, lived in Laurac. Blanche de Laurac, widow of the powerful lord, Sicard, kept houses there for women wishing to be converted. Her children were believers or sympathisers. Around 1226 Dulcie Faure of Villeneuve-la-Cantal left her husband and was sent first to Castelnaudary and then a year later to Laurac as a place better fitted for the education of neophytes.[31]

Raimonde Jougla, whose father threw her naked out of his house because of her suspected but unlikely affair with the Good Man, William of Gouzons, had many friends amongst the Good Women and went to Laurac to become one. Hers was a sad conversion. When she was arrested she immediately forswore her beliefs, '*par peur du feu*', 'for dread of the fire, and I was converted to the Catholic faith'.[32]

It was one matter to condemn ordinary men and women. It was very different when nobility were involved. Guillaume Arnaud summoned Bernard-Otho of Niort, lord of Laurac, a 'notorious heretic', his brothers William and Gerald and their mother to come to Carcassonne for questioning. Confident of their inviolability Bernard and William obeyed. They refused to admit anything and were released. Next day 'the seneschal of the King of France seized them and they were held in the city of Carcassonne and repeatedly interrogated'. Bernard, grandson of Blanche of Laurac and the same man who had abased himself before Louis VIII in 1226, remained silent. William did confess 'albeit not voluntarily'. He and his nephew were sentenced to life imprisonment. Bernard was condemned to death and the seneschal prepared to have him burnt.

There was instant alarm. War threatened. The absent brother, Gerald, closed the castles of Niort and Laurac and defied attack. It was an impasse. In the past Bernard had ambushed and executed a knight for arresting a Good Man who had attended Bernard during an illness. His defence of Cathars was well-known and he had many supporters ready to rise against the French. The likelihood of serious disturbances alarmed the royal forces in the Languedoc. The danger made it politic to free Bernard-Otho. His liberated brother and son returned to Laurac with him.[33]

The village was a troublespot and easily provoked, especially if any of its knights were angered. One of them, Raymond Barthe, lived in a former leperhouse with his mistress. An over-conscientious sergeant arrested six Cathars including Barthe's mother. The knight, who had already saved two Good Men near St.-Papoul, hanged the sergeant.[34]

These were 'bits and pieces' years, disrupted years of burnings, assaults and uprisings, of inauspicious signs in the skies that terrified superstitious medieval minds, years of unnatural deaths, murders and martyrdom, unwholesome years that were the prelude to the annihilation of the Cathars. Almost as a portent Guilhabert of Castres, the aged Cathar bishop of Toulouse, died in the castle of Montségur and was succeeded by Bertrand Marty. Burnings continued. Two Good Men were executed at Montgradail, two more at St. Martin-la-Lande, and a further pair at Villeneuve near Montréal. In November there was a violent storm and flooding.

1239 had been a year of omens. Before Easter in England there had been four months of heavy storms. On Friday, 3 June there was a solar eclipse that lasted six hours. Unprecedently, on 25 July, St James's Day, there was a second when it became 'so dark that the stars could be seen.[35]

All the signs were bad. The Inquisition began its work in Narbonne, whose loathed convent had been burnt years before by the resentful citizens. Their consuls did not hesitate to entreat the Count of Toulouse to protect them against the menace of the Inquisitors. Already hoping to recover his possessions in Provence Raymond VII sent a garrison under Oliver of Termes and Gerald of Niort to take control of the city. It was the beginning of yet another attempt by the count and the viscount of the Languedoc to expel the French soldiers and the Inquisition with them.[36]

There was a sinister beginning to 1240 when a dim comet trailed across the February sky. Amaury, son of Simon de Montfort, was captured in the Holy Land and imprisoned in Gaza. His health ruined, he was released but soon died in Rome. An enemy of his died in the same year. Gerald of Pépieux, tormentor and mutilator of crusaders, was captured by the French and hanged.[37]

Raymond VII led an army into Provence and besieged Arles throughout the summer. A greater city, Marseilles, begged him to become their lord. Raymond-Roger Trencavel, viscount of Bèziers and Carcassonne, gathered another host and with many knights including Oliver of Termes invaded the lands taken by the French king. Oliver of Termes raised his standard at Les Corbières near Mirepoix and marched towards Carcassonne. His men were welcomed at Limoux but Montelieu resisted and its inhabitants were massacred.

Reaching Carcassonne and joining the viscount the siege began on 7 September. Despite eight valiant attacks distinguished by the courage of Oliver of Termes but during which thirty-three priests were murdered on the outskirts of the city the arrival of a powerful French army on 11 October forced a retreat.[38]

The French under Jean de Beaumont pursued them. With the refugees scattering he no longer had an army to oppose him. The times were propitious. Castles, so long invincible, fell. Peyrepertuse on its mountaintop, one of the magnificent marvels of military planning, surrendered after a token siege of three days. Today its splendid ruins are approached by a modern marvel. French engineers have tunnelled a winding car-wide road under the rocky overhangs of the tortuous Gorges de Galamus.

Next year Oliver of Termes had to yield his castle of Aguilar and swore fealty to the French crown. It was the year when Pope Gregory IX died, 'almost a hundred years old', mused Matthew Paris, and was succeeded by the ailing Celestine IV, whose papacy lasted only a few weeks. There was argument over which candidate should be elected in his place although there was a general agreement that it should not be Romano Frangipani of St. Angelo, Bishop of Oporto, 'because he was said at one time to have debauched Blanche, the Queen of France'. There would be no Pope for almost two years until Innocent IV in 1243. On 6 October there was an eclipse of the sun, the second in three years, 'an event hitherto unheard of'.[39]

Even royal warfare could be almost farcical. A secret alliance between a desperate Raymond VII and Hugues de Lusignan, Count of La Marche, the unending enemy of the French crown, was joined by England. Henry III was enticed to invade by de Lusignan's assurance that a great and well-equipped army would be waiting for him.

Henry landed at Royan on 13 May 1242 with a small force of knights and foot-soldiers. Reaching Taillebourg a few miles to the north-east in July he was taken aback to learn that the 'well-equipped army' was little more than a battalion or so of La Marche's own men, a collection quite incapable of withstanding the powerful French force advancing upon them. Henry III scurried to the safety of Bordeaux. Hugues was abandoned and defeated at Saintes, now Saintonges. The royal army of Louis IX then followed Raymond VII as far as Penne-d'Agenais where an outbreak of disease compelled the pursuit to be abandoned. As an organised tripartite league against the might of France it had been a ludicrous and humiliating failure.

Yet the necessity of mustering some of the king's soldiers from the Languedoc had weakened French strength in the south and the opportunistic Count of Toulouse regained large areas of his ancestral lands: the Termenès region with its castles of Villerouge and Tuchan: the Minervois with Minerve itself and the three castles of Lastours; and the area of Razés around Limoux and Rennes-le-Château.[40]

Believing himself strong in men and popular with his people he proudly entered Narbonne and proclaimed himself its duke as though the Treaty of Meaux-Paris had been unilaterally annulled. He misled himself. His campaign against the king had been a miscalculation that had corroded his reputation. Former allies like the Count of Foix dissociated themselves from his actions. Worse still, an event of 27–8 May when he was far away at Taillebourg had left him with no future as a dominant figure in the politics of the Languedoc.

Avignonet was a walled town of about five thousand people in 1242, some five times its present population. At its entrance is a 'pepper-box' stone turret with an carved effigy holding a lance, '*le croisé*', 'the crusader of Avignonet' standing on a ledge. History demands that the figure should be a martyred Dominican friar.

Guillaume Arnaud, cold-hearted Inquisitor of Cahors and Moissac, probably the most energetic and most hated of all his fellows, came to Avignonet with ten companions on 28 May, ironically the evening before Ascension Day. With the Dominican Inquisitor was the Franciscan, Étienne de St Thibéry, the Benedictine prior of Avignonet, an archdeacon, two more Dominicans and a Franciscan, a scribe, a clerk and two officers of the Inquisition. It was a sizeable group but it had no bodyguards.

May was the seventh month of a long Inquisitorial tour of the Lauragais, questioning, recording names, passing sentences, and the tribunal's progress from village to village was widely known even as far as Montségur over thirty miles to the south. There Peter-Roger of Mirepoix gathered some men, added more at Gaja and reached Avignonet at night, concealing themselves in a spinney near a leperhouse.

Arnaud and his comrades were lodging in the castle whose guardian was Hugues d'Alfaro, distant relative of Raymond VII and a veteran who had defied Simon de Montfort at the siege of Penne d'Agenais in 1212. He was also a Cathar sympathiser who detested the Inquisition. When he was sure that the Catholics were asleep he sent William-Raymond Golairans to open the town-gate and admit twelve of the waiting party, all of them armed with heavy battle-axes. Inside Avignonet they were joined by some townsmen with clubs and cleavers.

It was a massacre. Startled from their rest, on their knees, crying 'Salve Regina', every one of the friars and monks was bloodily hacked to death. Cold-bloodedly, their murderers stole their belongings, horses, books, candlesticks, a pot of ginger. Lists were burnt.

The news spread. Austorgue, wife of the lord of Lanta, Peter of Rosenges, and herself a Good Woman rejoiced. 'All is free. All are dead'. Her husband disagreed.

The man who had admitted the assassins, Golairans, said that the killers had hoped that 'the affair of the Inquisition would be extinguished, and the whole land would be freed, and there would not be another Inquisition'.

Outside Avignonet Peter-Roger of Mirepoix impatiently asked his returning men which of them had the head of Guillaume Arnaud that he wanted as a goblet. '*Elle est brisée*', William Azéma informed him. Broken or not, he was told, 'I would have bound it with a ring of gold and drunk from it all my days'.[41]

Both the Good Woman and Golairans were mistaken. The affair of Avignonet was not an end but a beginning. Just as the murder of Pierre de Castelnau had resulted in the Crusade, so the atrocity at Avignonet enraged the Catholic world and caused the downfall of Montségur. There would be no safe hiding-place for Cathars after the death of Guillaume Arnaud.

There was still no pope. Innocent IV would not be elected until 1243.

By the October of 1242 Raymond VII accepted that resistance was futile and at the end of the month he formally submitted to Louis IX. In January 1243, he went to Paris to pay homage and at the Treaty of Lorris he gave the king the bastides of Bram and Saverdun. He was treated mildly, partly because Blanche had a liking for him, mainly because it would be foolish to harm lands in southern France that her son would inherit. But Montségur, a teeming nest of heretics, must be extirpated.

Raymond VII was reduced to a nonentity. The glorious days of Beaucaire were in the long past. He had become a minor figure, a man of mistakes, a man with all the trappings of the Count of Toulouse but with no power. Outside the priory of the Knights Hospitaller his father's neglected corpse decayed. Raymond VII lived but only as a figurehead. Cravenly but characteristically he promised Louis IX that he would capture Montségur and its Cathar community. In the autumn he arrived at the foot of the mountain with a large body of soldiers but with little determination. His lacklustre siege achieved nothing and by the end of the year it was abandoned.

The affair typified his declining years. No longer involved in momentous events he was reduced to petty local squabbles such as his argument with the Count of Foix over the ownership of the castle of Roquefixade. It was in that castle that Raymond of Péreille, the lord who had renovated Montségur, married Corba of Lanta at the beginning of the century. Forty years later she would die at Montségur.

Roquefixade and Montségur are characteristic of the castles of the Languedoc revealing the awesome labour that had gone into their construction and the care that had been taken in the choice of their almost inaccessible sites, remote from cities and standing at the peaks of steep mountains. Even in their prime they were never comfortable places for everyday living. Today, in ruin, they are demanding.

The guidebook to the amazement of Peyrepertuse states, 'The visit can be dangerous in hight winds and is stictly forbidden in storms [*sic*]'. Roquefixade, '*roca fisada*', 'the split rock' requires a walk up a path on to pleasant open grassland but to enter the castle one is confronted by a longish, narrow and unprotected ledge against a fearsome drop. Montségur is worse. Asking at the little museum in the village, '*Le sentier aux château, il est dangereux pour les anciennes?*', one is assured that many old ladies stroll up to the castle and return unscathed and untroubled. An affinity with ibexes seems probable. Less sanguine – if the word is appropriate – another guidebook states without qualification, 'The climb really is quite dangerous and the descent is worse'.

Statistics are instructive. Walks to the castles can be analysed from the height at which the ascent begins up to the summit (Table 1). Distances are less straightforward. The 'paths' meander from convenient ledge to conspicuous boulder so that although the direct line from car-park to the castle of Montségur is only about 350m the actual trail is over twice that. But it is not the distance that matters but the steepness of the climb, often at a very demanding angle. It is then that the efforts of the medieval masons are appreciated with breathless astonishment.[42]

For Montségur, 1243 was a bad year. There were more omens of a troubled future. In July there was a very clear Milky Way in which thirty or forty falling stars were observed, a portent, it was thought, of the ending of many lives somewhere.

Peter-Roger of Mirepoix, known to have been the instigator of the murders at Avignonet, was also known to be the chief defender of Montségur, that 'synagogue of Satan'. He and the fortress were to be destroyed. '*Caput draconis*', 'behead the dragon', ordered Blanche, the Queen Mother.[43]

TABLE I. *Heights and distances to the mountain-top castles of the Languedoc*

SITE	Height at the start	Height at the castle	Metres climbed	Distance walked	Angle of ascent	1 metre in?
Lastours	232m	350m	118m	600m	11°	5
Montségur	1026m	1207m	181m	725m	14°	4
Peyrepertuse	708m	796m	88m	450m	11°	5
Puivert	565m	595m	30m	375m	5°	13
Puylaurens	708m	796m	88m	525m	9°	6
Quéribus	628m	728m	100m	375m	15°	4
Roquefixade	760m	919m	159m	600m	15°	4
Termes	384m	461m	77m	300m	14°	4

Hugues d'Arcis, French seneschal of Carcassonne, was determined to take Montségur but its position made it almost impossible to capture. Nor could it be starved out. The castle had been well-stocked by sympathisers. It also had plentiful water from its '*avens*' or natural wells in the limestone.

With the Archbishop of Narbonne, Pierre Amiel, and the Bishop of Albi, Durand de Beaucaire, and with an army of several hundred knights and some six thousand men d'Arcis besieged the castle whose garrison was fewer than a hundred soldiers. Many historians regard the campaign as having the 'character of a crusade' that should have been over in less than a week.[44] But Montségur possessed formidable natural and architectural defences.

Its castle on a spur of the Massif of St Barthélémy stood on a *pog*, the Occitanian word for a hill or mountain, the Latin *podium*. In shape the mountain was like a monstrous mouse-nibbled wedge of hard cheese lying on its side, a long rise from the south-west, near-vertical sides and rear. Montségur was exhausting. The present path, almost on the original line, through trees on the lower slopes deteriorates into a track here and there made easier by the cutting of wide, shallow treads, 'donkey-steps', but the way worsens to a stumble and scramble between weathered boulders and scree. After rain it is perilous. For a man laden with armour and weapons it was almost impossible.

The only sensible approach was from the south-west and many crossbow bolts and stones have been found there, evidence of brief but deadly skirmishes. On 13 May the French army camped on the Col de Tremblement barricading the best way down. Hugues d'Arcis was to stay there for ten months, a siege longer than any other in the Languedoc. Carcassonne fell in a fortnight, Lavaur in two months; Minerve and Termes in four.

There were never sufficient men to surround Montségur and from its surrounding villages friends brought nocturnal provisions along undefended paths, baskets and bundles hauled up by waiting ropes. By day there were forays, assaults, feints, strong resistance, women winching and loading siege-machines, as others had done at Toulouse, their robes 'torn and stained with blood'. Through it all the castle at Montségur remained untouched.[45]

Contrasted with enormities like Termes it was a midget. Like other border fortresses it was cramped and unevenly divided into two. In plan it resembled the outline of a shoe with backward sloping heel, long instep and short big toe. The major entrance was through the sole with a second almost opposite. Everything was diminutive. The pentagonal inner ward measured no more than about 70m by 20m, about the area of a hockey-rink or five tennis-courts, the 'big toe' a mere 20m by 9m, about half a tennis-court, with a cistern at its north-west end. To the south-east was a chamber with its famous (for the escapist) or notorious (for the sceptic) 'solar windows'.

Fernand Niel calculated three alignments to sunrise in the castle's design. Nelli mistook this to mean orientations to the major seasons of the year, Spring, Summer, Autumn and Midwinter. Aubarbier and colleagues mistook Niel to mean alignments to the midsummer. Niel's own diagram showed three parallel alignments from north-west to south-east across the castle and through arrow-slits to the midwinter sunrise implying that Cathar beliefs included a cult of the sun. He was mistaken. After 1244 Montségur was levelled and any hypothetical sightlines were the responsibility of the improbably astronomical Catholic Frenchman, Guy de Lévis, who rebuilt the castle. By the beginning of the twentieth century it was a ruin and in

1946 the Department of Ancient Monuments undertook its partial reconstruction.[46]

Everything about the old castle was claustrophobic and yet it was the virile centre of a community of four to five hundred men, women and children. From 1209 until 1243 Montségur had been a community of many well-born Cathars. In 1232 Guilhabert of Castres, the Cathar bishop of Toulouse, had proclaimed it 'the seat of the Languedocian church' and during the years of the Inquisition many believers had gone there for protection. Over half were Good Men or Women and no fewer than forty of its four hundred or so civilians were four generations of the Mirepoix-Péreille family. There were many Good Women. One was Azalaïs or Hélis of Mazerolles whose sister-in-law, Fabrissa of Mazerolles, had a house for Cathar women at Montréal. Azalaïs was the mother of Pierre, one of the assailants at Avignonet.[47]

The castle could not have accommodated a tenth of the Cathars. Instead, beyond its north postern there was a village on rock-cut terraces, houses perched on cliff-edges, narrow streets, rough steps. There was a baker, miller, tailor, a blacksmith but this was not a peasant settlement. It was a religious and defensive centre. It had two wells. One was near the steps. Another, 35m deep, close to a barbican below the castle, was excavated in 1958. In it were spear-heads and five skeletons, one a woman, all of them killed during the fighting. Two of the skeletons now lie side by side exhibited in a case of the attractive museum at Montségur.

Despite the outbreaks of hand-to-hand fighting the army of Hugues d'Arcis made no progress. The castle seemed beyond reach and the thought of assaulting it was daunting. Before today's linguistic corruption a better word would have been 'dreadful'. Any soldier staring up at the far-off castle would have dreaded the prospect of attacking it and its forbidding defences. The castle was not the only obstruction. There were three others: the pog; the tower; and the barbican.

The distorted mountain with its precipitous sides and constricted approach was forbidding and made more hazardous by the existence of the Roc de la Tour at the north-east, a natural platform 600m from the castle. A tower had been built on it and could not be by-passed. Guarded by 80m high, giddying cliffs, it protected the slope leading to the barbican. That was the second defence, a sturdy circular bastion blocking access to the castle 200m away. All this could be seen by the French. A direct assault would be a failure. Different tactics were needed.

Just before Christmas, in the darkness of a winter night, Gascons, or possibly Basques, scaled the near-vertical cliff, broke into the tower and slaughtered its sentries. Next morning they saw 'with astonishment the terrible route by which they had climbed during the night, which they would never have dared to try in full daylight'.[48]

The way to the castle had been unlocked. The French began to carry up sections of a dismantled trebuchet designed by Durand, Bishop of Albi, yet another of those monks like Guillaume de Tudela and Guillaume, archdeacon of Paris, who seemed more preoccupied with sieges and slaughter than with the saving of souls. With a range of 200m, once the barbican had been taken, the machine would be able to bombard the castle with heavy stone balls.

A year later, testifying to the Inquisition, Imbert of Salas said that it had been around that Christmas that treasure was smuggled out of Montségur. The sergeant-at-arms who had been responsible for the killing of two inquisitors in 1233 and who had fought his way into Montségur with many reinforcements at the beginning of the siege had sometimes eaten with the Good Men and learned some of their plans.

He remembered that two Cathar preachers, Peter Bonnet, deacon of Toulouse, and another named Matthew had taken a huge amount of treasure, gold, silver and money, '*pecuniam infinitam*', which they were to hide in the labyrinth of the Sabarthes caves not far from Foix. That was all that he knew.[49]

By February 1244, the French had struggled almost to the barbican. A firing-platform for the assembled trebuchet was constructed. There was ferocious fighting. Inside Montségur, Bernard of Baccalaria had a catapult put together to fire at the trebuchet but in the middle of the month the barbican was overrun. The castle was still out of reach, accessible only across a perilous ridge between two suicidal chasms of rock. But it could be bombarded.

There was a last desperate effort to help the defenders. Bernard of Alion from Montaillou and his brother, Arnold of Usson, had often brought food to Montségur. Now they offered to bribe a Catalan mercenary, Corbario, to bring his Aragonese band of twenty-five élite fighters, the equivalent of highly-trained knights, to enter Montségur, drive off the French and wreck the trebuchet. He agreed, for the exorbitant sum of five hundred *sous*. Nothing came of it. Either he could not find a way through the tight siege-lines or his men refused to follow him to their deaths.[50]

Montségur surrendered. Men and women were being killed. Resistance had almost ceased. An unprecedented truce was agreed. There was to be a fifteen day period of peace from 2 March until the fifteenth. Montségur was to be the king's. The soldiers would be permitted to depart with their weapons on condition that they admitted their sins to the Inquisition and accepted a light penance. Ordinary men and women could go unharmed. So could any Cathar who recanted. Those who would not would die.

Arguments persist about such an extraordinary arrangement. Some believe that the fortnight's grace was to give Bertrand Marty time to administer the *consolamentum* to his flock. Others think that it was to allow the Cathars to observe one of their important feast-days just before the Catholic Easter. The truth died in the flames of 16 March.

The day before, there is a contradictory report that four Cathars, Amiel Aicart, Hugh, Poitevin and another, were hiding in a cave on the mountain top. Napoléon Peyrat disagreed. Instead, he rhapsodised over a maze of cellars and passages burrowed beneath the castle. Steps led down from the cistern into an immense complexity of a granary, an arsenal, dormitories, tunnels to the outside world. It was poetic. It was fantasy. There is no trace of his subterranean warren.[51]

The four men, if they existed, took the remains of Cathar wealth to the castle of Usson and then to the Sabarthes where it was secreted, perhaps in the fortified 'spulga' of Bouan as the walled caves of the Ariége are known. But in the extensive records of the Inquisition there is no mention of any treasure, 'of gold, of silver, and an infinity of coins'. Nor have the vigorous searches of Nazis and treasure-seekers recovered one *sou*. It is, as Moore wrote, 'like fairy gifts fading away'.[52]

On Thursday, 16 March over two hundred Cathars, Good Men, Good Women, believers led by Bertrand Marty and followers, fettered and bound, were shoved out of the castle. There was neither reverence nor respect for them. To their captors the Cathars were verminous devils. Arpaïs, daughter of the Good Woman, Corba of Péreille, watched as 'they were brutally dragged from the fortress of Montségur', men, women, some converted mercenaries, and thrown into the flames. '*Refusant la conversion à laquelle ils étaient invités* . . .' 'refusing the conversion offered them they were shut in a fence of stakes and posts, the pyre was lit and there they experienced the fire of Hell'.

A commemorative stele erected in 1960 at the beginning of the path to the castle does not mark the place. The burning field, '*Prat dels crematz*', was probably the wider, level space lower down.

'A fortress for the victors, a temple for the defeated', wrote the poet Joé Bousquet.[53]

NINE

1244 to 1328: Aftermath

In October, 1296, the Autier brothers, Peter and William, left Ax-les-Thermes to be ordained as Cathar preachers in Italy. They gave up everything, wives, children, possessions. Ax-les-Thermes was in the very south of the Languedoc, the only area in which many Cathar believers could be found in the late thirteenth century.

The Autiers departed more than fifty years after the surrender of Montségur. It had been half a century of political and religious events. In 1249 Louis IX and his wife, Margaret, sailed from Aigues-Mortes to join the Seventh Crusade. After a storm at Cyprus they reached the Holy Land in 1250 only for the ungovernable French army to be defeated, almost massacred, at Damietta. Hugues de la Marche, that long-standing enemy of the French crown, was killed.

A vast ransom was demanded for the release of Louis. After some haggling while Blanche, Queen-Regent once more in the absence of her son, gathered the money, the exorbitant sum was paid. It was rumoured that the crusaders cheated during the weighing of the coins. The ransom was huge but it was no more than half the royal annual income. Two years later Blanche died in Paris, one son far away, another dead, a third very ill. Her heart was sent to her abbey of the Lady of the Lily at Melun.[1]

Oliver of Termes had fought bravely at Damietta. Having made his peace with Louis IX his excommunication was lifted and he stayed with the king and queen until they sailed home from Acre in 1254. It was a long, dangerous voyage. The ship ran aground on a sandbank and was badly damaged. Jean, Sire de Joinville, chronicler of the crusade, reminisced that Oliver was the 'boldest man I have ever seen but he did not dare to stay with us for fear of drowning'. Instead, travelling overland, it took him a year and a half to reach home. Returning to the Holy Land he died there in 1274 and his body was taken to the abbey of Fontfroide that over the years had been enriched by his gifts.[2]

The crusade indirectly caused another death. In 1249 Raymond VII condemned eighty Cathars to be executed at Béoulaygues, a suburb of Agen on the west bank of the Garonne, perhaps in vindictive retaliation for the turmoil and tragedy the heresy had brought to his lands and to him. He then went to Aigues-Mortes to attend the embarkation of Alphonse, the king's brother, for the Holy Land, contracted a fever and died at Millau. His body was carried along the Tarn valley, then by barge through the Agenais and in the spring of 1250 he was buried in Fontevraud abbey in the valley of the Loire. On the long journey his mourning cortège wept because they 'knew that what they wept for was the end of their existence as a nation'.[3] In 1638 the tomb was destroyed by an abbess intent on enlarging the choir.

These were momentous affairs but they hardly touched the men and women of the villages and farms in the Languedoc. What did affect them was the Inquisition. The questioning never stopped. The red cross of the crusader had gone. The crucifix hanging from the necks of Inquisitors was always there, always threatening. The burning continued.

It has been calculated that in the century before Montségur there had been as many as fifteen hundred Good Men preaching openly in the cities and across the countryside. Over the following fifty years they almost disappeared and by 1300 there were perhaps no more than fifteen or sixteen, moving by night, trusting few, always watchful for the traitor or the equally dangerous coward.[4]

The reason was obvious, punishment for one wrong answer: a fine, a pilgrimage, loss of possessions, prison, the cruellest of deaths by burning. One terror had replaced another. Now there was no need to cower in the house as an army tramped through the streets.

There was no clash of swords, no crash of battle-axe and mace, no sunlit reflection on polished armour and weapons. The proudly prancing warhorse was almost forgotten.

Fear was not. Now it was the seated Dominican friar in his long black robe, a clerk with quill alongside him ready for the mistaken reply. Nervously facing the pair, standing, was a man in his day-to-day knee-length tunic and leggings, or a woman in her better kirtle, hair bundled in a kerchief, each of them scared of the thoughtless answer, worried about unclear memories.

The apprehension was justified. In 1246 thirty-four people were condemned in Toulouse in one day alone. Even in less remorseless periods the monthly average was twenty-five. Day after day there were summons to St.-Sernin, often of large groups, half of them from the devilish Lauragais, almost as many from Toulouse itself as flapping tongues released name after name. At the notoriously heretical Limoux more than a hundred and fifty people were made to wear the humiliating yellow crosses. Pierre Seila, Inquisitor of Moissac and Montauban, condemned some seven hundred heretics in three short years. Altogether in the Languedoc between 1237 and 1279 when an amnesty was announced it is recorded that well over five thousand men and women were examined. The real figure may have exceeded eight thousand.

To accommodate the more culpable Cathars, Louis IX ordered the establishing of special prisons for the guilty in Carcassonne, Albi, Toulouse and Béziers, all of them with individual cells to prevent communication, unlit, their forgotten inmates, the '*immurati*, fed on bread and water. 'Investigation and interrogation on this scale was unprecedented and must have struck fear into many people, perhaps helping to disrupt the networks of believers even when the heretics themselves escaped punishment by flight'.[5]

Some were ensnared without the need for the Inquisition. In Toulouse at Lent in 1247 the garrulous and gullible Peter Garcias confided to a relative, Guilhem Garcias, that he was a Cathar. He was but his kinsman was a Franciscan, a brother of the Order of Friars Minor. As a true Catholic he would not have minded hearing that Pere's wife was a fool and that Pere had not had sex with her for two years. Guilhem, however, would have minded being told that marriage was prostitution and that the Roman church was a 'harlot who gives poison', that the law of Moses was stupidity and the 'God that gave that law was a scoundrel'.

Unsuspected to the blabbing Pere it was a trap. Four eaves-dropping friars were within earshot but out of sight. As one attested, 'this witness was above, between them and the roof, in a place where he could see and hear them', perhaps in the rafters. The hiding-place is irrelevant. Their sworn statements were not. The nincompoop, Pere fled. His entire property was confiscated.[6]

More typical than the self-incriminating inanities of Garcias was the arrest, examination and sentencing of the wealthy Cathar believer, Alaman of Rouaix. He had welcomed Good Men to his home many times, had fed and sheltered them. He had even allowed a believer to be consoled in his cowshed. Although that woman was not rich, she made gifts to the Cathar church, as was customary: a tunic, twenty-two copper coins, a linen cloth, a gold coin, a fan and a cloak. Alaman of Rouaix sometimes acted as a banker for such sums. One of his counterparts, Ugo Rotland of Puylaurens, had a pot with six hundred silver coins buried under his doorway.

For his heretical associations Alaman was called to the Toulouse Inquisition in 1237 by Guillaume Arnaud. He did not attend. In 1229 he had already been ordered to go on a pilgrimage to the Holy Land. He did not go.

Either captured or giving himself up in June, 1248 in the pessimistic days after Montségur he recanted in the presence of the Bishop and the Count of Toulouse and was sentenced to lifelong imprisonment. From his goods fifty silver sous were to be paid annually to Pons, a colleague of Raymond Scriptor who had been murdered at Avignonet, and there was to be compensation to the Hospitallers of St John 'for the plunder he took from them'. Anything of value left after these penalties was taken by Raymond VII. It is assumed that Alaman died in prison.[7]

The middle of the thirteenth century was a dramatic time for France, the Languedoc and the Catholic church. In 1250 Louis IX had been captured at Damietta and Raymond VII, Count of

Toulouse, had been buried at Fontevraud-l'Abbé. Two years later, badgered by his impatient inquisitors, Innocent IV in his '*Ad Extirpanda*' permitted torture to be used against obdurate prisoners but only on condition that no holy man was present. Even this was rescinded. In 1256 a new Pope, Alexander IV, countermanded the edict.

Inquisitors could then enter the chamber where the instruments of persuasion were kept. There was a procedure. The suspect was to be showed the appliances and asked to confess. Stubborn refusal resulted in being stripped of clothes and once again urged to admit guilt. Failure to do so led to the infliction of pain: the rack that broke the body; the strappado that dislocated shoulders, torture by water, the burning of feet, anything that hurt as long as bones were not broken and blood was not drawn, always stopping a few agonising, semi-conscious seconds short of 'mutilation and danger of death'. What had begun years before as a haphazard search and interrogation steadily, intentionally corrupted into the sadism of a medieval SS.[8]

First, of course, a suspect had to be apprehended and this could be hazardous. Hearing of two Good Women living at Roquefort at the foot of the Montagne Noire the abbot of Sorèze sent an agent there to find them. The man arrested the women only for the other women of the village to beat him with cudgels and pelt him so heavily with stones that he fled. The Good Women escaped. The abbot came to Roquefort protesting at the indignity only to be made a fool. His incompetent servant, he was assured, had indeed picked on two women but two that were married and entirely respectable, certainly not Cathar preachers who had taken sincere vows of chastity.[9]

There was conflict and violence on a grander scale when Oliver of Termes, back from his first experience of a crusade, quarrelled with Chabert of Barbaira, 'the fighting lion', a famous though ageing knight well-known for his protection of Cathars. One, the deacon of Razès, Benoît of Termes, had stayed at the mighty castle of Quéribus whose commander was Chabert. Such heretical sympathies may have angered the reformed Catholic, Oliver, but whatever the cause he ambushed Chabert and imprisoned him in the castle of Aguilar. It seemed a matter of no importance but it led to the French possession of the last two great castles in the Languedoc, Puylaurens and Quéribus. Neither had been besieged, let alone assaulted by Simon de Montfort. Now their gates were opened without a blow.

They are astonishments. The elegant keep, round towers and tall walls of Puylaurens rise on the poetically-named Mont Ardu eight miles south-east of Quillan, reached through grotesque, steepling gorges along the valley of the Aude. Quéribus is a farther sixteen miles to the east-north-east.

It is even more awesome, higher, steeper and more hazardous as the visitor clambers past broken walls. 'The walls, in turn, are arduously accompanied by flights of steps suspended over the sheer drop . . . [it is] truly a castle built in the air'. The whole plain of Roussillon spreads out below, Peyrepertuse to the west, the snow-topped Canigou mountains to the south, the Mediterranean to the east. In the spaciousness the keep stubs up like the upraised fist of a monster. On its cramped summit the castle is congested, little more than a succession of terraces huddled together with a large Gothic chapel near the entrance, its elegant pillar puzzlingly off-centre.

Like Peyrepertuse, Quéribus would have been demanding and dangerous to capture but its garrison was small, its commander was absent and when Pierre d'Auteuil, seneschal of Carcassonne, besieged it in the Spring of 1255 it offered no resistance. Neither did Peyrepertuse. The capitulations have never been convincingly explained. There was unconfirmed gossip that Charbet de Barbaira had negotiated his freedom in exchange for the castles. Some years later at the Treaty of Corbeil on 11 May, 1258 the two 'citadels of vertigo' became royal fortresses that with Puylaurens guarded the boundary between France and Aragon.[10]

The French crown gained even more. In 1271 Alphonse de Poitiers, brother of Louis IX died after a persistent illness and his death was very shortly followed by that of his wife, Jeanne of Toulouse, daughter of Raymond VII. They had no children and by the Treaty of Meaux-Paris the County of Toulouse and the entire Languedoc became the property of the king.

In contrast England was losing its French possessions year by year. In 1271 they stretched northwards like a bloated and lopsided pear but within three centuries despite the victories at Crécy, Poitiers and Agincourt they shrivelled until the last tip of the stalk disappeared with the surrender of Calais in 1558.

1274 was a year of some interest. On the far side of the world the Mogul emperor, Kublai Khan, sent a fleet to attack Japan only for a storm to sink the ships. The Italian explorer, Marco Polo, watched Tartars eating raw beef, mutton and buffalo. Much nearer to France the philosopher and theologian, Thomas Aquinas, died in Italy. Edward I became King of England. In Florence the almost nine-year old Dante Alighieri fell in love with the eight-years-and-four-months-old Beatrice Portinari.

In France itself the colours and patterns of court and troubadour were being drained of light. 'In the wake of the Albigensian Crusade, the Languedoc and Provence fell under the control of both the Inquisition and the French monarchy, with their increasingly bureaucratic agents, puritanism and coercive laws'.[11]

In Toulouse in that same year of 1274 a man was examined by inquisitors for his liking and knowledge of the poems, *sirventes*, of the anti-Catholic troubadour, Guilhem de Figueira, who detested the Church for its avarice and pride. In 1228 he had accused the Pope of being guilty of the death of Louis VIII by inciting him to go to the Languedoc and wipe out the Cathars. Catholics were corrupt.

Roma, de gran tradossa	Rome, you traduce yourself
de mal vos cargatz.	By carrying so many evils.

and

quar faitz per esquern	the ills you are accused of are self-evident
dels crestians martire.	because you so derisively martyr Christians.

One can almost hear the growling sounds of the orgue-portatif behind the half-sung, half-shouted words of sorrow and contempt.

The fate of the accused man, who could recite long passages of the heretical versifier by heart, is unknown. Tolerance is unlikely.[12]

A troubadour, Kublai Khan, Marco Polo, Dante, Edward I, they were part of 1274. In the same year Robert Bruce of Scotland was born in England. And in that year Béatrice of Planisolles was born in the mountainous village of Caussou five miles west of Montaillou.[13] It was a time when, undeterred by the continuing activities of the Inquisition, Cathar preachers were quietly returning to the countryside and other believers were being ordained.

Around 1301 Béatrice married Bérenger de Roquefort, the lord of Montaillou. It was a notable occasion, perhaps conducted in the village church of Notre-Dame-de-Carnasses, and it was attended by nobles and well-to-do citizens from Pamiers, Foix and Ax-les-Thermes, one of them being William Autier, public notary, a profession shared by his elder brother, Peter. William apparently danced famously at the wedding. A few years earlier both he and Peter had become Good Men.[14]

In 1296 they left for Lombardy and the Cathar seminaries in Italy. Three years later, accepted as preachers, they returned along the pilgrim routes, pretending to follow the inescapable Catholic services, murmuring as they made the sign of the Cross, 'here's the forehead, here's the beard, now one ear and now the other'. To each other they derided the Catholic church for its rottenness and hypocrisy. Its priests were 'evil men' who would not even conduct a mass without payment. The papacy, they agreed, had done good a very long time ago but it was now like a cow that bountifully provided milk only to kick the pail over.

Their return to the Languedoc was cautious. Having sent Peter's illegitimate son, William Bonus, ahead of them to their home town of Ax-les-Thermes to make sure that it was safe from curious but unreliable neighbours they went there stealthily and stayed for almost a fortnight with their brother, Raymond. Once secure there they planned their future.

To anyone sensible they were mad. In their fifties they were a pair of defenceless men. There were no walled towns like Lavaur and Minerve to conceal them. There was no castle like Montségur to protect them. They were no more than two vulnerable human bodies tiptoeing into the web of the Inquisition and all they could do was hide, using the night for shelter, trusting the untrustworthy, supported only by their certainty that what they did was God's work. Their choice was an acceptance of a horrifying death.

The hilly region of the Sabarthès around Foix was a countryside that they knew well and it was there that they began, meeting friends, quietly letting it be known that there were Cathar preachers once more, at first only two but quite quickly ordaining a dozen or so in the locality including Prades Tavernier, a weaver, and a Good Woman from Limoux, Aude Bourrel.[15]

The preaching commenced. Peter and William worked in the Sabarthès but gradually, between about 1302 and 1305, they risked places farther north in the old areas of believers, the Lauragais, the valleys of the Agout and Tarn. Dressed in inconspicuous dark blue hooded cloaks and dark green tunics they held meetings, revisited demoralised adherents, even in Toulouse where a secret assembly was held in the church of Ste.-Croix.

There were dangers everywhere. The penalty for sheltering, even for not revealing, a Cathar was death. But information was rewarded. Preachers were always at risk of a chance recognition in a city crowd, of an overheard whisper.

There were unconsidered accidents. In Montaillou very early in the mission, perhaps in 1301, Alazais, wife of Arnald Fauré but former lover of Arnald Vital and later mistress of Pierre Clergue, saw Mengarde Clergue rinsing some shirts and handkerchiefs at *la laviera*, the communal washing-place. Washing clothes was not a commonplace in that village of shepherds. Washing clothes of cambric, a fine linen, unimaginably luxurious for any of its inhabitants, told her that there was a Good Man, probably William Autier, nearby. He often visited the Belots whose home was only five doors, just around the corner, from her own.[16] Autier's life depended upon her silence.

He and his brother and all their colleagues dreaded such unpredictable perils every day of their Cathar existence. They also knew companionship and comfort. In the Belot homestead William was accommodated not in a barn or a cowshed but in a loft-extension with 'a richly decked bed and on its pillow there sat a cushion of silk'. Vuissane Testanière who saw it was curious enough later to climb onto a dung-heap outside the house and peer through a crack to see William Belot, Bernard Clergue and William Autier in the loft on their knees at prayer.[17]

There were other safe houses like the three at Châteauverdun near Ax-les-Thermes and there were compensations for the skulking, nervous life. Believers were generous with their gifts of clothes, food and money. On one occasion bedding, wine and provisions were sent from Tarascon, across the Ariége to the little hamlet of Quié. There was no meat or fat but there were fish, apples, pears, figs, grapes, hazel-nuts and once, a succulent present, two large turbots.

The brothers were epicures. Peter was well-known for his love of honey from Bouan, spices, cheeses and wine. People remembered how Géraud d'Artigues had willingly gone out 'in search of a better and more renowned wine than the one kept in his own residence'.[18]

Against this were the demands of the year's three great feasts which demanded complete abstinence: 11 November to 24 December; 21 February to Easter; and Whitsuntide to 29 June. Of all the many virtues of the Good Men it was the rigorous observation of these periods of self-denial in contrast to the self-indulgence of bulbous Catholic priests, that impressed, reassured and convinced their followers.

It was inevitable that the Inquisition learned about the Autiers. Even in the anonymity of crowded streets of Toulouse Peter had been recognised by the son of one of his neighbours in Ax-les-Thermes. Long before going to Italy he had tried to convert the young Peter of Luzenac who had become a student at the university. He knew that the Autiers were Cathars. They bought his silence, fed him good meals, lent him money, hoped that he would say nothing in return for the bribes.

Not everyone was so amenable. William Dejean, a heretic of a different cult, was a double-dealer who pretended to be a believer while denouncing the preachers to the Inquisition in Pamiers. Warned by a friend William and Peter got away. Dejean did not. True believers found him, thrashed him so long and so brutally that he was unable to speak. The men took his half-dead remains to the

Larnat mountains and threw him down a ravine where his body would never be found. Ironically, the spot was a mere mile or two from Bouan and the favourite honey of the Autiers.[19]

The preaching continued. There were more than a thousand homes where the Cathars were welcomed, the majority of them families of craftsmen and peasants. The dying were consoled, even Roger-Bernard III, Count of Foix and many others by the Autiers and their companions, Pons Bayle of Ax-les-Thermes, Peter Sanche, Sanche Mercadier. More were needed. Peter Autier went as far away as Cahors to ordain two zealous believers but it was a rare event. The 'preachers' did little preaching, more consoling. They 'acted less as pastors of a flock than as visiting angels of death'.[20]

Amid these years of fear and faith there was a curious episode at Albi. Between December 1299 and 1301 its bishop, Bernard de Castanet, accused, tried and convicted thirty-five prominent men of heresy, imprisoned them and fined them heavily. Twenty-five of them came from Albi itself, not ordinary citizens but moneyed judges, lawyers, notaries, merchants, condemned, in what appears to have been a medieval 'kangaroo court, of their instant guilt. Of them probably only one was a Cathar and of the others 'some merely political opponents of the Inquisition'.

They were incarcerated in Carcassonne in conditions so foul that Bernard Délicieux, a Franciscan friar, persuaded a royal official to gather a mob, storm the dungeons and release them. He also accused de Castanet not only of conducting an unfair trial but of concocting fictitious accusations that his victims were helpless to disprove.

Despite his protests Délicieux failed to overcome the self-protecting Catholic establishment. Tried in July 1319 by Jacques Fournier, Bishop of Pamiers, who had begun interrogations at Montaillou the previous year, Délicieux was sent to gaol. It is claimed that the huge fines extorted by Bernard de Castanet contributed to the building of that Catholic fanfare of architectural exaltation, Albi's gigantic Ste.-Cécile cathedral.[21]

In the Languedoc ever more capable Inquisitors were appointed. Geoffroi d'Ablis became the Inquisitor at Carcassonne in 1303. The depositions he obtained at Montaillou in 1308 were used some years later by Fournier in his more thorough and successful examinations between 1318 and 1325.

Treachery continued, even from a believer. William-Peter Cavaillé, a *credente*, had been imprisoned but had remained commendably silent, naming no one, and was eventually set free. Without a home, without money he asked the Autiers for a loan and for some unknown reason was refused. In revenge he informed them that a Cathar woman was dying in Limoux. When they went there in September, 1305 James Autier and Prades Tavernier were arrested by the waiting officers and were imprisoned in Carcassonne. Somehow they contrived to escape.[22]

There was treachery of a different nature in 1307. In that year the Knights Templar were attacked by the French king, Philip IV, the Fair, not for religious or military reasons but through greed. He coveted the Order's wealth. Jacques de Molay, the Grand Master, was arrested in Paris and thousands of knights and sergeants were seized throughout France. Tortured ferociously they confessed to all the required sins: they had denied Christ, had spat on the crucifix, they were homosexuals, had summoned female demons from Hell and slept with them, they had worshipped cats.

In 1312 at the Council of Vienne the Pope, Clement V, suppressed the Order. Courageously Molay and Geoffroi de Charnay, Precentor of Normandy, retracted and were burnt alive in March, 1314. The kings of France and England took the Templar possessions.[23]

Already in 1307 the new Inquisitor at Toulouse, Bernard Gui, had proclaimed that the capture of Peter Autier was 'the foremost goal of the Catholic church in Languedoc' and he offered sums of money for the arrest of any Good Man.[24]

By order of the inquisitor, Geoffroi d'Ablis, in September, 1308, all the adult population of Montaillou was brought to Carcassonne, taken there by its gaoler accompanied by Arnaud Sicre. He was many things, a notary of Tarascon, a hater of Cathars, estranged husband of Sibylle d'En Baille, and father of a perfidious son of the same name who was to seek out, befriend and betray what is believed to have been the last of the Good Men.

In Carcassonne the frightened villagers were questioned about the Autiers and their whereabouts. From the information officers went to the farm of Bertrand Salas south-west of Montauban where Peter Autier and Peter Sanche were supposedly hiding but they had gone. Some months later both men were out of sight at the home of the Maurel brothers in Beaupuy-en-Lomagne miles north-west of Toulouse. So intense was the search for them that they were forced to hide for eight months because of the pressure. On 10 August Bernard Gui issued an order for the arrest of Peter Autier, Peter Sanche, and Sanche Mercadier.[25]

Escape was impossible. Early in September, 1309 Peter Autier and Sanche were delivered to the Inquisition, lucratively betrayed by the miserable and ungrateful Peter of Luzenac. They were taken to Toulouse and thence to the dungeons of Carcassonne where others of the group joined them: Peter Raymond, Amiel of Perles, James Autier, Prades Tavernier, Philip d'Alayrac, Pons Bayle, Peter Sans, Raymond Fabre. All were tried, all were burnt except for Sans Mercadier who, against all Cathar beliefs, committed suicide.[26]

Sibylla d'En Baille of Ax-les-Thermes, the protector of dying Cathar women, had already been burnt at an unknown date, perhaps at the instigation of her former husband and fervent Catholic, Arnaud Sicre. The last of the Good Women, Aude Bourrel, had also died, probably in 1307. Mortally ill she had hastened her death by deliberate exposure to cold, a sin to Cathars, for fear of being taken alive in her weakened state and executed. Gui found her body in '*terre consacrée du cimitière*', in the consecrated ground of the cemetery, had it dug up and burned for its abominable crime of heresy.[27]

Finally, in December, William Autier was discovered. For months he was questioned, tortured, re-examined. It was only after nearly a year of torment that on 9 April 1310, he was burnt at the stake outside the cathedral of St.-Sernin. He requested that he be allowed some words because 'if he were allowed to speak and preach to the people he would convert them to his faith'. He was denied.[28]

It was almost the end. The melancholy enterprise had begun in 1209 as a comprehensive crusade against Cathars in the whole of the Languedoc with its great cities of Albi, Béziers and Toulouse and its scores of dominating castles. A hundred years later the affair had shrunk into an investigation of one small village of a few hundred inhabitants, the unremarkable settlement of Montaillou a few miles from Ax-les-Thermes.

Today it is an insignificant place on the slopes of Mount Aillon in the foothills of the Pyrenees twenty-two miles south-west of Rennes-le-Château. Its name may derive from *Mons Alionis*, the hill of Agilo; just as the earthwork of Avebury near Stonehenge in England, was called 'Affa's burh' or stronghold. An alternative meaning of Montaillou would be the 'hill of the lion', because a silver lion on a red background was the eleventh century standard of the Alion family, owners of the land and castle.[29]

On the way to Montaillou from Quillan the road passes through Belcaire and a countryside studded thickly with towering needles of rocks as though giants had been using mountains as javelins. The land opens into warm Alpine meadows of chirping crickets, slender, sky-blue gentians, purple saxifrage creeping through the grasses, and bending yellow saxifrage rising among them, 'bear's ear' primulas, delicacies of dwarfed flowers decorating the pleasant hills beneath the mountains.

In the early fourteenth century Montaillou was small, some two hundred and fifty peasants, families of farmers and shepherds. Guarding them was the castle with its tower, courtyard and barbican, now no more than three ruined sides of a keep on a low hill amongst the mountains. To its east were a score of houses round a square, most with a small garden at their front.

Like many isolated and inward-looking communities it was filled with superstition. The violently slain disturbed their graveyards. Malevolent spells could harm cattle and sheep. Béatrice of Planisolles carried charms and love-philtres in her bag. Hair and nail-clippings were cut from dead bodies because they brought good luck to the household but only after the dead man's face had been washed. Alazaïs Azéma, testified that 'in Montaillou we do not wash the whole of the corpse'.

A well-to-do but aged and dying woman, Na Roqua or Roche, had been consoled in her son's barn by William Autier, and then wrapped in a blanket and carried to the home of Brune Pourcel to be watched over by three women during her *endura*. On the third day she died. Brune swore that at that moment two night-owls landed on the roof, 'the devils having come to carry off the old woman's soul'.[30]

It was a simple farming village in which animals shared life with humans. In their daily life villagers were jacks of all trade. Raymond Maury, the only weaver, also reared sheep. There was no smithy, no mill and little hygiene. 'In Montaillou people did not shave, or even wash, often. They did not go bathing or swimming'. Delousing was customary, traditionally done by women.[31]

Oats, wheat, hemp grew on terraces at the sides of the village. The surrounding forest provided hazelnuts, mushrooms and snails, wood for the fire and boards for buildings. But the major kind of farming was pastoral, flocks tended by specialist shepherds with their intimate knowledge of trails through the hills and mountains. In Montaillou itself women baked coarse bread, smoked pork, prepared day-by-day food of bread and meat with soup, a mixture of cabbages, pears, beans and turnips.

Today it is an unspoiled village with an occasional tourist office and a little exhibition centre with postcards and jars of homemade jams. Seven centuries ago it knew suspicion, informers and a dread of an agonising death.[32]

At that time and in that place there had been a strong revival of Catharism among the villages of southern Languedoc and Montaillou had been one of the main centres because of the Autiers, whose home had been at Ax-les-Thermes, only six miles to the south through a tortuous mountain pass. They had often visited the village, had relatives there, and almost everyone in it was a Cathar; a 'nest of heretics' it was called. There was nobody to check the spread of heresy.

The resident lord had died around 1299 leaving a widow, Béatrice, née Planisolles, who quitted the castle and took a house in the village.[33] There were no militant Catholics, just discreet Catholics. Except one, Arnaud Lizier. His dislike of the Autiers had been so intense that he worried William, who once remarked that 'there are only two people there [in Montaillou] that we have to guard against, namely a brother of Pierre Azéma and Arnaud Lizier'. Nothing of note happened to Azéma but Lizier was murdered by people unknown and his body was dumped outside the entrance to the castle. His widow, Raymonde, had a second marriage 'arranged by men as always'.

In a place as constricted as Montaillou it was easy to be disliked and it was dangerous to threaten or be suspected of treachery. Lizier was killed because he was unreliable. Mengarde Maury was disfigured because she was prepared to inform the Inquisition that the Clergue brothers were Cathars. 'In Montaillou the Clergues, bayle and priest, had Mengarde Maure's tongue cut out as punishment for denouncing them'.[34]

It was not incrimination by hostile Catholics that was the greatest danger to the Autiers. It was the realisation that any villager who knew them might unintentionally give them away under interrogation. Because of this the Good Men arrived in secret, departed almost furtively. Yet for all their precautions they were still recognised.

During her examination Raymonde Belot told the Inquisitor that 'when I was going for water Guillemette asked me in the street to bring her some tender cabbages from my garden which I did willingly. I went to the garden, cut the cabbages and took them to her in her farmyard. I did not know that she had asked them for the heretics'.

On the same day another woman cutting herbs for the evening meal saw Arnaud Vital lead two men, William Autier and Prades Tavernier, from the Belot house towards the woods, Tavernier having been smuggled during the day disguised as a pedlar. They went along the meadow by her garden and to the Combe del Gazel. From the axes over their shoulders they seemed to be woodcutters. In reality they were Good Men.[35]

The priest of Montaillou was the paradoxical Pierre Clergue, superficially a practising faithful Catholic but really a Cathar sympathiser, always outwardly devout, saying Mass, taking confessions, officiating at weddings and funerals, conspicuously attending synods, becoming very rich from gifts provided by an unsuspecting

Inquisition but mocking its rituals and rituals. He had an unclerical reputation. His brother, Bernard, was the bailiff, a servant of the Count of Foix, so that between them the two men controlled the spiritual and legal affairs of Montaillou. It gave them power.[36]

With the publication in 1975 of Emmanuel Ladurie's book, *Montaillou*,[37] the village became famous but not from any reputation as a well-protected retreat for heretics. Nor was it associated with legends of gold like Rennes-le-Château. It was famous for sex.

The village was rampant with it, normal and perverse. There was homosexuality. Arnaud de Verniolles abused youths, scaring them with his knife, explaining that intercourse between males was not a crime. 'I told Guillaume Ros . . . that the sin of sodomy and those of fornication and deliberate masturbation were, in point of gravity, just the same'. They became lovers.

There was rape. Bernard Belot, a sexual thug, attempted to force himself on Raymonde Autier. Béatrice of Planisolles was raped by Pathau Clergue, an illegitimate cousin of the priest. There was also enjoyable sex. The young Grazide Rives was approached by Pierre Clergue, who was very direct. 'Allow me to know you carnally'. Grazide, perhaps fourteen, was as direct. 'All right', she replied. Later she added, 'With Pierre Clergue I liked it. And so it did not displease God. It was not a sin'. Clergue was insatiable. He took women in the baths at Ax-les-Thermes. Inquisitorial records list at least a dozen women, wives, widowed or single, who had been his mistresses.[38] Fabrisse Rives rebuked him. 'You are committing an enormous sin by sleeping with a married woman'. The priest shrugged. 'One woman's just like another. The sin is the same whether she's married or not'. He was not a rapist. One of his conquests fondly remembered 'how, when he deflowered her among the straw in the family barn, he did not offer her any violence'.[39]

All this became known through the enquiries of the Inquisition, particularly those conducted by Jacques Fournier. From the records of his predecessor, Geoffroi d'Ablis, he had the sword testimony of dozens of people. He used it incisively.

Unattractive physically, he was exceptionally capable mentally. Spiritually, he was something of an enigma. He was so corpulent that opponents in Montaillou nicknamed their diminutive priest, Pierre Clergue, the 'little bishop' in mocking contrast to the overweight Bishop of Pamiers. Despite the obesity however Fournier was systematic and very shrewd. Being a native of Saverdun eight miles north of Pamiers he had the great advantage of speaking Occitanian fluently so that he could easily notice hesitations and ill-chosen words in the local dialects of his witnesses.

The years of his interrogations occurred in the middle of his very distinguished career. A Cistercian monk, he became Abbot of Fontfroide in 1311, Bishop of Pamiers in 1317, Bishop of Mirepoix the following year, a Cardinal in 1327 and finally elected Pope Benedict XII at Avignon in 1334. 'You have elected an ass', he claimed but became a friend of the poet, Petrarch and proved to be a severe ecclesiastical reformer.

At Pamiers he was also harsh and mercenary, unrelenting in his pursuit of unpaid church money, regaining taxes that had been ignored with a zeal that led to accusations that his investigations into heresy had less to do with Catholic orthodoxy than with a wish to enrich his Church. It has been claimed that he has been given a better press than he deserved.

He undertook twenty-five examinations of people from Montaillou between 1318 and 1325 following a proven method of discovering the truth. First there would be a message of denunciation delivered to the person's home, instructing them to attend a court at Pamiers. Statements were taken without an oath. Unsatisfactory explanations resulted in sharper questioning and sworn replies under penalty of prison, sometimes in the strict confinement of a small cell, fettered, fed on black bread and water. Yellow Crosses could be ordered to be sewn onto clothing, a pilgrimage might be demanded, property could be taken away. But in all this among all those questioned only one was tortured, William Agasse, a pathetic, almost raving leper.[40]

Of the people from Montaillou brought before him the one that most interested Fournier was Béatrice of Planisolles who had lived among heretics for so long and who had known the Autiers. From her the inquisitor eventually learned far more than he had expected.

He discovered not only heretics but very intimate details of village life.

She first appeared before him on Saturday, 26 July 1320. No oath was demanded and there were few questions. At a second, more demanding meeting she was accused of blasphemy. Years earlier she had laughingly asked Guillaume Roussel how, if God was present at the sacrament of the altar. He could allow Himself to be eaten by priests. She denied it. She had also failed to attend church until reprimanded by the vicar. She had jeered at Communion, saying that if Christ's body had been as big as a mountain it would already have been devoured ten times over by the priests and their congregations. It was untrue, she claimed.

Alarmed at the serious charges against her, sworn by witnesses, Béatrice fled from Pamiers before a third session on Tuesday 29 July 'although she was waited for patiently all the day'. She never reached the faceless safety of Limoux. Hoping to vanish briefly in the backwater of Mas-Saintes-Puelles near Castelnaudary she was arrested and brought back to Pamiers.

On Friday 1 August she was sharply questioned about the suspiciously heathen charms and philtres discovered in her bag and her dubious association with a sorcerers, the late Gaillarde Cuq. By Monday, 25 August, at her final and ninth interrogation, exhausted and ill she confessed her guilt to the Inquisition.

Twice married, twice widowed, with two sons and four daughters, in her mid-forties, physically she was a wraith. Little is known about her appearance, whether she was tall, slender, fair-haired, attractive, with a pleasant voice. Ladurie described her as 'a young and pretty bride in the 1290s' but it was guesswork. Azalaïs Azéma said she had large eyebrows but she is a phantom. There is no Napoléon Peyrat to give her the loveliness of flesh and blood even though her life was very much flesh and blood.

Sex was her constant pleasure, not with husbands but happily with Pierre Clergue, with Barthélemy Amilhat and others. Clergue had pestered her for three months and finally seduced her, making love to her on many occasions and in many places. The affair lasted for eighteen months from Lent in 1300 to August, 1301.[41] When she moved to Prades he made up a bed there and slept with her again. She admitted everything. 'He also knew me carnally one year on the night of Christmas and he nevertheless said mass the next day, even though there were other priests present'.

It was libidinous material but it was of slight significance to the inquisitor. Sins of the body were important. Sins of the soul were paramount, and what Béatrice of Planisolles told Jacques Fournier about the spiritual belief of Pierre Clergue was damning. He, a Catholic priest, was a Cathar.

Not only lusting for her body, he also attempted to convert her, and did so by denigrating the Catholic church and extolling the virtues of Catharism. Priests were 'dogs and wolves', he said, only hearing confessions and ordering penalties in exchange for money. Brothers and sisters should be allowed to marry, for that would avoid the expense of paying dowries. Most of the doctrines in the Bible were false. Only the Gospels and the Pater Noster were truth, the rest were fables. Neither the Pope nor his bishops had the ability to forgive sins. Only a Good Man could do that. He himself could do what he wished, for at his death the *consolamentum* would absolve him.

Physical bodies, he told her, were created by the Devil but the soul could be saved through a series of reincarnations. He would have agreed with the coarse sentiments of Raymond Delaire from Quié that the story of Christ's virgin birth was childish nonsense. Jesus was conceived, sneered Delaire, like any human being by *'foten e coardan'*, 'fucking and giving tail'. God Himself was the product of *'masan e foten ayshi co nos'*, 'plain fucking like the rest of us'. The Occitan phrases were recorded by the scribes of the Inquisition but not translated into Latin.

Most damning of all was Clergue's persistent argument, and possible temporary success, that Béatrice should abandon the Catholic church and join the true faith. 'He told me that if one day my heart inclined me to be received in the sect of the true Christians, that I should let him know at once, because he would see to it that there was a good Christian to receive me into the sect and save my soul'.[42]

228

Pierre Clergue had doomed himself and was sent to prison, suffering the most severe conditions as a lapsed priest. No record of his depositions has been found but it is known that he remained impenitent, refusing the sacraments of the Catholic church. He died a year later. His brother, Bernard, was briefly held, comfortably released and died in 1324. On Friday 13 January 1329, it was decided at Pamiers that Pierre Clergue's remains 'should be exhumed and posthumously burnt, as those of an impenitent proselytizer for heresy'.

Béatrice of Planisolles also spent fifteen months in a cell, and was released in 1322 but condemned to wear the Yellow Crosses.

Despite all the examinations and condemnations there was only one execution. William Fort had been very lightly treated by d'Ablis in 1315, simply made to wear very long yellow crosses, but on 1 August 1321 in front of Jean de Beaune, Inquisitor of Carcassonne and Bernard Gui of Toulouse, he insisted that he did not believe in the resurrection of the body. Bodies rotted. Such denial of a bedrock of Catholic belief was suicidal. He was condemned and the next day with Jean de Vienne and his wife he was burnt in the cemetery of St.-Jean in Pamiers.[43]

What had begun as a countrywide crusade had contracted into the investigation of villages in the Sabarthès. In turn that was reduced to the hunt for one man, William Bélibaste, the last and most unorthodox of the Good Men.[44]

After the arrests of the Autiers he too had been taken with the Good Man, Philip d'Alayrac, but they managed to get away from Carcassonne and cross the Pyrenees to the near-safety of Tarragona. D'Alayrac did not stay long, returned to the Sabarthès and was shortly discovered and executed. Bélibaste made his way to San Mateo. Refugees from Montaillou and Ax-les-Thermes had created an informal colony of believers there and they warmly welcomed the newly ordained Good Man, as William Bélibaste was.

Yet even almost two hundred miles south of Ax-les-Thermes discretion was still needed and as deception Bélibaste lived with a 'wife', Raimonde Piquier. He told the believers that she was actually a servant, that they had separate beds and when away from San

Mateo slept fully clothed so that naked flesh would never touch naked flesh.

Flesh, it appears, was weak. Before their departure for Tarragona the pair had stayed with Raimonde's sister, Blanche, in Prades, who 'had unexpectedly entered their room and found them in a compromising position'. Shamed, the Good Man had to be reconsoled before he could resume his preaching.[45]

It was as a preacher that he excelled. Uneducated, he brought to his teaching a fire of enthusiasm, full of imagery of lizards and demons, angels and eternity. Satan was the devil incarnate, not a fallen angel, and he brought evil and filth wherever he reached. On earth there were four fleshly devils: the Pope, the king of France who had allowed the crusade; Jacques Fournier, and the Inquisitor of Carcassonne. But believers should never know the sin of despair, the good God would always welcome them. Bélibaste, he told his listeners, was a sinner but without him no one could administer the *consolamentum*. If he, Good Man, should die or go away then the *melioramentum* would suffice and ensure them a true Cathar death. Years after his death his sermons were still remembered and honoured.[46]

Unknown to him there was a traitor in his group. Arnaud Sicre was a shoemaker and the son of Sibylle d'En Baille whose property had been sequestrated because she had been a heretic. Sicre, son of a bitter Catholic father, was told that he could regain it by trapping a Good Man for the Inquisition. Aware that d'Aylarac had been caught in the Pays de Sault he guessed that Bélibaste must be lurking somewhere in Tarragona and he searched the region. In 1317 he heard some women in San Mateo speaking with the well-known accents of Montaillou. Pretending to be a fugitive Cathar they trusted him and led him to Bélibaste.

Some suspected him. He made blunders such as bringing meat to the Good Man's table but slowly, living humbly amongst the group, following their ways, the fears and suspicions lessened.

In 1320 Sicre returned to Ax-les-Thermes on the pretext of visiting an ailing aunt. Instead, he informed Fournier of his discovery. All that was needed was somehow to lure Bélibaste to the

Languedoc. He went back to San Mateo with a lot of money, supposedly donated by his aunt, to help the believers there, but in fact Inquisition funds to catch their prey.

His lies were ingenious. Alazaïs, his aunt, was very ill and unable to come to Tarragona as she had hoped. Indeed her illness was so serious that the *consolamentum* might be needed. It was not a huge distance to Seu d'Urgell where she lived. As a Good Man Bélibaste should go to see her.

The believers were appalled. All their doubts about Sicre re-emerged. It could be a trap. Life was already uncertain even in San Mateo. To go so close to Foix and Pamiers would be madness. But Bélibaste had no choice. He had to go. He would take Sicre and Arnaud Maury with him.

They left in the spring of 1321. Everywhere the advice was negative and all the omens were unpropitious. At Beceite Mersende, one of his people, said that someone should go ahead to make sure that everything was safe. As the men departed two magpies flew across their path. A soothsayer measured from the hearth to the door of the Good Man's house with Bélibaste's shoe. It crossed the threshold. He would not return.

Everything foretold bad luck and the Good Man and Marty were uneasy. They plotted to intoxicate Sicre so that, drunk he might give himself away but he saw through the plan, pretended to drink and then tipsily vowed that he would protect Bélibaste with his life against any threat.

Unlucky portents recurred. At Pons a magpie crossed in front of them three times and it took all the cajolements of Maury and Sicre to persuade Bélibaste to continue.[47]

They reached Castellbo, a trivial place but one within the jurisdiction of the Inquisition. Sicre informed the bailiff. Next night, sleeping at Tirvia, a Catalan possession of the Count of Foix, the three were arrested. Sicre persuaded the officers to release Maury.

They were taken to Carcassonne for questioning but Fournier was deprived of ultimate victory. As Bélibaste had been born in Cubières he was liable to be tried under the jurisdiction of the Archbishop of Narbonne. He was sent to Villerouge-Termenès for his trial and predictable conviction. There is a splendid château there. In its courtyard there is a slab commemorating the spot where the last Good Man was burnt to death.[48]

On 13 January 1322, Arnold Sicre was exonerated of all blame for his association with heretics. The confiscated properties of Sibylle d'En Baille were returned to him.

There is one last shadow. Two miles south-east of Tarascon-sur-Ariège there is the biggest cave open to the public in the whole of France. Lombrive was believed to have been a Cathar refuge, even for bishops and deacons. The Montségur treasure may have been hidden in it. There is an old tradition that several hundred Cathars were walled up in the upper gallery in 1328 and allowed to starve. Centuries later, around 1580, Henry IV, the Count of Foix, had the wall demolished and the skeletons piously buried. There is no proof, only whispers in the wind.

APPENDIX

Coins, Codes and Crucifixions.
The Many 'Treasures' of Rennes-le-Château.

This is an exercise in gullibility. During the mid-twentieth century, that escapist age of UFOs, von Däniken, visitors from outer space, ley-lines and corn circles, there was a fairyland of books about Rennes-le-Château and its mysterious treasure. Saunière, its priest, discovered the fortune in 1891 but even today no one knows what it consisted of or whose it had been. Saunière spent extravagantly but whether with coin, jewellery, precious articles of silver and gold, or even without anything of form or substance, is unanswered. There have been many 'solutions' but no proof. Its original owners are lost to us, an uncertainty of Dark Age Visigoths, a medieval queen, the Knights Templar, the Cathars, possibly even an amalgam of all of them.

Looking for facts among these phantoms is like searching for the Yeti in the Amazon jungle or in the swamps of the Florida everglades, a quest for something that may never have existed in places where it never lived.

There is a long shelf of books about the treasure, lots of argument and assertion, but little critical judgement in the theories. Six major claims have been made: that the source of treasure was revealed in coded messages; that the date, 17 January, was significant; that the treasure did not consist only of simple coinage but also referred to an incredible spiritual revelation; that the mid-seventeenth century artist, Nicolas Poussin, painted a landscape whose geometry

233

contained an unsuspected disclosure; that great areas of the Languedoc were landscaped from village to distant village at the points of a vast pentagon; and, most amazing of these amazements, that Jesus Christ and his wife, Mary Magdalene, had come to southern France after the failure of his supposed Crucifixion.

These were suppositions. The fact are different. For decades after 1891 there had been questions about what Saunière had discovered and how, but the commonplace conclusions were transformed into fantasy with the 1967 publication of Gèrard de Sède's provocative book, *L'Or de Rennes*.

Its contents stimulated and challenged. There were codes that had been deciphered and codes that were not even mentioned. There were hints of a secret society somehow linked to a royal dynasty and, like an Agatha Christie masterpiece, there were red herrings and false clues in profusion. The book generated literary offspring in French and English, some serious, some silly, some desperate in their search for a solution to de Sède's mystery. This was not the obvious 'find the treasure'. It was much more subtle: what *was* the treasure?'

The puzzle of Saunièrc and Rennes -le-Château became a detective story. Even de Sède's excited claims of codes and arcane societies became magnified by disciples whose complex explanations revealed the locations of a treasure that fluctuated from ordinary money to the Holy Grail, even to the burial-place of an uncrucified Christ in the mountains of the Languedoc.

The story began simply. In 1891 during a restoration of his dilapidated church Saunière found that one of the Visigothic pillars supporting the altar was hollow. In it were four parchments. Two of them were genealogies, one of 1244, the time of Blanche of Castile, another of 1644. There were also two seemingly clearcut pious Latin texts – but only superficially. They were not straightforward pieties but compilations of indecipherable codes about a hidden treasure.

THE CODES

Doubts abound. The four manuscripts, if ever they existed, have disappeared and only 'facsimiles' were published in de Sède's book.

Their ciphers were fantastically complex, unpredictable and described as unbreakable. Some were. 'The most experienced code-breaker could not deduce the steps required'. Decipherment would have been impossible without full knowledge of the procedure used. Computers would be of no help, since the letter substitutions were made from an independent and irrecoverable text chosen by the code-maker.[1]

The family trees were uncontroversial. The texts were not. One was almost unreadable, with words linked together or with irrelevant words added. The other was worse, lines cut short, sometimes in the middle of a word. Yet from this chaos translations were provided. One read, '*A Dagobert il roi et a Sion est ce trésor et il est mort*' which has variously been translated as 'To Dagobert II king and to Sion is this treasure and he is dead', the last four ambiguous words also capable of an alternative reading, 'and it still lies there'. Dagobert was a fifth century Visigothic ruler of Rennes-le-Château.[2]

As always with hidden messages there are contradictions and confusions. 'Sion' may have been the holy city of Jerusalem. It could equally be a contraction of 'The Priory of Sion', a secret order of the Knights Templar dedicated to the restoration of the Merovingian dynasty to the throne of France. There is also an irrelevant Sion at the foot of the Swiss Alps.

The texts were supposedly documents craftily composed by the Abbé Antoine Bigou just before 1791. Yet for his codes he used a non-existent, twenty-six-letter alphabet. In his lifetime the official French alphabet contained twenty-five letters without a W. Even today the 'double-V', is rare, appearing in loan-words from German and English such as whisky, weekend, wigwam. In a large, up-to-date dictionary there are no more than thirty-three entries in 895 close-set pages, a note being added that 'This letter is borrowed from the northern languages, and only occurs in words taken from those languages' such as 'guerre' from 'war' and 'guèpe' from 'wasp'. It is most unlikely that the grudgingly amended alphabet of the nineteenth century was incorporated in a code in late eighteenth century southern France.

There is an obvious explanation. The person best qualified to break an unbreakable code is the person who devised it. He, or she, could then insert Poussin, Dagobert, a tomb, anything that enhanced the mystery of the money that Saunière is said to have found. If, as is probable, the forgery really is a twentieth century falsification then the use of a twenty-six-letter alphabet is an understandable blunder but an incriminating proof of deception. The sad likelihood must be that any deductions based on the falsities are mistaken. If not, then the forgeries were unnecessary.

17 JANUARY

For unconvincing reasons, it has been asserted that 17 January was a significant date in the history of the Rennes-le-Château treasure. It is true that Marie de Négri d'Ablès, Marquise d'Hautpoul de Blanchefort, died on that day in 1781. Her tomb in the churchyard of Rennes-le-Château supposedly had a sub-literate and presumably intoxicated mason's inscription carved on it. Much has been made of the wording. Translated it reads:

Here lies the noble M
arie de Negre
d'Arles Dame
d'Hautpoul de
Blanchefort
aged six
ty seven years.
Died the
XVII January
1781.
May she rest in   [Requies catin
peace.   Pace].

It was thought odd that the noblewoman should have been termed a 'catin' or whore but a commonsense reply is that the unlettered mason did not understand Latin and should have chiselled 'Requiescat in . . .

236

Scepticism is justified. Like the parchments, the epitaph is said to be encoded. In its 'transcription' the 'M' was separated from 'arie', Darles should be d'Ablès, the final 'E' of 'Negre' is lifted above the line and is a mistake for 'Negri'. When translated in conjunction with a second stone from the tomb a sentence appears, 'At royal Reddis in the store-rooms of the fortress' of Arques. What an ingenious hoaxer Bidou was![3]

The stone can be seen in the ossuary of the cemetery at Rennes but the inscription has gone, defaced it is said by Saunière when he realised that other investigators might translate it. Very strangely, he did not commit the mutilation until after 1905, at least fourteen years after his first discoveries. It is arguable that he did not even touch it. Years before his time the slab's inscription may have been eroded by weather, just enough remaining to permit ingenious alterations. Like the 'parchments' the wording could be fictitious, conveniently contrived to 'explain' Saunière's discovery.

Returning to 17 January, other than the death of Marie de Negri the date has little connection with the treasure. Saunière had a stroke on that day in 1917 but died on the 22nd. His housekeeper, Marie Denarnaud, died on 29 January 1953. Bigou himself, theoretically having created his ciphers, died near Barcelona on 26 March 1794. In such contexts, 17 January has as little to do with Rennes-le-Château as the birthdays of Benjamin Franklin in 1706 or Anne Bronte in 1820.[4]

THE POUSSIN LANDSCAPE

Optimists have convinced themselves that a landscape of about 1640–2 by the French artist Nicolas Poussin, 'The shepherds of Arcadia', was painted near Arques at the site of a tomb, now destroyed, not far from Rennes-le-Château. The work of art is important, supporters say, because the picture shows a countryside that obviously is today's, and the painting's geometrically devised pentagram, tilted to avoid detection, points to the whereabouts of the treasure.

The painting does have similarities to the actual skyline but there are considerable discrepancies. In it one can see hills and mountains on which places connected with the story stood: Rennes-le-Château, the ruined castle of Blanchefort. One can also see differences. The sharp peak of Cardou mountain is notched in reality but not in the painting. Blanchefort is too close. So is Rennes. Even more significantly, the skyline to the left, east, of the tomb is completely wrong. Believers are reluctant to admit that the horizon's 'similarity' is limited to the right-hand side of the work. On the other side of Poussin's work the land falls away. In real life it climbs from the peak of Toustounes, 500m high, to the 762m crest of Berco Grande half a mile to the east, and continues to rise along the mountain range. It is regrettable that published photographs show only the western half of the horizon.

Poussin's artistic life is well chronicled and proves that he never went near the Languedoc. Established as a great painter in Rome he was persuaded to go to Paris in 1640 and arrived there in December. Disillusioned he returned to Rome in November, 1642. Near that time the English diarist, John Evelyn, made part of the same journey in 1646, two hundred miles from Milan to Geneva, through the Alps by the Simplon Pass and its 'strange, horrid and fearful crags', sleeping in 'infamous, wretched lodgings' but enjoying a 'comfortable inn at Sion'. That relatively short distance took almost a fortnight to complete.[5]

Poussin would not have diverted from his journey to Paris at Milan, turning to Turin and then risking a nightmare through Hannibals's frightening mountain passes, to make a six hundred mile diversion to Arques. A five hundred mile ride from Paris to the same destination is equally unconvincing. Such immense journeys can hardly be considered 'a brief tour into the Languedoc' as though it were a day trip to Disneyland. The cryptic significance of Poussin's landscape is an illusion.[6]

The eminent art historian and authority on Poussin, Sir Anthony Blunt, was certain that the artist had never been to the Languedoc. His learning did not impress an enthusiast for cryptic clues, who dismissed Blunt's opinion as 'a not uncommon trait in the more pompously self-opinionated experts in many fields'. So much for scholarship, but a regrettable rudeness when a hoped-for confirmation is denied.[7]

LEY-LINES

For the present writer there is something of an archaeological irony. For years while studying prehistoric stone circles he had to consider only to reject the validity of ley-lines, those concoctions of castles, dew-ponds, standing stones and anything else that happened be on the same direct line.

Researching the problems of Rennes-le-Château, he was amused to read that Saunière's Tour Magdala stood on another precisely straight, six-mile long 'sunrise line' from Arques, through Blanchefort to Rennes. Any competent field-archaeologist knows how difficult it is to lay out even a 100m gridded square, precise to two or three centimetres, across rough ground. Yet in the Languedoc medieval churches were speculatively neatly land-scaped on the circumferences of miles-wide circles, and inexplicably laid out in vast pentagons. 'The Temple of Rennes-le-Château is perhaps the largest structure ever built by man upon the face of the earth'.[8]

Somehow the hypothetical distances to a variety of important and unimportant places in southern France, Rennes-le-Château, Blanchefort and also the insignificant La Soulane and Serre de Lauzet occur in exact whole and half multiples of English miles even though the sites were founded at the very latest in early medieval times. In England the mile of 1,760 yards was not established until 1592, in the reign of Queen Elizabeth. That distance was never accepted in France.

The likelihood is that many centuries ago French long distances were measured in variants of the Roman mile, its foot being 11.65 inches, five of which made the Roman pace. The mile consisted of a thousand paces, 'mille passus', or 1,618 'yards', changing the imaginary 3½ miles from Rennes to Montferrand into 3.8 Roman miles. It is no more than Murphy's Law that the imperfect 1.8

English miles from Rennes-le-Château to Blanchefort should be approximately two [1.96] Roman miles![9]

THE TREASURE

Like everything else in the fantasia of Rennes-le-Château it had a variety of sources: part of the Visigothic treasure of Dagobert; Blanche of Castile's ransom for her captive son, Louis IX; the accumulated wealth of the Knights Templar, even the uncountable riches of the Cathar church, smuggled out of Montségur, taken to the Sabarthés caves and later buried in a dozen hiding places around Rennes.

All these feasible although unproveable surmises steadily became inadequate. There was always something more arcane, more astonishing. The treasure had been the 'Holy Grail', in which Christ's blood had been poured after his Crucifixion. Even that idea was improved. The Grail was re-interpreted as the embalmed head of Jesus that had been taken to the Languedoc by Mary Magdalene.[10]

More iconoclastic yet was the transformation of Mary from a notorious but reformed harlot into the wife of Jesus who, as a rabbi, was compelled to marry by the laws of Judah. 'An unmarried man may not be a teacher', the laws proclaimed. Then, after Christ's physical death on the cross, some writers have suggested that Mary went to France. It raised logistical questions. 'There was always, however, the awkward question of how Mary Magdalen's body had come to its resting place in Burgundy, so far from her birthplace in Judaea'.[11]

Questions can be answered. After the crucifixion there had been panic and persecution. Some apostles fled, went into hiding. Orthodox Jews put Mary and seven to thirteen companions, Joseph of Arimathea and St Maximus among them, into a boat without sails at Jaffa, the port of Jerusalem. Lacking oars or food the castaways endured months of fifteen hundred drifting miles through the Mediterranean and the Tyrrhenian Sea and eventually, miraculously, landed at the harbour of Saintes-Maries-de-la-Mer in the Camargue, some fifty miles WSW of Aix-en-Provence. The exhausted company parted. Mary Magdalene went to St Maximin-la-Ste Baume near Aix where she lived in solitude in a cave. Legend claims that the church stands on the site of her death. Buried in the crypt, her sarcophagus with her skull was hidden against invading saracens in 726, and uncovered in 1279 in the new monastery. St Maximus is also buried there. The story is romantic but it is a romance.[12]

'The authors breathlessly bend to their purpose whatever information comes their way, and the book offers no new insights into the historical figure of Mary Magdalen, but concentrates on trying to assemble proof for some of the more far-fetched of the legends which have accumulated around her over the centuries, using as their guiding principle the idea that there is no smoke without a fire'.[13]

A rare and welcome fact amid the frenetic speculation is that today's château and church at Rennes-le-Château are on Visigothic foundations. If Saunière really did discover material treasure then almost certainly it came from the church in Rennes-le-Château, buried when the Languedoc was invaded by Franks in the seventh century AD.

Notes to the Appendix

1. Codes: Andrews & Schellenberger, 15–23, 46–7; Baigent *et al.*, 5–6; Hopkins *et al.*, 32–3.
2. Royal Reddis: Lincoln, 1991, 47–9.
3. The tomb of Marie d'Ablès: Lincoln, 1991, 46–51.
4. January 17: Baigent *et al.*, 9–10, 164.
5. John Evelyn: *The Diary of John Evelyn*, I–III, Macmillan, London, 1906, 329–45; G. de Beer, *Early Travellers in the Alps*, Orchard House, New York, 1967, 63–6.
6. 'Brief detour': Lincoln, 1991, 59. Nicolas Poussin: Blake & Blezard, 15–17; *Yale Dictionary of Art and Artists*, eds. Langmuir, E. & Lynton, N., New Haven, 2000, 559–61.
7. Sir Anthony Blunt: Lincoln, 1991, 57–8.
8. Temple of Rennes-le-Château: Lincoln, 1991, 17, 95. Alignments: *ibid.*, 90–2. Pentagons: *ibid.*, 109–16.
9. English miles: Berriman, 170. Roman miles: Zupko, 6–7.
10. The treasure: Baigent *et al.*, 214–19. Dagobert: Laidler, 91–3. Hidden places: Patton & Mackness, 3–5, 10–11. The Holy Grail: Laidler, 142–61.
11. Awkward question: Haskins, 117.
12. Mary Magdalene: Blake & Blezard, 131–41; Hopkins *et al.*, 73–83; Laidler, 85–6.
13. Mary Magdalene: Haskins, 375.

Books cited in the Appendix

Andrews, R. & Schellenberger, P., *The Tomb of God. The Body of Jesus and the Solution to a 2000-year-old Mystery*, Little Brown & Co., London, 1996.

Baigent, M., Leigh, R. & Lincoln, H., *The Holy Blood and the Holy Grail*, Jonathan Cape, London, 1982.

——, *The Messianic Legacy*, Jonathan Cape, London, 1986.

Berriman, A.E., *Historical Metrology*, J.M. Dent, London, 1953.

Blake, P. & Blezard, P.S., *The Arcadian Cipher. The Quest to Crack the Code of Christianity's Greatest Secret*, Sidgwick & Jackson, London, 2000.

Corbu, C. & Captier, A., *L'Héritage de l'Abbé Saunière*, Bélisane, 1985.

Droumergue, *Rennes-le-Château, le Grand Héritage*, Lacours, Nîmes, 1997.

Haskins, S., *Mary Magdalen. Myth and Metaphor*, HarperCollins, London, 1994.

Hopkins, M., Simmons, G. & Wallace-Murphy, T., *Rex Deus. The True Mystery of Rennes-le-Château . . .*, Element, Shaftesbury, 2000.

Jarnac, P., *Histoire du Trésor de Rennes-le-Château*, Bélisane, 1985.

Laidler, K., *The Head of God. The Lost Treasure of the Templars*, Weidenfeld & Nicolson, London, 1998.

Lincoln, H., *The Holy Place. The Mystery of Rennes-le-Château – Discovering the Eighth Wonder of the Ancient World*, Jonathan Cape, London, 1991.

Patton, G. & Mackness, R., *Web of Gold. The Secret History of a Sacred Treasure*, Sidgwick & Jackson, London, 2000.

Rivère, J., *Le Fabuleux Trésor de Rennes-le-Château – le Secret de l'abbé Saunière*, Bélisane, 1983.

Séde, G. de, *L'Or de Rennes*, Juillard, Paris, 1967. It was reissued as a paperback in 1968 as Le Trésor Maudit, Editions J'ai Lu, Paris.

——, *Rennes-le-Château, le Dossier, les Impostures, les Phantasmes, les Hypothéses*, R. Laffont, Paris, 1988.

Zupko, R.E., *British Weights and Measures*, University of Wisconsin, Madison, 1977.

Notes

There are two important contemporary chronicles of the crusade, one by Guillaume de Tudela and his anonymous successor, the other by Pierre des Vaux-de-Cernay. An explanation is needed for their references in the Notes.

Tudela's *Son* was composed in 214 verses or Laisses and are cited as Tudela [L 1-131], *Laisse* no, and page no. After the death of Tudela references are Anon [L 132–214] *Laisse* no. and page no.

Vaux-de-Cernay's chronicle was written in 620 sections. References are given in *Section no.* followed by the pages in Sibly and Sibly, e.g. *280*, 140.

A third, rather later, cleric, Guillaume de Puylaurens, writing of events from about 1145 to 1275 but not knowing anything at first hand earlier than 1210, divided his *Chronicle* into fifty parts, I to L. They are cited as Part and pages, e.g. the siege of Montségur, XLIV, 182–7.

Introduction

1. St Paul-Fenouillet: Sumption, 48.
2. Yellow crosses: Weis, 10–11.
3. Troubadours, husbands and sex. Bruckner *et al.*: husbands, 64–5, 130–1; rejected knight, 10–11; Chaytor, 11, 65; Paterson, 262–3.
4. Béatrice of Planisolles. The spelling is medieval improvisation. Ladurie, 16, preferred 'Planissoles'. So did Brenon, 20, and Lambert, 249. Costen, 92, chose 'Plannisoles'. In Caussau, her birthplace, there is a house called 'Planisolles', Weis, xxxvii, and that name is used in this book. Béatrice and Limoux: Weis, 355–8. Pierre Clergue: Ladurie, 39, 163–8. The black Madonna is in a barred recess in the north chancel.
5. Ordination of the Autier brothers: Lambert, 233–9; Oldenbourg, 373–5; O'Shea, 231–4; Weis, 77–87.
6. Béatrice of Planisolles and transubstantiation: Weis, 70. Transubstantiation: Klaminski, 27.

247

7. Last rites of the *Consolamentum*: Lambert, 76. Sibylla Pauc: Lambert, 237, 239; A. Pales-Gobilliard, *L'Inquisiteur Geoffrey de'Ablis et les Cathares du Comte de Foix, 1308–9*, Paris, 1984, 67–71; Oldenbourg, 368–72.
8. Sibylla d'En Baille: Brenon, 307, 320–1; Barber, 184.
9. The abstinence of the *Endura*: Barber, 104; Weis, 97. Cassagnas: Weis, 97.
10. Pierre Clergue and women: Ladurie, 39, 153–68; Weis, 129.
11. Modern treasure: Kletzky-Pradere, 21. Gold in the Corbières: Patton & Mackness, 63–4.
12. Saunière's expenses: Lincoln, 1991, 11.
13. His sudden spending: 171, 183; de Sède, 1967, 46–7; Aué, 192, 84.
14. The Society's 'beautiful' visit to Rennes: Patton & Mackness, 117.
15. Parchments: Andrews & Schellenberger, 15; Baigent, Leigh and Lincoln, 1982, 5. Discovery of a tomb: Lincoln, 128; Andrews & Schellenberger, 230.
16. Accusations: Andrews & Schellenberger, 172.
17. The new Bishop of Carcassonne: Andrews & Schellenberger, 443; Baigent, Leigh and Lincoln, 9; Patton & Mackness, 92–3.
18. The siege and looting of Jerusalem: Flavius Josephus (Joseph ben Matthius), *The Jewish War*, 3rd ed., trans. G.A. Williamson, revised, E.M. Smallwood, London, 1981, 355–75, 385–6.
19. The sack of Rome: T. Hodgkin, *The Barbarian Invasions of the Roman Empire, II. The Huns and the Vandals*, Folio, London, 2000, 167–75. The Missorium: E. Gibbon, *The History of the Decline and Fall of the Roman Empire, III*, London, 1883, 457; Patton & Mackness, 8.
20. Drystone walls: Lincoln, 152–3.
21. Dagobert: Baigent, Leigh and Lincoln, 214–18; Blake and Blezard, 2000, 165–75; Patton & Mackness, 17–19.
22. The Knights-Templar. Their income: Burman, 74–97. Their Estates: M.M. Postan, *Essays in Medieval Agriculture . . .*, Cambridge, 1973, 98. And the crusade: Selwood, 46–7. Their treasure: K. Laidler, *The Head of God. The Lost Treasure of the Templars*, London, 1998, 91–5. Digging near Blanchefort castle: Baigent, Leigh and Lincoln, 13; Patton & Mackness, 33, 39–45. But see: Andrews & Schellenberger, 264–5.
23. The vanished Templar treasure: T. Wallace-Murphy & M. Hopkins, *Rosslyn. Guardian of the Secrets of the Holy Grail*, Shaftesbury, 1999, 104.
24. No money: Read, 289. Fall of Cyprus: Burman, 173
25. Blanche of Castile: Patton & Mackness, 10. Louis IX at Damietta: Perry, 178–85; Labarge, 114–3`. Rebellious barons: Strayer, 135.
26. Aigues-Mortes: M. Guitteny, *Aigues-Mortes*, trans. R. I. McLaren, Société Ajax, Monaco, 1996. Adultery: Labarge, 103, note.
27. Rennes-les-Bains: Baigent, Leigh and Lincoln, 122; Patton & Mackness, 10; Aué, 1992, 84.

28. The treasure of Montségur: Oldenbourg, 323, 353; Baigent, Leigh and Lincoln, 29–32; Patton & Mackness, 265.
29. Cathar wealth: Barber, 184–5; Weis, 87.
30. Gentille d'Ascou: Weis, 127–9; Lambert, 240, 317. Gentille of Planisolles: Ladurie, 165.

Chapter One

1. Occitania: Bonner, 14.
2. Occitanian society: Sumption, 25–7.
3. Payments to minstrels: Bullock-Davies, 179, 177, 148, 203, 162, 68–9, 161.
4. Troubadours and minstrels: Sumption, 29. In Occitania: Kienzle, 49–51.
5. Marcabru: Bonner, 44–60; Press, 41–3. Rudel: Chaytor, 24; Aubrey, 7; Rowbotham, 261.
6. Music: Bonner, 25–7; M. Switten, 'Music and versification', in Gaunt & Kay, 141–63; 'Performance', Aubrey, 237–73.
7. Raymond de Péreille and Montségur: Costen, 158.
8. The Cathar church organisation: Barber, 74–5; Holmes, 19–20; Sumption, 48–50; Wakefield, 31–4. For differences between Cathar sects, see: R. I. Moore, 'The origins of medieval heresy', *History 55*, 1970, 21–36.
9. Fornièra and Azalaïs: Brenon, 254.
10. Good Women: Lambert, 249. D'Avrigny: Read, 192. Foulques of Marseilles: Oldenbourg, 318.
11. Esclarmonde's *consolamentum*: Lambert, 62.
12. Rebuked by a Cistercian: Costen, 73; Lambert, 62; Oldenbourg, 60; Vicaire, 133.
13. Esclarmonde: Peyrat: vol. II, ch. 7, 197ff; ch.9, 352, 369. Rahn: *Kreuzzug Gegen Den Gral*, 1933.
14. Ermessinde Viguier: Brenon, 107, 190–2, 216, 220, 270; Lambert, 150–1; Oldenbourg, 52.
15. Maternal instincts: Lambert, 151.
16. Transubstantiation: Klawinski, 27.
17. Zoroastrianism: Barber,15. Manicheism: Barber, 10, 11; Guirdham, 1977, 10–11. Bogomilism: Guirdham, 1977, 11–12; Lambert, 23–9; O'Shea, 22–3; Sumption, 42; Wakefield, 27ff.
18. 'Cathar' as a term of abuse: Oldenbourg, 256; Lambert, 19, 20–3; Rouquette, 40. Licentious Albigensians: Sismondi, xiii.
19. Soissons: Lambert, 7, 16;. Vezélay: Sumption, 41. Cologne: Lambert, 32, 36. Hildegard: F. Maddocks, *Hildegard of Bingen. The Woman of Her Age*, Headstone, London, 2001, 167, 217–18; Brenon, 70; Kienzle, 4, 110.

20. Innocent III: Strayer, 18–19. Monks and women: Binns, 121. Syphilis: *British Archaeology 53*, 2000, 22.
21. Gormonda: Bruckner, 107; Paterson, 264. Jongleurs: Bruckner, 185.
22. Land ownership in the Languedoc: Sumption, 19–21.
23. Peter of Bruis and Henry: Eales, 230–2; O'Shea, 27–8; Sumption, 43–4; Wakefield, 23–5.
24. Alberic: Eales, 233–4. Bernard of Clairvaux: Eales, 1890; Frayling, 83. In the Languedoc: Eales, 234–9; Costen, 53; Kienzle, 78–108; Lambert, 39–41; Sumption, 43–5. Verfeil: Kienzle, 98–100. Bernard and Abelard: Eales, 163–84; Frayling, 119–57; Lloyd, *Peter Abelard. The Orthodox Rebel*, Latimer, London, 1947, 191–4; R. Pernoud, *Heloïse and Abelard*, trans. P. Wiles, Collins, 186–99.
25. Lombers: Aué, 1992, 7; Costen, 59–60; Holmes, 37; Lambert, 46–7; O'Shea, 30–1; Sumption, 46–7.
26. Cathar church organisation: O'Shea, 21–6, 31.
27. Raymond V's letter: Vicaire, 68. A forgery? Rouquette, 77.
28. Enemies of Toulouse: Barber, 44–50; Sumption, 22–3.
29. Alamanda de Castelnau: Bruckner et al, 160, n.62.
30. Béatrice of Planisolles: Ladurie, 39, 252. Sybille Teisseire: Ladurie, 39; Weis, 69. Simon: O'Shea, 77; Sumption, 89–90.
31. Jews: Costen, 27; O'Shea, 53, 77; Strayer, 8; Sumption, 89–90.
32. 'Labours of the Months': K. Roberts, *Bruegel*, Phaidon, London, 1982, 23–34.
33. Peasant houses in Montaillou: Fayet, 15–18.
34. Lavaur, a Cathar town: Puylaurens, II–III, 34–7; Lambert, 61.
35. Siege of Lavaur: Strayer, 42.3; Vicaire, 68.
36. Alexander III: Sumption, 86.
37. Pons Adhémar: Chaytor, 79–82; Oldenbourg, 54, 99; Sumption, 113.
38. Character of Innocent III: Binns, 185–208; Lambert, 92–3, 97–8; Sayers, 1–3.
39 Zara: Armstrong, 299; Sumption, 143–4.
40. Pierre de Castelnau and his mission: O'Shea, 62–3; Guirdham, 1977, 53–4.
41. Robin Hood. If the outlaw ever existed it is likely that it was in the thirteenth century, see: Bradbury, 1985, 58–70; R. B. Dobson & J. Taylor, *Rymes of Robin Hood. An Introduction to the English Outlaw*, Heinemann, London, 1976, 5, 13, 15; J.C. Holt, *Robin Hood*, 2nd ed., Thames & Hudson, London, 1989, 62–81, 75; S. Knight, ed., *Robin Hood. Anthology of Scholarship and Criticism*, Brewer, Cambridge, 1999, 198.
42. Dominic in Montpellier and his reforms: Costen, 112–13; Sumption, 70–1.
43. Barefoot Catholic preachers: Barber, 119; Costen, 112–14; Lambert, 101; Sumption, 71.
44. Lengthy debates: Klawinski, 90–1; Lambert, 101; O'Shea, 62–4.
45. Babylon: Puylaurens, IX, 56–9; Oldenbourg, 94.

46. Prouille: Oldenbourg, 391; Vicaire, 106, 110.
47. The Devil at Prouille: Vicaire, 121.
48. The ghost-town of Fanjeaux: O'Shea, 110.
49. Dominic the martyr: O'Shea, 64–5. Criticisms of him: Rouquette, 96.
50. Raymond VI and his excommunication: O'Shea, 65; Sumption, 72–4.
51. Innocent III asked for a crusade: Sibly & Sibly, Appendix F, 305–7; Armstrong, 296; Oldenbourg, 95; Sumption, 75; Vicaire, 146. Translation of the entire letter: Riley-Smith, L. & J., 78–80.
52. St.-Gilles meeting: Sumption, 75–6; Vaux-de-Cernay, 57, 32.
53. The assassination of Pierre de Castelnau: Strayer, 51; Vaux-de-Cernay, 55–60, 32–3. Planned by Arnaud Amaury? Rouquette, 83–4; Tudela, *Laisse 14*, 13.
54. St Gilles: D. H. Farmer, *Oxford Dictionary of Saints*, Oxford, 1987, 184–5; *Pilgrim's Guide*, 29–35.
55. The assassin: O'Shea, 283–4; Strayer, 51, 283–4; Wakefield, 6, 15. Tudela, *Laisse 4*, 13.
56. Suspicions that Raymond ordered the murder: Armstrong, 297; Lambert, 120; O'Shea, 67–8; Strayer, 51; Sumption, 75–6.
57. Rabastans: Lambert, 80; O'Shea, 68; Oldenbourg, 53–4.
58. The Papal conference about the war: Tudela, *Laisse 5*, 13.
59. The Crusade: Costen, 21; O'Shea, 68–9; Strayer, 52; Sumption, 76, Wakefield, 93–4.
60. Mercenaries: Oldenbourg, 105.
61. Humiliation of Raymond VI: Lambert, 122; O'Shea, 66–70; Vaux-de-Cernay, 77–8, 44–5.

Chapter Two

1. The crusade assembled: Sumption, 85. Arnaud Amaury: Kienzle, 152–61.
2. The papal promises: Sumption, 78.
3. The crowd: O'Shea, 71. Ignorant multitude: Sismondi, 16. Use of mercenaries: Sibly & Sibly, Appendix D, 299–301.
4. Horses: Nicolle & McBride, 16. Squires: Paterson, 49–50.
5. Scutage and mercenaries: Slope, 26. Ribauds: O'Shea, 71–2.
6. The Orders of Hospitallers and Templars: Read, 182, 194. Hearth Tax: Mundy, 1991, 105, 201.
7. Tudela, *Laisse 17*, 19; O'Shea, 79; Sismondi, 18.
8. Assault on a priest: Vaux-de-Cernay, *85*, 49.
9. List of heretics: Barber, 65–6.
10. Tonneins: Sismondi, 18.
11. Casseneuil: Oldenbourg, 109–10; O'Shea, 18; Sumption, 85. Body-armour: Sumption, 203. The Count: Tudela, *Laisse 14*, 18.

12. Villemur-sur-Tarn: Tudela, *Laisse 14*, 18.
13. Simon de Montfort's 'cat': Bradbury, 271.
14. Garrisons and surrender: Tudela, *Laisse 21*, 21.
15. Mary Magdelene and Jesus: see the Appendix.
16. The attack on Béziers: Tudela, *Laisses 19–21*, 21; Sibly & Sibly, Appendix B, 289–93.
17. 'Kill them all'. Spoken by Arnaud Amaury: Wakefield, 197. The quotation: Costen, 123. Sources: *Timothy II*, 2, 19; and *Numbers, 16*, 5. Lambert, 103.
18. Bones in Ste.-Marie-Madeleine: O'Shea, 85. Vaux-de-Cernay, *91*, 51.
19. The arson: Tudela, *Laisse 22*, 21–2.
20. Number of deaths: Barber, 66, c.14,500; Costen, 123, c.10,000. Amaury's letter: Sismondi, 20.
21. Gormonda and the Feast Day: Bruckner *et al.*, 184, n. 210. Guiraut Riquier: Chaytor, 92, 118–19; Gaunt & Kay, 64, 233, 286. For books about the troubadours, see: Aubrey; Bonner; Bruckner et al; Chaytor; Gaunt & Kay; Paterson; Press; Riot. Indexes in most of these are inadequate. Paterson is more a social history than a musicology. Riot describes the instruments and is very good. For the music itself there are recordings. Those known to the author include: *L'Agonie du Languedoc*, C. Marti, Studio der Frühen Musik, EMI Electrola, Cologne, 1976; *A Medieval Banquet. Music from the Age of Chivalry*, Martin Best Medieval Consort, Nimbus NI 17533, 1999; *Music of the Troubadours*, Ensemble Unicorn, Naxos 8.554257, 1999; *Troubadours*, Clemenic Consort, Harmonia Mundi 90396, 1977; *Lieder der Troubadoure aus Aude und Roussillon*, Ensemble Convivencia, Antes LC 7985, n.d.; *Gérard Zuchetto chante les Troubadours XIIe et XIIIe Siécles*, Gallo CD-529, Carcassonne, 1988; *Troubadours et Trouvères dans le Cours d'Aliénor d'Aquitaine, Richard Coeur-de-Lion*, Alla Francesca LC 5718, Paris, 1996.
22. Carcassonne. The visitor: A. H. Burne, *The Crécy War*, Eyre & Spottiswoode, London, 1955, 254. B. Emerson, *The Black Prince*, Weidenfeld & Nicolson, London, 1976 m 95.
23. The history of Carcassonne: Morel, 5–21; Devèze, 4–24. Prosper Merimée, *Notes d'un Voyage dans le Midi de la France*, 1833. The city had already been condemned. Viollet-le-Duc, Morel, 21–2.
24. The defences of Carcassonne: Sumption, 96.
25. The attacks and capitulation of Carcassonne: O'Shea, 22–6; Sismondi, 21; Sumption, 94; Vaux-de-Cernay, *92–100*, 51–5; Wakefield, 45–6.
26. Pedro II and Raymond-Roger: Sismondi, 21; Sumption, 99.
27. The evacuation of Carcassonne: Tudela, *Laisse 33*, 26; Vaux-de-Cernay, *98*, 54. Raymond-Roger: Sismondi, 22–3.
28. The wells of Carcassonne: Oldenbourg, 122–5. Horses and mules: Tudela, *Laisse 33*, 22–6.

29. The booty: Oldenbourg, 125.
30. Reluctance to become leaders: Sumption, 100–101.
31. Alice, wife of Simon de Montfort: O'Shea, 255; Sumption, 141; Vaux-de-Cernay, pages 59, 96, 161, 296.
32. The troubadour, Biétris de Roman: Bruckner et al, 33, 153–4.
33. Simon de Montfort: Sibly & Sibly, Appendix C, 294–8; Oldenbourg, 134–6; Sumption, 129; Rouquette, 88.
34. Worries at Carcassonne: Tudela, *Laisse 36*, 27. Also: Sumption, 101–2, 104, 129.
35. Death of Raymond-Roger Trencavel: Sumption, 102–3; Tudela, *Laisse 40*, 29. His widow: Vaux-de-Cernay, 68, n.6; Decamps, 30; Oldenbourg, 139–40. Money: the names of medieval French coins, *livre*, *sol* and *denier* derive from the Latin *libra*, *solidus* and *denarius*. Before British decimalisation these were abbreviated *to L.S.D.*, pounds, shillings and pence.
36. Trencavel motto: Devèze, 20. Sans Morlane: Lambert, 226; Nelli, 1993, 5.

Chapter Three

1. The lieutenants of Simon de Montfort: Tudela, *Laisse 37*, 28.
2. Cassoulet: traditionally this should be made with water from Castelnaudary, the white beans coming from Lavenalet, everything very slowly cooked in an earthenware pot over a fire of gorse twigs from the Montagne Noire. A day is recommended. Today it is sold in tins.
3. The 'Cathar' cross: Aué, 1992, 87; Nelli, 1993, 9–11.
4. Fanjeaux and Catharism: Lambert, 68, 74, 79, 132, 134. Women there: Brenon, 140.
5. Fanjeaux and the autumn campaign: Vicaire, 99–100, 143–4.
6. Preixan: Costen, 130; O'Shea, 102; Sumption, 106.
7. Castres: Oldenbourg, 130; Sumption, 102.
8. Castres. The miracle: Vaux-de-Cernay, *113*, 62–3. Pierre's personal history: ibid, xxiv–xxv.
9. Carcassona fo preza: CD OC, 'La musique Occitane . . .', 3053542, Wagram, 1999.
10. Lastours: M-E. Gardel, *Les Châteaux de Lastours*, Archaéologie du Midi Médiéval, Carcassonne, 1981.
11. Peire Vidal. The song: O'Shea, 104. The troubadour: Aubrey, 219–20, 222, 225; Bonner, 164–7, 288–91; Chaytor, 71–3, Gaunt et al, 288. There is music for twelve of his forty-nine poems. The legend: Bonner, 166; Brenon, 143, 147–8; Decamps, 29, Nelli, 1993, 15; Rowbotham, 223–5. Raymond of Miravel: Chaytor, 82, 118–19; Gaunt & Kay, 44, 290; Rowbotham, 287–9.

12. The ambush: Sumption, 110; Tudela, *Laisse 41*, 30; Vaux-de-Cernay, *123*, 68–9.
13. Murder of the abbot: Vaux-de-Cernay, *130*, 71–2.
14. Gerald of Pépieux: Barber, 132; Sumption, 110; Tudela, *Laisse 41*, 30; Vaux-de-Cernay, *125–6*, 69–70.
15. Revenge: *Romans 12*, 17–19.
16. The losses of de Montfort in 1209: Barber, 124; Sumption, 111.
17. Excommunication: Sumption, 107–8; Tudela, *Laisses 42–3*, 30–1.
18. Letter of the pope to Philippe-Auguste, 17 November 1207: Riley-Smith, L. &c. J., 78–80.
19. Tonneins: Tudela, *Laisse 13*, 18; Sismondi, 18. Oldenbourg, 113, stated that 'several heretics' were executed at Casseneuil, perhaps confusing that place with Tonneins a few miles to the west.
20. Foulques: Puylaurens, XV, 70–3; Kienzle, 165–71. In Toulouse: Oldenbourg, 153–4; O'Shea, 123; Sumption, 111–14.
21. Vengeance of the Lord: *Nahum I*, 2.
22. Montlaur: Sumption, 111; Vaux-de-Cernay, *141*, 78. Bram: Oldenbourg, 136; O'Shea, 106; Sumption, 111. The Montréal priest: Vaux-de-Cernay, *135*, 73–4. The mutilations: *ibid*, *142*, 78–9.
23. 'Rendability' of the castles to Pedro II: Barber, 36–7; Vaux-de-Cernay, *149*, 81.
24. P. J. Casey, *Carausius and Allectus. The British Usurpers*, Yale U.P., New Haven, 1994, 22. 'The products of incompetent historians who hung out their ignorance and prejudices like tattered banners'.
25. For Minerve see: *Minerve. Cité Cathare*, by Philippe Assie, 1997. For Pantagruel: François Rabelais, *Gargantua & Pantagruel*, Book 5, Chapter 48.
26. Good Man house: Aué, 1992, 102; Roquefort & Serrus, 12.
27. Trebuchets: Bradbury, 259–69. Suitable stone: Tudela, *Laisse 92*, 51.
28. Malevoisine: Vaux-de-Cernay, *152*, 83.
29. Night sortie: O'Shea, 113–14; Sumption, 117; Vaux-de-Cernay, *153*, 83–4.
30. The mass pyre: Sumption, 118; Tudela, *Laisse 49*, 33; Vaux-de-Cernay, *155–6*, 84–5.
31. Termes. The siege: Vaux-de-Cernay, *171–91*, 91–100; Oldenbourg, 142–3; Sumption, 121–5; L. Bayrou, *Le Château de Termes*, Archéologie du Midi Médiéval, Carcassonne, 1988. Destruction of the castle: Aué, 1992, 81; Serrus, 1990, 89. Strength of the castle: Serrus & Roquefort, 28–9. Tudela, *Laisse 50*, 33.
32. Oliver and Bernard of Termes: Langlois, 18, 64–71.
33. Siege-train skirmish: Tudela, *Laisse 55*, 35.
34. Guillaume, archdeacon of Paris: Vaux-de-Cernay, 175, 93, 94, n.87.
35. Sumption, 122.
36. Miraculous escapes of de Montfort: Vaux-de-Cernay, *190–1*, 99–100. Valiant knight: *ibid*, *179*, 95.

37. Termes, dysentery: Tudela, *Laisse 57*, 37.
38. The ladies: Tudela, *Laisse 57*, 37.
39. Bouchard de Marly: Sumption, 128–9; Tudela, *Laisses 63–6*, 39–40.
40. Capture of Puivert: Vaux-de-Cernay, *191*, 100.
41. Meeting of troubadours: Bonner, 77, 78, 83, 254; Viera, 13. Alpaïs: Vaux-de-Cernay, 100, n.119; Brenon, 210, 249. The chaplain, Costen, 73.
42. Peire d'Auvergne: Bonner, 77–8, 250–6; Press, 86–9; Gaunt & Kay, 21–2.
43. Proficiency of a jongleur: Rowbotham, 157. The instruments: Rowbotham, 157–65; Riot, 70–101.
44. The flood: Aué, 1992, 54; J. Tisseyre, *Le Château de Puivert*, Archéologie du Midi Médiéval. Carcassonne, 1982, 13.

Chapter Four

1. Guillaume de Puylaurens: Duvernoy, 1996, 7–27. Barber, 44, 58. Synagogue: Puylaurens, II, 34–5.
2. The demands at St.-Gilles: Oldenbourg, 144–5.
3. Montpellier: Oldenbourg, 146–7; Sumption, 126–7; Vaux-de-Cernay, *212*, 108–9.
4. Declaration of war: Tudela, *Laisse 61*, 39. Excommunication and Innocent III: Costen, 134.
5. Miracle at Cabaret: Vaux-de-Cernay, *144*, 79.
6. The siege of Lavaur: Barber, 38–43; Tudela, *Laisses 67–8*, 72–1; Vaux-de-Cernay, *215–7*, 111–12, *222–9*, 115–17; Puylaurens, XVI–XVII, 73–8; Barber, 34, 111.
7. The defences: Tudela, *Laisse 68*, 41.
8. Horsemen on the ramparts: Vaux-de-Cernay, *222*, 115.
9. Lavaur untakeable: J. Shirley, 1997, 49, 64–5.
10. Arnauda of Lamothe: Brenon, 19–23, 34–5, and many other references.
11. Guirauda of Laurac: Brenon, 20, 133, 164, 181. O'Shea, 289–90; Barber, 35, 'Heretic': Vaux-de-Cernay, *215*, 111.
12. Raymond VI and Foulques at Toulouse: Vaux-de-Cernay, *221–2*, 114. White Brotherhood: Sumption, 130.
13. Montgey: Tudela, *Laisses 69–70*, 42; Sumption, 131; Plaque: O'Shea, 289. The Count of Foix's hatred: Tudela, *Laisse 145*, 75.
14. Guirauda: 'Dame Guiraude de Laurac', pamphlet, Office de Tourisme, Lavaur; Guirdham, 1977, 64; Puylaurens, XVI, 76–7; Tudela, *Laisse 68*, 41; Vaux-de-Cernay, *227*, 117.
15. Rue de la Brèche: *Lavaur, Pont du Tarn. Cité d'Histoire*, Albi, 1995, 45. The procession: Vicaire, 141.
16. 'Joy in our hearts': Sumption, 132; Vaux-de-Cernay, *227*, 117.

17. Dante Alighieri, *The Divine Comedy 1: Hell*, trans. Sayers, D., Penguin, London, 1949, *XI*, 49–50, 135; *XVII*, 56–7, 175.
18. Les Cassès: Aué, 1995, 12; Nelli, 1993, 7; Vaux-de-Cernay, *233*, 119–20; Tudela, *Laisse 84*, 47–8. In 'The taste of good and evil . . .', Montaigne referred to 'fifty heretical Albigeoises, with a resolute courage suffered themselves to be burned alive together in one fire, before they would renounce their religion'. He mistook Les Cassès for 'Castlenau-Darry' or Castelnaudery eight miles to the SSE. *Essays*, trans. C. Cotton, Murray, London, 1870, 162–76.
19. Baudouin: Sumption, 133–4. Montferrand: Tudela, *Laisses 72–4*, 43–4.
20. Baudouin and Bruniquel: Sumption, 133–4.
21. Tudela, *Laisse 1*, 11.
22. Chaytor, 85, 117–18. Peire Cardenal: Press, 298; Bonner, 197–8; Villon, *The Legacy XXXII*, 259–60; A. Burl, *Danse Macabre. François Villon: Murder and Poetry in Medieval France*, Sutton, 2000, 108.
23. The Count of Foix and Foulques: Tudela, *Laisse 145*, 75.
24. The first siege of Toulouse: Sumption, 135–7; Tudela, *Laisses 78–83*, 45–7.
25. 'From the sky': Roquebert & Serrus, 1993, 6.
26. The 'fish' at Foix: Nelli, 1993, 11.
27. Raymond-Bernard III: Roquebert & Serrus, 8; O'Shea, 235; Weis, 125.
28. Reputation of the count of Foix: Tudela, *Laisse 142*, 72, *Laisse 119*, 139; Vaux-de-Cernay, *134*, 73.
29. Alet-les-Bains: Aubarbier et al, 121–2; Costen, 111–12; Wakefield, 72.
30. Trencavel as page, squire and knight: Decamps, 19, 26, 28. Knighthood, Slope, 6.
31. Louve and the death of Raymond-Roger Trencavel: Decamps, 28–9.
32. Pilgrims' stopping places: Hoggart, xi, 7–8. Roux, 19–22.
33. The cruelty of the Count of Foix: Vicaire, 67, 157; Vaux-de-Cernay, *197–209*, 103–7, *361*, 169.
34. Raymond VI and the rebellion: Tudela, *Laisse 87*, 49; Sumption, 137.
35. The southern army: Tudela, *Laisse 88*, 49.
36. Raymond VI's jester: Vaux-de-Cernay, *261*, 133.
37. The battle of St Martin-Lalande. Puylaurens, XVIII, 80; Sumption, 138–41; Vaux-de-Cernay, *264–75*, 133–8. Significantly, the most detailed description of the fighting and the combatants is given by that 'unmilitary' monk, Guillaume de Tudela, *Laisses 87–106*, 49–55.
38. De Pépieux: Tudela, *Laisse 96*, 52.
39. Attack, massacre, and the count of Foix: Tudela, *Laisse 102*, 53–4.
40. The trebuchet: Tudela, *Laisse 106*, 55. De Montfort: Vaux-de-Cernay, *275*, 138–9.
41. The southern rebellion: Madaule, 70.
42. The count of Foix and rumours: Vaux-de-Cernay, *278*, 139.
43. Lagrave: Vaux-de-Cernay, 141; Tudela, *Laisses 108–9*, 55–6.

44. Traitors to de Montfort: Vaux-de-Cernay, *438*, 199.
45. Coustaussa: Vaux-de-Cernay, *280*, 140.

Chapter Five

1. Plan of de Montfort's campaign in the north: Wakefield, 107.
2. Places captured but no record of Cathar executions: Vaux-de-Cernay, 144–201; Tudela, *Laisses 106 – 131*, 54–65.
3. Confused state: Vaux-de-Cernay: 201.
4. St Marcel-Campes: Tudela *Laisse 111*, 56; Vaux-de-Cernay, 145–7.
5. Destruction of St Marcel: Vaux-de-Cernay, 151–2. Cordes: J. G. Jonin, Cordes-le-Ciel, OMT, Cordes, 1998; Aubarbier et al, 71–4; Costen, 87; Lambert, 133; Oldenbourg, 235. Inquisitors: O'Shea, 200; Strayer, 157.
6. Childrens' Crusade: Armstrong, 299–301; Matthew Paris, II, 452.
7. Hautpoul: Vaux-de-Cernay, *301–4*, 148–9; Sumption, 146. Catharism: Aubarbier et al, 79; Barber, 72; Lambert, 147.
8. Miravel castle: Paterson, 97. Cathars: Lambert, 106. Raymond de Miravel: Bonner, 185; Brenon, 144, 147–9. Chaytor, 29, 85; Rouquette, 92. Admirer of Louve: Brenon, 147–8. Pedro II: Paterson, 93.
9. St Antonin: Vaux-de-Cernay *314*, 152–3; Sumption, 145, 146–7; Tudela, *Laisses 112–14*. 57. Made a canon: Tudela, *Laisse 1*, 11.
10. The anonymous chronicler: Shirley, 1996, 5.
11. Mercenaries and crossbows: Paterson, 52, 60. Winched crossbows: Kottenkamp, 47–54.
12. Penne d'Agenais: Vaux-de-Cernay, *319–25*, 155–7; *328–34*, 158–9; Tudela, *Laisses 114–15*, 58–9; Aubarbier et al, 43; Sumption, 148–9.
13. Biron and Martin Algai: Oldenbourg, 138–9; Vaux-de-Cernay, *337*, 160; Tudela, *Laisse 116*, 59; Sumption, 149. Ravens, vultures: Shirley, 1997, 89. Algai and John: W. L. Warren, *King John*, Eyre & Spottiswoode, 1962, 91.
14. Alice of Montmorency: Vaux-de-Cernay, *339*, 161.
15. Moissac: Vaux-de-Cernay, *340–53*, 161–6; Tudela, *Laisses 117, 118–24*, 59–62; Costen, 36, 40; Sumption, 149–52.
16. The cloisters: M. Schapiro, (1985) *The Sculpture of Moissac*, G. Braziller, New York; Sirgant, P. (1986) *Moissac. Abbaye Saint-Pierre*, Montmurat-Montauriol, Montauban.
17. After Moissac: Vaux-de-Cernay, *355–9*, 166–8; Tudela, *Laisse 125–6*, 62–3; Sumption, 149–50; Costen; 136–7. Pastoureaux: Aubarbier et al, 56; Weis, 256. Heretical filth: Vaux-de-Cernay: *362*, 170.
18. The Statute of Pamiers: Costen, 138–9; Oldenbourg, 157–60; Strayer, 87–9; Sumption, 154–5; Tudela, *Laisse 127*, 63; Vaux-de-Cernay, *362–4*, 169–71. Costen, 36, 40; Sumption, 149–52.

19. Battle of Las Navas de Tolosa: O'Shea, 132–3; Puylaurens, XIX, 82–3; Sayers, 178. Innocent III: Riley-Smith, 59–61.
20. Letters of Innocent III. To Arnaud Amaury: Strayer, 90–1. To Simon de Montfort: Oldenbourg, 161.
21. The Council of Lavaur: Oldenbourg, 162; O'Shea, 138; Strayer, 192; Wakefield, 108. Letters to the Pope: Sumption, 157–8. The Catholic delegation: Binns, 133; O'Shea, 139–41; Sumption, 158. Letter to the King of Aragon: Barber, 137.
22. Amaury's knighthood: Sumption, 161–2.
23. Pujol: Anon, *Laisse 132–4*, 66–70; Vaux-de-Cernay, *424*, 195, *434–5*, 197–8; Puylaurens, XIX, 82–5; Sumption, 161.
24. The Toulousian army: Sumption, 163. Turkish bows: Paterson, 52.
25. Omens. De Montfort: Vaux-de-Cernay, *449*, 205. Raymond VI: ibid, *212*, 109.
26. Pedro's letter: Puylaurens, XX, 87.
27. Boulbonne: Vaux-de-Cernay, *449*, 205.
28. Pedro's ruse: Anon, *Laisses 187–8*, 69.
29. Second attack on Muret: Anon, *Laisse 139*, 70.
30. Michael of Luesia: Anon, *Laisse 139*, 70.
31. Pedro a womaniser: Sibly & Sibly, 213, note 54; Sumption, 167.
32. Jaime, son of Pedro: Paterson, 89, note 56.
33. Secret exit from Muret: Sibly & Sibly, 210, note 41.
34. The battle: Anon, *Laisses 139–41*, 69–71; Oldenbourg, 166; O'Shea, 144; Puylaurens, XXI, 91; Sumption, 168; Vaux-de-Cernay, *463–5*, 210–12.
35. Towton: A. W. Boardman, *The Battle of Towton*, Sutton, Thrupp, 1994, 114–45. Number of deaths at Muret: O'Shea, 148–9; Sibly & Sibly, 212, note 52; Vaux-de-Cernay, *466*, 213. A. Couget, *Vestiges du Champ de Bataille de Muret*, Revue de Gascogne, Auch, 1882.
36. Death of Pedro: Oldenbourg, 167; Vaux-de-Cernay, *465*, 212. Obelisk: Klawinski, 124.
37. The victory: Vaux-de-Cernay, *466*, 213; Anon, *Laisse 141*, 71; Barber, 55.
38. The fate of troubadours: Bonner, 16–17; Paterson, 98, 102; Chaytor, 82–3.

Chapter Six

1. Innocent III: his wishes, Burman, 117–18. De Montfort, Sumption, 171–2.
2. Philippe-Auguste: Oldenbourg, 171.
3. *Faidits and rebellions*: Sumption, 172.
4. English troops at Marmande: Sumption, 176–7.
5. The battle of Bouvines and Louis in the Languedoc: Oldenbourg, 175; O'Shea, 100–1; Sumption, 177.
6. The death of Baudouin: Oldenbourg, 173–5; Puylaurens, XXII, 92–5; Rouquette, 62; Sumption, 173; Selwood, 44; Vaux-de-Cernay, *495–9*, 222–5.

7. Robert de Courçon: Oldenbourg, 171; Sumption, 177; Wakefield, 110.
8. Campaigns in the Agenais and Perigord: Griffe, 6, and map. Silence: Anon, *Laisse 141*, 71; Puylaurens, XXIII, 94–9. Details: Vaux-de-Cernay, *505–42*, 228–41.
9. Volunteers: Vaux-de-Cernay, *505*, 228.
10. Waldenses: Costen, 55–7; Lambert, 97–8. Innocent III: Sayers, 141–50. At Morlhon: Vaux-de-Cernay, *513*, 231.
11. Castelnau: Vaux-de-Cernay, *514*, 231; Mondénard, ibid, *514*, 232; Montpézat, ibid, *516*, 232; Marmande, ibid, *518*, 232–3; Casseneuil, ibid, *519–27*, 233–7. Dominic: Sibly & Sibly, 237, note 95.
12. The faith of Simon de Montfort: Joinville, 147.
13. The four castles of Perigord: Vaux-de-Cernay, *529–35*, 237–9.
14. Bernard of Cazenac: Vaux-de-Cernay, *530*, 27–8; Anon, *Laisse 199*, 158; *Laisse*, 204, 169.
15. Sévérac-le-Château: Barber, 157; Vaux-de-Cernay, *540–1*, 240–1. Bishop of Rodez: Sumption, 175.
16. Council of Montpellier: Sumption, 178; Vaux-de-Cernay, *543–8*, 242–5.
17. Contrition at Narbonne: Sumption, 172.
18. Foulques: Dante, *Paradise*, Canto IX, 47–142.
19. The Fourth Lateran Council: Anon, *Laisses 143–52*, 72–83; Lambert, 108–11; Oldenbourg, 177–84; O'Shea, 150–6; Sumption, 179–81; Vaux-de-Cernay, *570–2*, 253–5.
20. Foix and Foulques: Barber, 138; Oldenbourg, 180.
21. The guilt of Simon de Montfort: Anon, *Laisse 149*, 79.
22. Condemnation of Toulouse and Foix: Madaule, 75–8; Sumption, 181.
23. Excommunication of de Montfort: Sismondi, 69; O'Shea, 159.
24. De Montfort in Paris: Madaule, 165; Barber, 131.
25. Celebrations at Avignon: Anon, *Laisses 153–5*, 83–7; Barber, 56; Oldenbourg, 187–80; Sumption, 183.
26. The wall: Anon, *Laisse 158*, 89.
27. Flowering olive tree: Anon, *Laisse 161*, 94.
28. An enchanter's dream: Anon, *Laisse 163*, 96.
29. Cannibalism: Anon, *Laisse 166*, 101; The third assault: ibid, *Laisse 165*, 99.
30. The siege of Beaucaire: Anon, *Laisse 156–71*, 87–105; Klawinski, 146–8; Oldenbourg, 188–90; Sumption, 183–8; Vaux-de-Cernay, *574–84*, 257–62.
31. Death of Innocent III: Sumption, 186–7.
32. Toulouse. Thrown from battlements: Anon, *Laisse 173*, 110.
33. Foulques' promise: Anon, *Laisse 174*, 110–11.
34. Destruction: *Laisse 178*, 116. Silence of Vaux-de-Cernay, *585*, 262–3.
35. De Montfort and Petronilla: Sibly & Sibly, 263, n. 42. Bigorre, Foix: Sumption, 188–9.

36. De Montfort in Provence: Vaux-de-Cernay, *592–600*, 266–270.
37. Raymond's arrival in Toulouse: Oldenberg, 194–9; Rouquette, 107–8; Sumption, 76–8; Wakefield, 118. Alice: Anon, *Laisse 185*, 128.
38. Citizens and the defence of Toulouse: Sumption, 193.
39. Guy, son of de Montfort: Anon, *Laisse 188*, 133.
40. The attack: Anon, *Laisse 195*, 149.
41. Death of de Montfort: *Laisse 205*, 172. Details of the siege of Toulouse: Anon, *Laisses 187–207*, 130–76; Sumption, 192–8; Vaux-de-Cernay, *601–14*, 270–8.
42. Song of joy: Aué, 1995, 20; Oldenbourg, 201.
43. Burial of de Montfort: Shirley, 1996, 176, note 1.
44. The 'epitaph' of the chronicler: Anon, *Laisse 208*, 176.
45. The Berzy brothers: Puylaurens, XXXI, 114–15, 'Bergy'.
46. Death of Pierre des Vaux-de-Cernay: Oldenbourg, 133; Sibly & Sibly, xxv.

Chapter Seven

1. Vilification of Blanche of Castile: Peyrat, Book I, chapter 4, 77, 79.
2. Baziége: Costen, 150; Sumption, 202–3. Raymond and chivalry: Anon, *Laisse 211*, 183.
3. Massacre at Marmande: Anon, *Laisse 212*, 188, 189; Frayling, 97. Guillaume le Breton: Oldenbourg, 203.
4. Louis' army: Anon, *Laisse 213*, 189. Genocide: *ibid., Laisse 213*, 194.
5. De Berzy released: Oldenbourg, 204; Sumption, 205. The Cathar revival: O'Shea, 173–4.
6. The de Berzy brothers: Sumption, 205. Seraglio: Sismondi, 87.
7. Oliver and Bernard of Termes: Langlois, 18, 64–7.
8. Death of Raymond VI: O'Shea, 175; Read, 195; Rouquette, 111; Sumption, 208.
9. Excommunication and Joan of Arc: W. S. Scott, *The Trial of Joan of Arc*, Folio Society, London, 1956, 173.
10. Death of the Count of Foix: O'Shea, 176. Of the Count of Comminges: Puylaurens, XXXII, 122–3, n. 196.
11. Amaury and the end of the Crusade: Sumption, 208–11.
12. Council of Montpellier: Oldenbourg, 208–9.
13. Council of Bourges: Aué, 1995, 24; Oldenbourg, 209; Sumption, 214–15.
14. The second crusade: Madaule, 87–9; O'Shea, 182.
15. English prophesy of the death of Louis VIII: Sumption, 217; by Gormonda: Bruckner, 108–9, VI, 61–66.
16. Figueira: Chaytor, 88–9. Gormanda and Merlin: Bruckner, 109, VI, 62–6. And Rome: Bruckner, 107, III, 23–5. Figueira and the Inquisition: Brucker, 185; Paterson, 264.

17. Jacques Fournier, later Benedict XII: Ladurie, vii, xi–xvii; Lambert, 230–3; Weis, 1–3.
18. Siege of Avignon: Oldenbourg, 122–13; O'Shea, 182–5; Puylaurens, XXXIII, 124–7; Sumption, 217–22.
19. Surrender in Languedoc: O'Shea, 184; Sumption, 217. Bernard-Otho: Lambert, 136. Blanche of Laurac: Brenon, 129–35, 141–3; Lambert, 72, 74, Sicard de Puylaurens: Sumption, 220. Jordan of Cabaret: Langlois, 72; Peal, 112.
20. Humbert de Beaujeu: Sumption, 222; Wakefield, 126.
21. Death of Louis VIII: Puylaurens, XXXIV, 128–31, '*une jeune fille, belle et noble*'; Sumption, 222.
22. Rosamund Clifford: A. Kelly, *Eleanor of Aquitaine and the Four Kings*, Cassell, London, 1952, 150–2; R. Barber, *Henry Plantagenet. A Biography*, Barrie & Rockcliff, London, 1964, 65–6. John Leland: E.T. Smith, ed., *The Itinerary of John Leland in or about the Years 1535–1543, Parts I – III*, 5 vols, Illinois University Press, Carbondale, 1964, I, Appendix III, 328–9.
23. Blanche and Urraca: A. Kelly, Note 21, 356–61; Parsons, 75.
24. Blanche of Castile: Labarge, 25; Perry, 108–10, 124, 127. As regent: Parsons, 1, 75ff, 214–16. Her psalter: Evans, 150.
25. Antagonism to Blanche: Labarge, 38; Perry, 27–8, 44.
26. Council of Pieusse: Madaule, 97, 166; Oldenbourg, 232; Sismondi, 88.
27. Massacre at Labécède: Barber, 160; O'Shea, 186; Sumption, 222.
28. Foulques as a bishop of devils: Puylaurens, XXXV, 132–3.
29. Toulouse scorched earth policy: O'Shea; 186–7; Puylaurens, XXXVI, 138–9.
30. Castelsarrasin: Puylaurens, XXXVI, 134–7; Oldenbourg, 215–16.
31. Oliver de Termes: Costen, 182; Langlois, 78–9; Madaule, 125; Peal, 112, 116.
32. Treaty of Meaux-Paris: Sumption, 223; Wakefield, 126–9.
33. Treaty of Paris: Labarge, 46, 72; Langlois, 80–1; Madaule, 89–95; Nickerson, 188–9; Oldenbourg, 239–53. O'Shea, 187–90; Puylaurens, XXXVII, 138–43; Sumption, 223–5; Wakefield, 127. Salaries of Toulouse lecturers: Evans, 162.
34. Female troubadour: Bruckner, 104–5, V, 45–9. Bernard Sicart: Oldenbourg, 282.
35. *Besant de Dieu*: Evans, 98.
36. Youngsters to inform on Cathars: Saylor, 145.

Chapter Eight

1. Pagan of Labécède: Puylaurens, XL, 154–5; Oldenbourg, 278; Wakefield, 132. For his general background, see: Brenon, 194–5, 202, 218, 221.
2. Dominicans: Barber, 147; Frayling, 104. Pélhisson: Wakefield, Appendix 2, 206–36.
3. Houses of the Dominican friars: Vicaire, 168–9; Barber, 146–7.

4. Clandestine network: Madaule, 129–31. Puylaurens, XXXVIII, 142–9.
5. 'Gestapo': Barber, 144–5, 149; Wakefield, 134.
6. Jean Teisseire: Pélhisson, 213–14; Lambert, 139. Juliana: Wakefield, 231, note 42.
7. Raymond di Cremona at Piacenza: Lambert, 129.
8. Orders for the inquisitors: Sismondi, 144.
9. Methods of the Inquisition: Klawinski, 198–200; Lambert, 128; Madaule, 99–104; Sismondi, 130–4, 143–5.
10. Establishment of the Inquisition: Holmes, 53–5; Guirdham, 1977, 70–7.
11. The lack of zeal by Raymond VII: Costen, 155–6. His Statutes Against the Heretics: Sismondi, 142–4.
12. Raymond VII to the Pope: Madaule, 104–5. Cordes: Oldenbourg, 394; Sumption, 231.
13. Inquisitors in the Languedoc: Barber, 148–9; Wakefield, 140–1.
14. The interrogation: O'Shea, 197.
15. Exhumation at Albi: Pélhisson, 211, 226–8; Barber, 151; Costen, 171; Lambert, 125; Sumption, 121. At Cahors: Pélhisson, 214.
16. Raimon du Fauga, Bishop of Toulouse; Pélhisson, 215–16; Brenon, 221; Costen, 139; Guirdham, 1977, 106–7; Lambert, 169; Oldenbourg, 290.
17. Pélhisson, 217; Barber, 153–4; Costen, 125.
18. Good Friday: Pélhisson, 216–17; Barber, 148, 151–2; Lambert, 127.
19. Roland di Cremona: J. H. Mundy, *The High Middle Ages 1150–1309*, Longman, London, 1991, 345; Lambert, 129; Oldenbourg, 276–7; Wakefield, 139.
20. The four friars: Pélhisson, 220.
21. Eviction from Toulouse: Pélhisson, 219–23; Costen, 169; Lambert, 127; Sismondi 145; Sumption, 231.
22. Arnold Giffre: Barber, 152. Exhumations in Toulouse: Pélhisson, 224.
23. Matthew Paris: Vaughan, vii–xiii. Jews: I, 277; Blanche, III, 7.
24. Inquisitorial methods before torture became allowed: Lea, 174–83; Nickerson, 203–5; Rouquette, 126–7.
25. Robert le Petit: Matthew Paris, I, 28; II, 452; Duvernoy, 1979, 126–8, 133–5. 'Buggers': Frayling, 83.
26. Christopher Marlowe: C. Nicholl, *The Reckoning*, Jonathan Cape, London, 1992, 65–8; M. J. & T. Trow, *Who Killed Kit Marlowe?*, Sutton, Thrupp, 2001, 8–10. John Aubrey and Ben Jonson: *Brief Lives*, ed. O. L. Dick, Secker & Warburg, London, 1949, 178.
27. Mont Aimé and Robert le Petit: Barber, 147; Duvernoy, 1979, 126–8; Labarge, 67–8; Lambert, 122; Oldenbourg, 256; Paris, I, 156–7.
28. Cathar apostates: Duvernoy, 1979, 303.
29. Anaesthetics: J. Trager, *The People's Chronology*, Heinemann, 1979, 106.
30. Laurac: Aubarbier et al, 130; Lambert, 71; Oldenbourg, 304, 334; Sumption, 57; Vicaire, 99.

31. Blanche of Laurac: Lambert, 79.
32. Raimonde Jougla: Lambert, 149; Brenon, 265–8.
33. Bernard-Otho: Oldenbourg, 279–81; Pélhisson, 218; Wakefield, 132.
34. Raymond Barthe: Guirdham 1970, 141–2; Oldenbourg, 304.
35. The year 1239: Paris, I, 164, 171, 193; Puylaurens, XLI, 162–3.
36. Narbonne: Langlois, 92–103; Peal 116–17; Oldenbourg, 295–6.
37. Comet: Paris, I, 257. Amaury de Montfort, Wakefield, 129, n.4. Gerald of Pépieux, ibid, 205, n.18.
38. Arles: Puylaurens, XLI, 162–3. Carcassonne: Costen, 182; Langlois, 104–10; Madaule, 106–9; Peal, 112–13, 118.
39. Frangipani and Blanche: Paris, I, 384. Eclipse: Paris, I, 388.
40. The triple alliance: Labarge, 75–7; Paris, I, 409–32; Peal, 113; Perry, 110–23.
41. Avignonet: Aubarbier et al, 81–2. The massacre: Puylaurens, XLIII, 176–7, Note 303; Lambert, 154; Costen, 157; Oldenbourg, 334–8; O'Shea, 208–10. Austorgue of Rosenges: Brenon, 104–5.
42. Roquefixade: Serrus, 1990, 88. Raymond VII and Montségur: Sumption, 237.
43. Milky Way: Paris, I, 451. Synagogue: Puylaurens, XVIV, 184–5. 'Behead the dragon': Nelli, 1993, 18.
44. Montségur's garrison: Lambert, 168. For details of Montségur: J. Peyrou & M. Henry-Claude, *Montségur. Last Refuge, Last Rampart of the Catharist Church*, trans. Degans, B., Fragile, Tiralet, 1998.
45. Supply of food: Madaule, 106, 113–17. Length of sieges: Oldenbourg, 341. Women fighting: Sumption, 239.
46. Solar alignments: F. Niel, *Montségur. Temple et Forteresse des Cathares d'Occitanie*, Grenoble, 1967; Nelli, 1993, 22; Aubarbier et al, 105; O'Shea, 258; Peyrou & Henry-Claude, 8.
47. Women at Montségur: Barber, 156–7; Brenon, 140, 243, 246.
48. Roc de la Tour and the bastion: Note 44, Peyrou & Henry-Claude, 5. The climb to the tower: Puylaurens, XVIV, 184–5.
49. Imbert de Salas: Barber, 204; Oldenbourg, 343, 353; Sumption, 238.
50. Corbario: Oldenbourg, 354; Sumption, 239.
51. Subterranean chambers: Peyrat, III, 441–2.
52. The four Cathars: Labarthe, 79; Guirdham, 1977, 87; Madaule, 102, 113–14. 'Spulga': Aué, 1995, 30. 'Dans les entrailles du pays Cathares', *Pays Cathars* 20, 2000, 18–20. Fairy gold: Thomas Moore, *Irish Melodies*, 1807.
53. The pyre: Puylaurens, XLIV, 186–7; Brenon, 258–60; Frayling, 116; Lambert, 169; Oldenbourg, 363. For Montségur, see: Peyrou & Henry-Claude, Note 44; Aubarbier et al, 101–5; Nelli, 1993, 18–24. For the 'astronomy': F. Niel, *Montségur. Le Site, Son Héritage*, Presses Universitaires de France, Vendôme, 1997, 114–16.

Notes

Chapter Nine

1. Damietta: Labarge, 127, 129; Paris, 103; Perry, 158, 159; 165. Blanche: Labarge, 151.
2. Oliver of Termes: Joinville, 293. Langlois, 121–68; death, *ibid.*, 232; Peal, 117.
3. Béoulaygues: Puylaurens, XLVI, 194–5; Aubarbier et al, 45. Death of Raymond: Madaule, 167; Oldenbourg, 365; Sumption, 244; Wakefield, 165.
4. Numbers of Good Men: Costen, 174.
5. The years of interrogation: Toulouse: Klawinski, 200; Lambert, 215–18, Wakefield, Appendix 4, 237–41. The scale of the enquiries: Costen, 170–1.
6. Pere Garcias: Costen, 171; Lambert, 159–60; Wakefield, 242–9.
7. Alaman of Rouaix: Wakefield, 237–8, 239–41. For the *consolamentum* and the banking: Lambert, 68, 126, 156–7.
8. Torture: Barber, 175; Carew, 33, 50–2; Nickerson, 203.
9. Roquefort and Sorèze: Lambert, 154; Oldenbourg, 313.
10. Peyrepertuse: Viera, 18–19; Roquebert & Serrus, 18–20. Quéribus: M. & J.B. Gau, *Le Château de Quéribus. Guide des Ruines*, C.A.M.L., Carcassonne, 1982. Charbet de Barbaira and Oliver of Termes: Langlois, 150–9. Corbeil: Sumption, 251.
11. After the Albigensian Crusade: Paterson, 363.
12. Guilhem de Figueira: Bruckner, 182–5; Paterson, 264, 342.
13. Birth of Béatrice of Planisolles: Weis, 9–10.
14. Her wedding and William Autier: Weis, 11–15.
15. The beginning of the Autiers' campaign: Barber, 180; Lambert, 234; O'Shea, Aude Bourrel: Brenon, 332–5.
16. Alazaïs Fauré: Weis, 21, 202–3. As a lover: Ladurie, 32, 155, 228.
17. Vuissane Testanière: Weis, 160–1.
18. Connoisseurs of good food: Weis, 113–14.
19. Peter of Luzenac: Weis, 86–9. Dejean: Barber, 180; Lambert, 237–8.
20. The consoling: Barber, 184–90; Lambert, 239–44. 'Angels of death': O'Shea, 235.
21. Bernard Délicieux: Barber, 191–2; Lambert, 227–9; O'Shea, 4, 233.
22. Treachery: Lambert, 256; O'Shea, 237; Weis, 152–4.
23. Jacques de Molay: Burman, 154–7, 175; Nicholson, 200–2, 220–1, 236–7; Read, 262, 266–8, 276–8, 299–300. For a general history of the Knights Templar see also: Selwood, Seward.
24. Bernard Gui: Weis, 89.
25. In hiding: Barber, 181.
26. The arrests and executions: Lambert, 257–8; O'Shea, 237; Weis, 237, 239–40.
27. Sibylle d'En Baille: Brenon, 319–23. Aude Bourrel: Brenon, 322–5.
28. William Autier: Weis, 240.

29. Place-name of Montaillou: 'Agilo', Weis, 14–15; 'lion', Fayet, 3–6. The castle: Fayet, 7–14. For plans of the village see: Weis, xvi, xvii.
30. Superstitions: Ladurie, 31, 42, 294. Na Roche: Ladurie, 219–20; Weis, 172–3.
31. Hygiene and delousing: Ladurie, 141.
32. Nothing was known of it until Ladurie's researches in the Vatican, Rome.
33. Absent lord. Montaillou as a Cathar centre: Ladurie, 27. Its relatives of the Autiers: Weis, 100–1.
34. Arnaud Lizier: Weis, 109, 171–2. Raymonde: Ladurie, 180. Mengarde Maury: Weis, 170–1; Ladurie, 330.
35. Raymond Belot and the Good Men: Ladurie, 75–6; Weis, 208–9. Good Men at Montaillou: Ladurie, 54, 75, 76, 78, 256–7. Weis, 23n.
36. Pierre Clergue, Inquisition agent: Ladurie, 58, 65; Lambert, 262–3.
37. *Montaillou* by Ladurie. Despite a rather heavy translation into English and the absence of a proper index the book became an understandable best-seller. Twenty-five years later the story of Montaillou and its inhabitants has been much extended by the detailed researches and fieldwork of René Weis in his *The Yellow Cross*. It has an index.
38. Sex in Montaillou: homosexuality, Ladurie, 146. Rape: Ladurie, 149–50. Grazide: Ladurie, 157–9. In Ax-les-Thermes: Ladurie, 129. Married women: Weis, 246. Incomplete list of Clergue's mistresses quoted in Ladurie, 155.
40. Fournier: Lambert; 232–3; Weis, 3. William Agasse: Weis, 360.
41. Béatrice of Planisolles and Pierre Clergue: Ladurie, 39, 164–6; Lambert, 262–8; Weis, 1–8, 357–9.
42. Raymond Delaire: Weis, 57. Pierre Clergue attempts to convert Béatrice: Testimony in the Vatican Register, trans., N. P. Stork; Lambert, 264–8; Weis, 5–7.400.
43. Pierre Clergue: Weis, 390–2. William Fort: Weis, 11n, 373–4.
44. For an account of Bélibaste's career see: Rouquette, 146–68.
45. The Good Man and his 'wife' at Prades: Rouquette, 156; Lambert, 253.
46. The teachings of Bélibaste: Lambert, 253–4; O'Shea, 241–2.
47. Three magpies: Weis, 344.
48. Trap and execution of Bélibaste: O'Shea, 243–5; Rouquette, 160–6; Weis, 342–5.

Bibliography

Alexandre-Bidon, Bon, Philippe, P. & Boitel, P., *Guide de la France Médiévale*, Librairie Générale Française, Paris, 1997.

Anonymous. See: Hogarth; Shirley; Tudela.

Armstrong, K., *Holy War. The Crusades and their Impact on Today's World*, Macmillan, London, 1988.

Aubarbier, J-C. & Binet, M., *Le Pays Cathars*, Editions Ouest-France, Sarlat, 2001.

Aubrey, E., *The Music of the Troubadours*, Indiana University Press, Bloomington, 1996.

Aué, M., *Discover Cathar Country*, trans. Pleasance, S., MSM, Vice-en-Bigorre, 1992.

——, *The Cathars*, trans. Hebborn, A., MSM, Vic-en-Bigorre, 1995.

Barber, M., *The Cathars, Dualist Heretics in Languedoc in the High Middle Ages*, Longman, London, 2000.

Baudreu, D., Bayrou, L., Dauzat, M. & Sarret, J-P., *Châteaux Medievaux de l'Aude*, Archéologie du Midi Médiéval, Carcassonne, 1986.

Bayrou, L., *Le Château de Villerouge-Termenès*, Archéologie du Midi Médiéval, Rouffiac, 1988.

Binns, L.E., *Innocent III*, Methuen, London, 1931.

Bonner, A., ed. & trans., *Songs of the Troubadours*, Allen & Unwin, London, 1973.

Bradbury, J., *The Medieval Archer*, Boydell, Woodbridge, 1985.

——, *The Medieval Siege*, Boydell, Woodbridge, 1992.

Brenon, A., *Les Femmes Cathares*, Editions Perrin, Mesnil-sur-l'Estrée, 1992.

Bruckner, M.T., Shepard, L. & White, S. (2000) eds. and trans., *Songs of the Women Troubadours*, Garland, New York, 2000.

Bullock-Davies, C., *Register of Royal and Baronial Domestic Minstrels 1272–1327*, Boydell Press, Woodbridge, 1986.

Burman, E., *The Templars, Knights of God*, Aquarian Press, Wellingborough, 1986.

Capdeville, M. *et al.*, *Montaillou*, Imprimerie Vogels, Arques, 1998.

Cardew, Sir A.G., *A Short History of the Inquisition*, Watts, London, 1933.

Bibliography

Chaytor, H.J., *The Troubadours*, Cambridge University Press, Cambridge, 1912.

Corfis, I.A. & Wolfe, M. eds., *The Medieval City Under Siege*, Boydell Press, Woodbridge, 1999.

Costen, M., *The Cathars and the Albigensian Crusade*, Manchester University Press, Manchester, 1997.

Coulton, G.C., *Life in the Middle Ages, IV. Monks, Friars and Nuns*, Cambridge University Press, London, 1930.

Decamps, M., *Trencavel. Entre Légende et Réalité*, Imprimerie Tinéna, Quillan, 2000.

Devèze, L., *The City of Carcassonne*, Lily Devèze, Carcassonne, n.d.

Duvernoy, J., *Albigeoisme ou Catharisme*, Cahiers du Sud, 387–8, 1966.

——, *L'Histoire des Cathares. Le Catharisme*, Editions Privat, Toulouse, 1979.

——, trans., *Guillaume de Puylaurens. Chronique 1145–1275*, Pérégrinateur, Toulouse, 1996.

Eales, S.J., *St Bernard, Abbot of Clairvaux, AD 1091–1153*, Society for Promoting Christian Knowledge, London, 1890.

Evans, J., *Life in Medieval France*, Oxford University Press, Oxford, 1925.

Fayet, A., *In Search of Montaillou*, privately printed, Montaillou, 2000.

Frayling, C., *Strange Landscape. A Journey through the Middle Ages*, BBC Books, London, 1995.

Garban, J-M., *et al.*, *Lavaur. Porte de Tarn*, Office du Tourisme, Lavaur.

Gaunt, S. & Kay, S., *The Troubadours. An Introduction*, Cambridge University Press, Cambridge, 1999.

Giles, Rev. J.A., trans., *Matthew Paris's English History from the Year 1235 to 1273, I–III*, H.G. Bohn, London, 1852–4.

Griffe, M., *Les Cathares. Chronologie de 1022 à 1321*, Editions T.S.H., Le Cannet, 1997.

Guébin, P. & Maisonneuve, H., *Histoire Albigeoise*, Librairie Philosophique, J. Vrin, Paris, 1951.

Guirdham, A., *The Cathars and Reincarnation*, Spearman, London, 1970.

——, *The Great Heresy*, Spearman, St Helier, 1977.

Hamilton, B., *The Albigensian Crusade*, Historical Association, London, 1974.

Haskins, S., *Mary Magdalen. Myth and Metaphor*, HarperCollins, London, 1994.

Herrin, J. ed., *A Medieval Miscellany*, Weidenfeld & Nicolson, London, 1999.

Hogarth, J., trans., Anon. (1140–50) *The Pilgrim's Guide. A 12th Century Guide for the Pilgrim to St James of Compostella*, Confraternity of St James, London, 1992.

Holmes, E., *The Albigensian or Catharist Heresy. A Story and a Study*, Williams & Norgate, London, 1925.

——, *The Holy Heretics. The Story of the Albigensian Crusade*, Watts & Co. London, 1948.

Kienzle, B.M., *Cistercians, Heresy and Crusade in Occitania, 1145–1229.*

Bibliography

Preaching in the Lord's Vineyard, University of York, Boydell & Brewer, Woodbridge, 2001.

Klawinski, R., *Chasing the Heretics. A Modern Journey through the Medieval Languedoc*, Ruminator, Saint Paul, 1999.

Kletzky-Pradere, T., *Rennes-le-Château. A Visitor's Guide*, Tatiana Kletzky-Pradere, Rennes-le-Château, 1997.

Kohn, G.C., *Dictionary of Wars*, Checkmark, New York, 1999.

Kottenkamp, F., *The History of Chivalry and Armor*, trans. Löwy, A., Portland House, New York, 1988.

Labarge, M.W., *Saint Louis. The Life of Louis IX of France*, Eyre & Spottiswood, London, 1968.

Lambert, M., *The Cathars*, Blackwell, Oxford, 1998.

Langlois, G., *Olivier de Termes. Le Cathare et le Croisé (vers 1200–1274)*, Editions Privat, Toulouse, 2001.

Le Roy Ladurie, E., *The Peasants of Languedoc*, trans. Day, J., University of Illinois, Urbana, 1974.

——, *Montaillou. Cathars and Catholics in a French Village, 1294–1324*, trans. Bray, B., Scolar Press, London, 1978.

Lea, H.C., *The Inquisition of the Middle Ages. Its Organisation and Operation*, Eyre & Spottiswood, London, 1963.

Madaule, J., *The Albigensian Crusade. An Historical Essay*, trans. Wall, B., Burns & Oates, London, 1967.

Mâle, E., *The Gothic Image. Religious Art in France of the Thirteenth Century*, 3rd ed, trans. Nussey, D., Fontana, London, 1961.

Morel, P., *The Sights of Carcassonne*, trans. Catford, A-G., Arthaud, Paris, n.d..

Mundy, J.H., *The Repression of Catharism at Toulouse. The Royal Diploma of 1279*, Pontifical Institute of Medieval Studies, Toronto, 1985.

——, *The High Middle Ages, 1150–1309*, Longman, London, 1991.

Munthe, A.J., *A Note that Breaks the Silence*, Bodley Head, London, 1977.

Nelli, R., *La Vie Quotidienne des Cathares du Languedoc au XIII Siècle*, Hachette, Paris, 1969.

——, *The Cathars*, trans., Moyon, A., Editions Ouest-France, Rennes, 1993.

Nickerson, H., *The Inquisition. A Political and Military Study of its Establishment*, John Bale, Sons and Danielsson, London, 1923.

Nicolle, D. & McBride, A., *French Medieval Armies 1000–1300*, Osprey, Oxford, 1991.

Niel, F., *Albigeois et Cathares*, Presses Universitaires de France, Paris, 1955.

Norman, A.V.B. & Pottinger, D., *Warrior to Soldier. 449 to 1660*, Weidenfeld & Nicolson, London, 1966.

Oldenbourg, Z., *Massacre at Montségur*, trans. Green. P., Weidenfeld & Nicolson, London, 1961.

——, *Cities of the Flesh*, trans. Carter. A., Victor Gollancz, London, 1963.

O'Shea, S., *The Perfect Heresy. The Life and Death of the Cathars*, Profile Books, London, 2000.

Paris, Matthew, 1235 to 1257, see: Giles, Rev. J.A; 1247 to 1250, see: Vaughan, R.

Parsons, J.C. ed., *Medieval Queenship*, Sutton Publishing, Thrupp, 1998.

Paterson, L.M., *The World of the Troubadours. Medieval Occitan Society*, c. *1100–c. 1300*, Cambridge University Press, Cambridge, 1993.

Peal, A., 'Oliver de Termes and the Occitan nobility in the 13th century', *Reading Medieval Studies XII*, 109–29, 1986.

Pélhisson, Guillaume de (1229–c. 1250) *Chronicle*. See: Wakefield, Appendix 3, 207–36.

Perry, F., *Saint Louis (Louis IX of France). The Most Christian King*, Putnam, New York, 1901.

Peyrat, N., *Histoire des Albigeois. Les Albigeois et l'Inquisition, I–III*, Christian Lacour, Nimes, imprimé 1996, 1870–2.

Peyrou, J. & Henry-Claude, M., *Montségur. Last Refuge, Last Rampart of the Catharist Church*, trans. Degans, B., Collection La Mémoire des Pierres, Gavaudun. 1998.

Picaud, Aimery, *Le Guide du Pélerin de Saint-Jacques de Compostelle*. see, Hogarth, J., 1130–50.

Poux, D., *Cathare Country. The Cathare Religion*, Editions APA POUX, Albi, 1995.

Press, A.R., ed. & trans., *Anthology of Troubadour Lyric Music*, Edinburgh University Press, Edinburgh, 1985.

Puylaurens, Guillaume de. See: Duvernoy, 1976.

Read, P.P., *The Templars*, Weidenfeld & Nicolson, London, 1999.

Reeves, C., *Pleasures and Pastimes in Medieval England*, Sutton, Thrupp, 1995.

Riley-Smith, L. & J., *The Crusades. Idea and Reality, 1095–1274*, Arnold, London, 1981.

Riot, C., *Chants et Instruments. Trouveurs et Jongleurs au Moyen Age*, Rempart, Paris, 1998.

Roquebert, M., *Cathar Religion*, trans. Wagner, A., Editions Loubatières, Portet-sur-Garonne, 1994.

Rouquette, Y., *Cathars*, trans., Depledge, R., Editions Loubatières, Portet-sur-Garonne, 1992.

Roux, J., *The Roads to Compostela*, trans., Freyche, J., MSM, Vic-en-Bigorre, 1999.

Rowbotham, J.F., *The Troubadours and Courts of Love*, Swan Sonnenschein, London, 1895.

Sayers, J., *Innocent III. Leader of Europe, 1198–1216*, Londman, London, 1994.

Selwood, D., *Knights of the Cloister. Templars and Hospitallers in Central-southern Occitania, 1100–1300*, Boydell, Woodbridge, 1999.

Serrus, G., *The Land of the Cathars*, trans., Depledge, R., Editions Loubatières, Portet-sur-Garonne, 1990.

Bibliography

——, & Roquebert, M., *The Cathare Castles*, trans., Assrour, F., Editions Loubatières, Portet-sur-Garonne, 1993.

Seward, D., *The Monks of War. The Military Orders*, Folio Society, London, 2000.

Shannon, A.C., *The Medieval Inquisition*, Liturgical Press, Collegeville, Minnesota, 1991.

Shirley, J., trans., *The Song of the Cathar Wars. A History of the Albigensian Crusade*, by Guillaume de Tudela, [*Laisses 1–13*], and Anonymous [*Laisses 132–214*] (*c.* 1220), Scolar Press, Aldershot, 1996.

——, trans. Anon. (late 12C). *Daurel and Beton*, Llanerch, Felinfach, 1997.

Sibly, W.A. & M.D., trans. *Historia Albigensis*, by Pierre des Vaux-de-Cernay, (*c.* 1212–1218). Boydell, Woodbridge, 1998.

Sismondi, Simonde, J.C.L. de., *History of the Crusades against the Albigenses in the Thirteenth Century*, 1826, trans., Anon., Gazarii Libris, Trowbridge, 1996.

Slope, N., *The Book of Medieval Wargames*, Harper & Row, New York, 1984.

Song of the Cathar Wars. See: Shirley, 1996.

Strayer, J.R., *The Albigensian Crusades*, University of Michigan, Ann Arbor, 1992.

Sumption, J., *The Albigensian Crusade*, Faber & Faber, London, 1978.

Tuchmann, B., *A Distant Mirror*, Macmillan, London, 1979.

Tudela, Guillaume de and Anonymous. See: Shirley, 1996.

Turnbull, S., *The Book of the Medieval Knight*, Cassell, London, 1985.

Vaughan, R., trans., ed., *The Illustrated Chronicles of Matthew Paris. Observations of Thirteenth-Century Life* [1247–50], Sutton, Trupp, 1993.

Vaux-de-Cernay, Pierre des. See: Sibly & Sibly.

Vicaire, M-H, *Saint Dominic and His Times*, Darton, Longman & Todd, London, 1964.

Viera, A. de la., *The Castles of the Cathar Country*, trans. Macdonald-Plénacoste, A., MSM, Vic-en-Bigorre, 1996.

Wakefield, W.L., Heresy, *Crusade and Inquisition in Southern France 1100–1250*, University of California, Berkeley, 1974.

Walker, C., *Sites of Mystery and Imagination*, Chancellor Press, London, 1990.

Warner, Rev. H.J., *The Albigensian Heresy, I, II*, Society for Promoting Christian Knowledge, London, 1990.

Warner, P., *Sieges of the Middle Ages*, Penguin, Harmondsworth, 1968.

Weis, R., *The Yellow Cross. The Story of the Last Cathars, 1290–1329*, Viking, London, 2000.

271

Index

Important references are shown in bold print.

Index

Index

Index

Index